MANHATTAN

FOR SALE OR RENT

Jenny Henry
© Aaron Publishing, Inc.

GW00338811

ACKNOWLEDGEMENTS

Special thanks to all of the following for their invaluable assistance:

- Laura Torres for designing the cover and building directory.
- Sarah Johnson for her contribution to the text and to the overall production of this book.
- Mark Lorenz for his contribution to the text.
- Jennifer Whalen and Sandra Naidich for their assistance in copy-editing
- Chia Tsao for contributing immensely in every way to the final product and without whom this book may not have been possible. I am deeply in her debt.

This publication is intended to provide accurate and authoritative information in regard to the subject matter covered. Due diligence was taken by the publisher in the acquisition, editing and reporting of the information therein, but the publisher disclaims any liability to any party for any loss or damage caused by errors or omissions or for any other cause. We make no warranty or guaranty, express or implied, as to the accuracy of the information believed to be accurate at the time of publication. Telephone numbers and other information are subject to change.

This book is published and put on sale with the understanding that the publisher is not engaged in rendering legal, accounting, financial, or other professional service. If expert assistance is required, the services of a professional should be sought.

ISBN #0-9660096-3-0

Library of Congress Catalog Card Number: 99-93249

Printed in the United States by:
Morris Publishing . 3212 East Highway 30 . Kearney, NE 68847

Dear Reader:

Welcome to one of the most exciting cities in the world. Manhattan offers the largest variety of shops, theatres, art galleries, bookstores, restaurants, music venues, museums, and businesses. It's the place where new things are happening in film, fashion, theatre, broadcasting, publishing, advertising, banking, computer technology, and finance.

The best, the brightest, and the most talented people in the world relocate here. They come because they have something they want to do, and this is the best place on earth to do it. As you search for your new residence, you join the ranks of these highly ambitious people.

New Yorkers enjoy one of the highest per capita incomes in the country, but the price of real estate in Manhattan is sky-high. Rental and sale prices are daunting, making the search for an affordable apartment incredibly frustrating. <u>This guide was written to provide you with all the help you need to find an affordable no-fee apartment in Manhattan, and to settle comfortably into your new home.</u>

It will show you how to:

- Locate short-term housing while you search for your new home
- Select a neighborhood - each neighborhood is fully described; schools, shops, restaurants, houses of worship, services, parks, entertainment and cultural institutions are noted
- Find a no-fee rental, co-op or condominium apartment
- Make your move and set up utilities: phone, mail, and other services
- Find fun and interesting things to do in your new community

MANHATTAN FOR SALE OR RENT <u>offers the most up-to-date and complete listing of Manhattan's top co-op, condo, and rental buildings ever compiled.</u> Building descriptions, amenities and apartment features are given for more than 500 downtown apartment buildings. For newer Rental buildings with On-site Agents, and for older buildings with available apartments, price ranges are given for Studio, One-bedroom and Two-bedroom units.

Major developers, landlords, and management companies are also listed, leading the reader to thousands of rental units with no brokerage commission. Rental policies, application requirements, and rent stabilization laws are given.

Whether you are a single person looking for your first home, a newly married couple, or a family, this guide will be an invaluable resource. You'll find easy-to-read maps, worksheets, checklists and sample documents, and you'll learn how to calculate what you can afford for housing in Manhattan.

Good luck and welcome to "The Big Apple!"

Sincerely,

Jenny Henry
Author

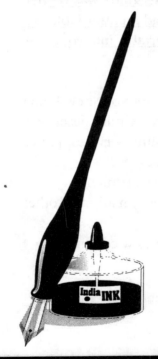

For
Aaron Michael
And
Raquel Jenna

MANHATTAN STATISTICS

Manhattan has:

- 1,487,536 residents; 700,573 males and 786,953 females

- 75.3 percent of its population are high school graduates; 42 percent hold bachelors degrees

- 16.6 percent are under 18 years old, while 13.3 percent are over 65 years old

- The median age is 35.9 years

- The median income is $27,682 per person; $32,265 per household

- There are 785,127 housing units; 1.99 persons per household

- There are 23.7 square miles; 15,170 acres, 42 zip codes

✳ Data presented here is taken from the 1990 Dicennial Census

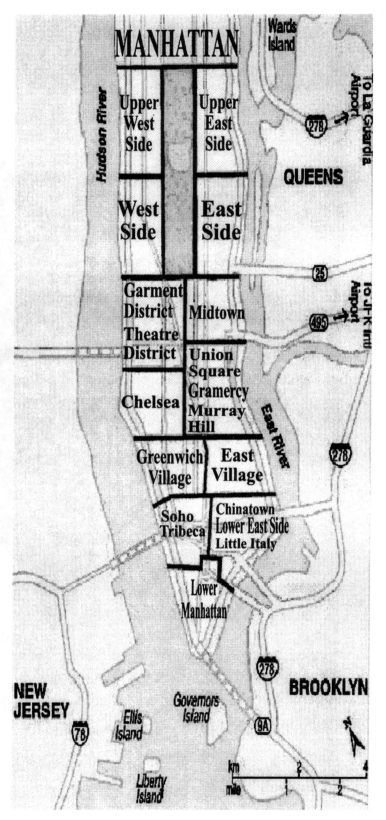

CONTENTS

PART I INCLUDES:

PART II INCLUDES: **161**

PART III INCLUDES: **168**

LOWER MANHATTAN AND THE HARBOR: A BRIEF HISTORY

CHRONOLOGY OF THE EARLY HISTORY OF NEW YORK
THE DUTCH SETTLE NEW AMSTERDAM

1609-
Henry Hudson stops in Manhattan, then continues up the Hudson.

1626-
Peter Minuit buys Manhattan from local Indians for $24 worth of goods.

-1638
William Kieft becomes the new director-general, and imposes the first known city ordinances (port regulations, drinking laws). He raises tensions with the Indians.

1647-
Kieft is replaced as director-general by Petrus Stuvesant, whose first ordinance is to close taverns at nine o'clock.

1655-
Indians attack New Amsterdam, killing and capturing settlers.

1658-
The first street, named Stone Street, is paved with cobblestones.

-1524
Giovanni da Verrazano sails into New York Bay.

-1624
The first Dutch West India Company settlers arrive in Manhattan.

-1628
Manhattan has 270 inhabitants, 30 houses, 6 farms.

-1639
First English immigrants arrive in Manhattan.

-1643
Settlers have their first serious clash with Indians

-1653
New Amsterdam forms a new municipal government, a forerunner of today's city council. City Hall is established in a tavern. The wall that gave Wall Street its name is built.

-1656
Population: 1,000; 120 Homes. Sunday laws forbid drinking, dancing, laboring, bowling, and boating during church hours.

-1660
Settlers and Indians establish peace. A hospital is built.

BRITISH NEW YORK

1664-

The English take over New Amsterdam and rename it New York.

1683-

Thomas Dongan, New York's first governor, calls a representative assembly. The Dongan Charter, or Charter of Liberties and Privileges, becomes New York's first constitution.

1698-

Census counts 4,937 inhabitants.

1725-

The city's first newspaper, The New York Gazette, is published.

1754-

King's College (Columbia University) is founded. New York Society Library, the first public library is established.

-1670

First merchant exchange is established when businessmen begin meeting Fridays at noon.

-1693

Fearing an attack by the French, the city sets up a battery of cannons at the southern tip of the island (the Battery).

-1705

First free grammar school is instiued.

-1732

Bowling Green park is fenced off and used for bowling.

-1763

Samuel Fraunces opens his tavern on Pearl Street.

AMERICAN REVOLUTION AND INDEPENDENCE

1765-

British pass the Stamp Act; colonists meet in City Hall at Stamp Act Congress and issue The Declaration of Rights and Grievances.

1775-

American Revolution begins; Washington makes Richmond Hill house in Greenwich Village his headquarters; British position themselves around the city.

-1770

Skirmish between British soldiers and colonists on Golden Hill (John Street) predates Boston Massacre by a few days.

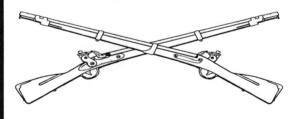

**NATIONAL FLAG
1775 - 1800**

**NATIONAL FLAG
JUNE 1777 - APRIL 1795**

**NATIONAL FLAG
JUNE 1777 - APRIL 1795**

New York ratifies the
new U.S. Consitution
and becomes the
federal capital.

-1776

The Declaration of Independence is read publicly from City Hall and America's flag is flown on July 18th.

August 27: Americans retreat after losing the battle of Long Island; British take Brooklyn Heights.

September: Americans win the battle of Harlem Heights and move north; British take possession of New York City, (the city remains Loyalist until 1783); American troops and patriots begin to leave the city.

September 21: Nearly a fourth of Manhattan is destroyed by fire ; losses include Trinity Church.

September 22: The British hang Nathan Hale, 22, as a spy without giving him a trial.

-1783

November 25, Evacuation Day : American troops, led by Washington, reenter New York. Loyalists and British leave.

December 4: At Fraunces Tavern, George Washington bids his comrades farewell.

-1784

New York State legislature begins to meet at City Hall. The Bank of New York is established, (New York's first bank). King's College is renamed Columbia University.

-1785

The U.S. Congress meets in New York City.

-1789

George Washington is inaugurated President on the balcony of Federal Hall in Manhattan.

LOWER MANHATTAN AND THE HARBOR: A BRIEF HISTORY

The southern tip of Manhattan is where the city began, and where its economic powers still lies. Its deep, broad harbor at the mouth of the Hudson River is one of the finest natural harbors in the world and is ideally suited to be a seaport.

The Dutch discovered New York harbor in 1624 and settled there, establishing the town of "New Amsterdam." It was a perfect spot for small boats and wagons to transfer raw materials to European trading vessels and to pick up imported, manufactured goods. In 1664, the English seized the colony and renamed it "New York."

New York flourished upon its harbor and became both a shipping and a shipbuilding center. In 1746, with a population of about 7,000, New York became the third largest population center in the country. Unlike Puritan Boston and Quaker Philadelphia, New York was not founded by religious leaders, nor governed with an eye toward religious ideals. Commerce was New York's guiding principal from the start, and money was its measure. Any new idea that could turn a profit was welcome.

Businesses made great profits, and bankers invested wisely in the New York and Harlem Railroad, the Erie Canal, the steamboat, and local real estate. A building boom was on, and New York quickly grew upward and expanded outward.

By 1800, the population of New York was 60,000, with most people living south of Canal Street. The area north of Canal was still completely rural. Sailing ships docked in the East River; shippers, importers, wholesalers, retailers, banks, and insurance companies were located on Pearl, Front, and South Streets. Merchants lived in townhouses on the Battery, Bowling Green, Greenwich Street, and lower Broadway. New York was a small town that you could walk across in about twenty minutes.

In 1818, a shipping line revolutionized transportation by starting America's first regularly scheduled service to Europe. Later, the Erie Canal, which was built in 1825, linked New York harbor with America's heartland, causing New York to become the most preeminent port in the country. In that

13

year, Governor DeWitt Clinton predicted that the city would, in the course of time, become "the emporium of commerce, the seat of manufacture, the focus of great moneyed operations, and the concentrating point of vast, disposable and accumulating capital." His vision was prophetic.

By the 1830's, New York became the nation's shipbuilding, meat packing, manufacturing, and financial capital. Then came the mass European immigrations of the late 1830's and 40's which changed forever the look and feel of the city.

As the city expanded to accommodate its exploding population, a grid system of streets and avenues was created throughout the entire island, leveling its hills and valleys and urbanizing what had once been rural forest land. Rivers and streams running through the island were filled in, streets were built, gas street lights were installed, and sewer and water supply systems were built.

There was a constant racket in the streets, congestion, and general bedlam. Factories fouled the air and the waters. The city was no longer a pleasant place to live.

Those who could, fled uptown to the emerging suburbs of Greenwich Village. Merchant homes were replaced with banks and office buildings, and twelve-story "skyscrapers" went up on Broadway and Wall Street.

In 1850, 515,547 people lived in Manhattan. By 1900, there were almost two million, and the city's northern boundary had expanded first to 14th Street, then to 23rd Street, and from there to 34th Street.

As the city grew, it became a kind of cultural center, run by commercial interests and catering to popular American tastes. In the early 1900's, Vaudeville, Tin Pan Alley, and new media, like radio and television, were centered here. The most prominent writers, artists, and musicians in the country moved to Manhattan to have proximity both to one another and to the sophisticated New York audiences.

By the end of World War II, with Europe in ruins and America a world power, New York became the world's capital, and Wall Street became the economic center of the capitalist world.

LOWER BROADWAY AND WALL STREET:
THE FINANCIAL DISTRICT

The Financial District - bordered by Fulton and Vesey streets in the north, Battery Park in the south, and bounded from east to west by Water and West Streets - is home to the New York Stock Exchange, various international banks and corporations and the Federal Reserve Bank of New York.

Throughout New York's history, this area has remained the center of commerce and the financial capital of the United States. From 1913 to 1930, it was also the site of the tallest building in the world; the Woolworth Building, which was known as the "Cathedral of Commerce". In the 1980's, New York reclaimed that title with the World Trade Center. Each of the World Trade Center's twin towers is 1377 feet high and together they dominate the lower Manhattan skyline.

The area from Trinity Church (which stands at the corner of Broadway and Wall street) to the southern tip of the island delineates the old Dutch village of New Amsterdam. In 1653, Governor Peter Stuyvesant built a wooden wall across the town's northern boundary to protect his people from the Indians and the English. Unfortunately, the English arrived by sea in 1664, and took New Amsterdam without firing a single shot. The English removed the wall in 1669, but the street came to be known as Wall Street in its memory.

Diagonally across from Wall Street, at 20 Broad St., is the New York Stock Exchange; the nation's largest organized market for stocks and bonds. The exchange was founded in 1792 by a group of 24 brokers who grew tired of conducting business "on the street." Until that time, all trading had

taken place at tables set up under the trees.

Eventually, after financing The War of 1812 and the Erie Canal, the Stock Exchange came to be taken seriously. Its present lavishly decorated building, designed in 1901, reflects the increased status of the Exchange by the turn of the twentieth century.

The Exchange's glory days, however, did not last long. On October 24th 1929, "Black Tuesday," the market collapsed because of investor and trader shortsightedness in allowing stock shares to be bought "on margin." This meant that the buyer only needed to pay a small part of the total cost of the stock, and could then borrow the rest while using those same shares as security. When the inevitable downturn occurred, a panicked chain reaction ensued and within days the "crash" had taken place.

Fortunes disappeared overnight and millions of people lost their life savings. Banks, businesses, and industries closed their doors as unemployment spiraled out of control. The Great Depression had begun. As a result, safety nets, put into place after the 1929 crash, today surround the market's operations, ensuring that a debacle like "Black Tuesday" can never happen again.

LANDMARKS AND HISTORIC SITES

The lower tip of Manhattan is where one can still get a feel for the city's origins and for the city as a port. Here are a few of the places that make the downtown area such a great place to live or visit:

THE SOUTH STREET SEAPORT

The South Street Seaport, with it's historic ocean-going Clipper ships, recreates a period in time during the nineteenth century when the East River was the country's busiest port, when ships laden with goods, sailed for Europe. After 1825, Clipper ships also sailed inland, through the Erie Canal, to deliver goods to the interior of the emerging nation. The Seaport was a bustling, thriving waterfront community then, and commerce was conducted in the warehouses, counting houses, and market buildings that lined its streets.

When, in 1890, steampowered ships became dominant and the deeper Hudson River became the main gateway to the city, the South Street Seaport began to decline in importance. The area deteriorated until the 1960's, when much of the district was razed to make way for new high rise buildings. In 1967, the South Street Seaport Museum was created to rehabilitate and preserve an 11 block area: from John Street to Dover Street, and from Pearl Street to the East River. The Seaport Museum encompasses the largest

fleet of historic, high-masted ships in the world, the famous Fulton Fish Market; and Schermerhorn Row. Schermerhorn Row, which runs from 2 to 18 Fulton street, is an original group of warehouses dating from 1811, built by Peter Schermerhorn. These warehouses, which now house restaurants, gift, and clothing shops, are the heart of the Seaport and, except for a few changes, have survived intact for almost two centuries. They give us an idea of what much of the area was like until just a few decades ago.

ELLIS ISLAND IMMIGRANT MUSEUM

Ellis Island, located just north of the Statue of Liberty, was the primary point of entry for immigrants coming into the

United States between 1892 and 1925. Recently restored to its original Beaux-Arts grandeur, it is one America's most historic landmarks.

The museum's cavernous main building exhibits displays with photographs of immigrants, personal documents, letters, and artifacts. An oral history tells of the entire immigration experience, from the beginning of the journey through to the arrival in America. There are two theaters, a library, special exhibit galleries, and the Learning Center, which contains a 16 screen interactive "videowall".

THE STATUE OF LIBERTY

At the base of The Statue of Liberty is Emma Lazaus' poem, "The New Colossus". "Give me your tired, your poor . . ." it reads, "I lift my lamp beside the golden door!" Frederic August Bartholdi's 'Liberty Enlightening the World', has stood 151 feet tall on her pedestal in New York harbor since 1884. Presented to the United States by France, it has been a powerful symbol of liberty and personal freedom for countless European immigrants. For many, it symbolizes the promise of a new life, and a new start in America.

Restored for its centennial in 1986, its pedestal museum contains exhibits on American immigration and on the history of the statue from its creation to its placement in New York harbor. One can climb the steps to the crown for the quintessential view of New York's skyline.

Both Ellis Island and the Statue of Liberty can be reached by ferry from Battery Park in Lower Manhattan.

THE BROOKLYN BRIDGE

Opened in 1883, the Brooklyn Bridge was one of the greatest engineering milestones of the 19th century. It was the first bridge to cross the East River, and the longest in the world when built.

Composed of two Gothic-style granite towers, from which four huge steel cables and a vast network of wires were suspended, it was built at a cost of 25 million dollars and 20 lives. Despite the cost, its construction opened a new era for the emerging city, and for the city's office workers. Thousands of people could walk from Brooklyn to their jobs in Manhatttan across the bridge's middle "boardwalk," which was elevated above traffic. The walk afforded beautiful views of both the river and the lower Manhattan skyline.

The Brooklyn Bridge remains one of the world's greatest suspension bridges, and is as spectacular an example of human industry and ingenuity today as it was when it was first built.

BACK IN MANHATTAN:

BATTERY PARK

At the tip of downtown Manhattan lies Battery Park: twenty three acres of greenery, statuary, and harbor views along its riverfront esplanade. It takes its name from the battery of cannons that once protected Manhattan on this spot. From the promenade, one can see Brooklyn Heights, Governor's Island, Staten Island, Liberty Island, and Ellis Island. Looking toward the city, the dramatic skyline of Lower Manhattan unfolds.

Inside the park there is a monument to Giovanni da Verrazano, the Italian navigator who first sailed into New York Harbor in 1524. Another monument, Castle Clinton, was originally built as West Battery Fort to provide protection against the British in the War of 1812. It was subsequently used as an Immigrant Landing Depot, from 1855-1890, a concert hall, and later an aquarium. Today, tickets for the Statue of Liberty and Ellis Island can be purchased here.

BOWLING GREEN PARK

Bowling Green Park, the city's first park, was the site of the transaction between Peter Minuit (first director general of the Dutch colony of New Amsterdam) and the Manhatto tribe of Native Americans. Supposedly the Dutchman bought the whole island for approximately $25 worth of trinkets. The Native Americans, however, didn't actually own the island, and had no concept of ownership similar to that of the Dutch.

By the 18th century, colonial Brits were bowling on the green and a statue of King George III had been erected. After the Declaration of Independence had been read in 1776, however, the statue was melted down for bullets and musket balls which were later fired at the British troops. In 1788, Bowling Green was the site of joyous celebration when New York ratified the new Constitution.

CITY HALL PARK AND CITY HALL

Two hundred years ago, when New York was a town of only 25,000 people, City Hall Park was the village common. On this spot, couriers brought news of revolution, and, in 1776, the Declaration of Independence was read to George Washington and his army. After City Hall was constructed, this triangular plot of land was renamed City Hall Park.

City Hall, because of its elegant proportions and details, may be the finest example of Federal period American architecture still in existence today. Built between 1802 and 1811, it reflects the idealistic vision of the early republic as Thomas Jefferson conceived it.

Used as the seat of New York's government since 1811, it's as lovely inside as out. Centering around a domed circular hall that holds a sweeping, curving double staircase, the building appears sculpted. Today, the second floor Governor's Room functions as a museum and portrait gallery.

FEDERAL HALL

When New York became the nation's capitol in 1789, the original Federal Hall became the place where George Washington was sworn in as the nation's first president. It was also the first capitol building under the new Constitution. When the capitol moved to Philadelphia in 1790, the old building was demolished. The present structure, reminiscent of a Greek Doric temple, was built in 1842. Built of marble and granite, it once served as a U.S. Customs House and Sub-Treasury building, before it was proclaimed a National memorial. The museum contains inaugural artifacts, including the actual bible Washington used upon his swearing in.

FRAUNCES TAVERN MUSEUM

Housed on the site of Fraunces Tavern and four adjacent buildings, the Museum contains the site of Washington's farewell to his officers in 1763, as well as a collection of prints, paintings, decorative arts, and artifacts relating to American history. A ten-minute audio-visual presentation also chronicles the city's early days.

TRINITY CHURCH AND ST. PAUL'S CHAPEL

The present edifice, built in 1846, is the third Episcopal Church on this site. Its neo-Gothic complex has the look of an English church, and its cemetary has tombstones which are over three centuries old. Famous Americans buried here include Alexander Hamilton, Robert Fulton, and William Bradford, publisher of our first newspaper, *The New York Gazette*.

When this church was built, its spire was the tallest structure in Manhattan. Every hour the church bell rings, as it has done for over a century and a half, providing an acoustic backdrop to the hum of business being conducted in the surrounding area.

ST. PAUL'S CHAPEL

St. Paul's Chapel, modeled on St. Martin's-in-the-Fields of London, was built in 1766 in the Georgian-classic revival style. The interior is gracefully proportioned and bathed in sunlight. The steeple was added in 1799, when the city was 150 years old. George Washington worshipped here and his pew has been preserved for posterity.

Points of Interest and How to Get There

HISTORIC ORCHARD STREET BARGAIN DISTRICT
Orchard Street between Canal & E. Houston Streets.
Tel: (212) 995-8258
Subway: Line **F** to Delancy St. Station,
Lines **J, M, Z** to Essex St. Station,
Lines **B, D, Q** to Grand St. Station,
Bus: M9, M14, M15, M101, M102, B39.

GREENWICH VILLAGE, WASHINGTON SQUARE
Subway: Lines **A, B, C, D, E, F, Q** to W. 4th St. & Washington Square,
Line **6** to Bleecker St. Station,
Line **1** to Christopher St. Station.
Bus: M1, M2, M3, M5, M6, M8, M18, M21.

SOHO
South of Houston Street.
Subway: Lines **C, E** to Spring St. Station,
Lines **N, R** to Prince St. Station.
Bus: M1, M5, M6, M21.

LITTLE ITALY
Mulberry St.
Subway: Lines **J, M, N, R, Z, 6** to Canal St. Station,
Lines **B, D, Q** to Grand St. Station.
Bus: M1, M101, M102, B51.

CHINATOWN
From Canal St. to City Hall.
Subway: Lines **J, M, N, R, Z, 6** to Canal St. Station,
Lines **B, D, Q** to Grand St. Station.
Bus: M1, M9, M101, M102, B51.

WORLD TRADE CENTER
West, Church, Versey, and Liberty Streets.
Observatory open 9:30am to 3:30pm.
Tel: (212) 453-7377
Subway: Lines **C, E** to World Trade Center Station.
Bus: M1, M6, M9, M10, M22.

WALL STREET, FINANCIAL DISTRICT
New York Stock Exchange:
20 Broad St., 3rd fl. Open Mon-Fri 10am to 4pm. (free)
American Stock Exchange:
78 Trinity Plaza. Open Mon-Fri 9:45am to 4pm. (free)
Federal Reserve Bank of New York:
Liberty St. across from Chase Manhattan Plaza.
Open Mon-Fri. Closed Bank Holidays. Tours by reservation only.
Tel: (212) 720-6109
For those locations listed above:
Subway: Lines **J, M, Z** to Broad St. Station,
Lines **2, 3, 4, 5** to Wall St. Station.
Bus: M1, M6, M15.

SOUTH STREET SEAPORT
Fulton and South Streets.
Subway: Lines **A, C** to Broadway & Nassau St. Station,
Lines **J, M, Z, 2, 3, 4, 5** to Fulton St. Station.
Bus: M15.

CITY HALL and CIVIC CENTER
Foley Square.
Subway: Lines **N, R** to City Hall Station.
Bus: M1, M6, M9, M15, M22, M101, M102, B51.

STATUE OF LIBERTY/LIBERTY ISLAND/ELLIS ISLAND
Statue of Liberty & Liberty Island:
Ferries from Battery Park every hour from 9am to 4pm. Closed Christmas Day.
Ellis Island Immigration Museum & National Monument:
Ferries from Battery Park every hour from 9:30am to 3:30pm. Closed Christmas Day.
For both islands:
Subway: Lines **4, 5** to Bowling Green Station,
Lines **1, 9** to South Ferry Station,
Lines **N, R** to Whitehall St. Station.
Bus: M1, M6, M15.

Manhattan Community Districts

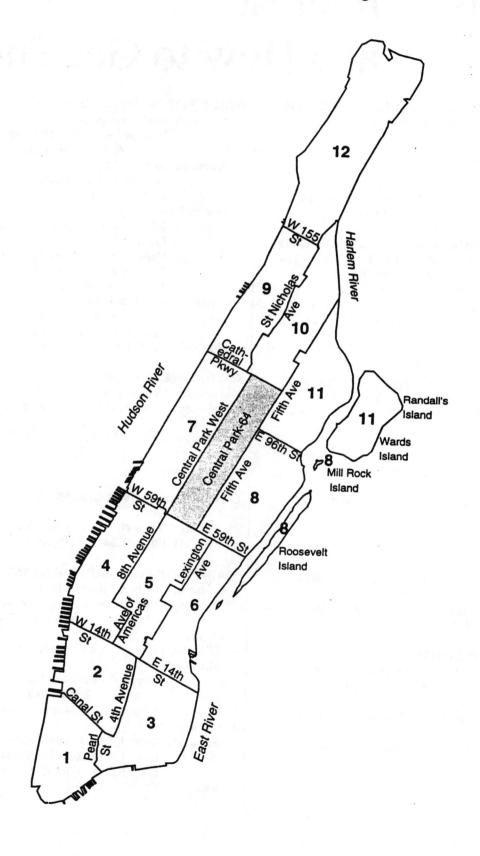

THE NEIGHBORHOODS

CHAPTER 1

Community District 1

Battery Park to Canal Street ~ East River to the Hudson River

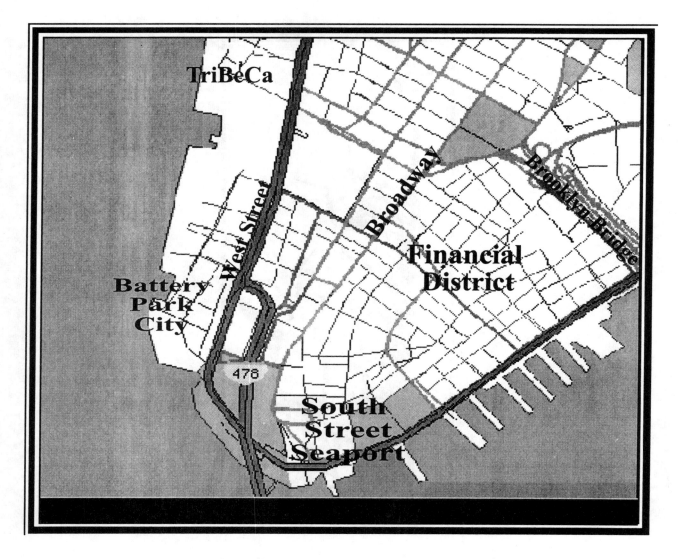

**Includes: Battery Park City,
Civic Center, Financial District,
South Street Seaport, TriBeCa.**

24

Manhattan Community District 1
Battery Park to Canal Street ~ East River to the Hudson River

DEMOGRAPHICS
Data presented here is taken from the 1990 Decennial Census

	Number	Percent
POPULATION		
Children (under age 10)	2,365	9.4
10-19 years	1,332	5.3
20-29 years	5,408	21.4
30-39 years	7,433	29.3
40-49 years	4,370	17.2
50-59 years	1,752	6.9
60+ years	2,706	10.7
TOTAL	25,366	100%
Male	13,988	55.1
Female	11,378	44.9
Median Age	*34.8*	
MARITAL STATUS		
Age 15 & Over		
Never married	9,418	42.1
Married	9,484	42.4
Separated, widowed, divorced	3,477	15.5
EDUCATION		
Less than 9 years	923	4.7
High school graduate	17,246	88.2
College graduate	10,937	56.0
Graduate Degree	5,505	28.8
INCOME		
Family	$54,590	
Per Capita	$37,228	
HOUSING UNITS		
TOTAL	13,127	100%
Vacant - for rent or sale	644	4.9
*Renter occupied	8,432	72.8
*Owner occupied	3,144	27.2

*Renter & owner occupied figures add up to the total <u>occupied</u> units,
therefore they do not equal the figure for total housing units.*

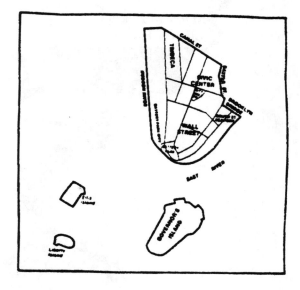

Neighborhood Amenities

Manhattan Community District 1

Parks and Playgrounds

Battery Park
**Battery Place, State and
Whitehall Streets**

City Hall Park
**Broadway, Park Row,
Chambers Street**

George Soilan Park
**Liberty and Marginal Streets,
Pier A**

Natural Areas & Others

Ellis Island
Ellis Island

Statue of Liberty
Liberty Island

Triangles, Malls, Strips and Sitting Areas

Beach Street Park
West Broadway, Beach Street

Bowling Green
Broadway, Whitehall Street

Foley Square Court House Plots
**Worth, Pearl and Centre
Streets**

Hanover Square Park
Hanover Square & Pearl Street

Park (Civil Court)
**Leonard, Centre and
Lafayette Streets**

Public Place
**Hudson River South of
Liberty Street**

Sitting Area (Duane Street)
Hudson and Duane Streets

Vietnam Veterans Plaza
**South and Broad Streets,
Old Slip**

Neighborhood Amenities

Police Precincts

Precinct 1
16 Ericsson Place
(212) 334-0611

Precinct 5
19 Elizabeth Street
(212) 334-0711

Precinct 6
233 West 10th Street
(212) 741-4811

Precinct 7
19 Pitt Street
(212) 477-7311

Precinct 9
321 East 5th Street
(212) 477-7811

Precinct 10
230 West 20th Street
(212) 741-8211

Precinct 13
230 East 21st Street
(212) 477-7411

Fire Department Facilities

Engine 3 - Ladder 12
146 West 19th Street

Engine 4 - Ladder 15
42 South Street

Engine 5
340 East 14th Street

Engine 6
49 Beekman Street

Engine 7 - Ladder 1
100 Duane Street

Engine 9 - Ladder 6
75 Canal Street

Engine 10 - Ladder 10
124 Liberty Street

Engine 14
14 East 18th Street

Engine 15
269 Henry Street

Engine 16 - Ladder 7
234 East 29th Street

Engine 17 - Ladder 18
25 Pitt Street

Engine 18
132 West 10th Street

Engine 24 - Ladder 5
227 Sixth Avenue

Engine 28 - Ladder 11
222 East 2nd Street

Engine 33 - Ladder 9
42 Great Jones Street

Engine 55
363 Broome Street

Ladder 3
108 East 13th Street

Ladder 8
14 North Moore Street

Marine Company 1
North River Pier A,
Bloomfield Street

Marine Company 6
East River, Grand Street

Post Offices

Knickerbocker
128 East Broadway
(212) 227-0089

Cooper
93 Fourth Avenue
(212) 254-1389

Bowling Green
25 Broadway
(212) 363-9490

Wall Street
73 Pine Street
(212) 269-2161

Church
90 Church Street
(212) 330-5247

Peter Stuyvesant
432 East 14th Street
(212) 677-2112

Madison Square
149 East 23rd Street
(212) 673-3771

Old Chelsea
217 West 18th Street
(212) 675-2415

Prince
103-05 Prince Street
(212) 226-7868

Canal Street
350 Canal Street
(212) 925-3378

Village
201 Varick Street
(212) 989-9741

Neighborhood Amenities

Hospitals

Bellevue Hospital Center
446 First Ave at 27th Street
(212) 562-4141

Beth Israel Medical Center
First Avenue at 16th Street
(212) 420-2000

Cabrini Medical Center
227 East 19th Street
(212) 995-6100

Hospital For Joint Diseases
301 East 17th Street
(212) 598-6000

New York Downtown Hospital
170 William Street
(212) 312-5000

**The New York Eye and
Ear Infirmary**
310 East 14th Street
(212) 979-4000

**St. Vincent's Hospital and
Medical Center**
153 West 11th Street
(212) 604-7000

Museums

Alternative Art Museum
594 Broadway
(212) 966-4444

Forbes Magazine Galleries
62 Fifth Ave at 12th Street
(212) 206-5548

**The Guggenheim Museum
SOHO**
576 Broadway @ Prince Street
(212) 423-3500

**The Lower East Side
Tenement Museum**
66 Allen Street
(212) 431-0233

Museum for African Art
593 Broadway
(212) 966-1313

**National Museum of the
American Indian
George Gustov Heye Center**
1 Bowling Green
(212)514-3700

**The Museum of Contemporary
Art**
583 Broadway
(212) 219-1355

New York Fire Museum
278 Spring Street
(212) 691-1303

Fraunces Tavern Museum
54 Pearl Street
(212) 425 1778

South Street Seaport Museum
South Street at Fulton Street
(212) 748-8600

**Museum of Chinese in the
Americas**
70 Mulberry Street
(212) 619-4785

Exit Art
548 Broadway
(212) 966-7745

Public Libraries

Hamilton Fish Park Library
415 East Houston Street
(212) 673-2290

Tompkins Square Library
331 East 10th Street
(212) 228-4747

Ottendorfer Branch Library
135 Second Ave at Ninth Street
(212) 674-0974

Seward Park Branch Library
192 East Broadway
(212) 673-4528

Muhlenberg Branch
209 West 23rd Street
(212) 924-1585

**Andrew Heiskell Library
for the Blind & Physically
Handicapped**
40 West 20th Street
(212)206-5400

Chatham Square Branch
33 East Broadway
(212) 964-6598

Epiphany Branch
228 East 23rd Street
(212) 679-2645

Hudson Park Branch
66 Leroy Street
(212) 243-6876

New Amsterdam Branch
9 Murray Street
(212) 732-8186

Jefferson Market
425 Sixth Avenue
(212) 243-4334

Columbus Branch
742 Tenth Avenue
(212) 586-5098

Neighborhood Amenities

Senior Centers

Bowery Resident Senior Nutrition Program
30 Delancey Street

Caring Community Senior Center
20 Washington Square

Community Lounge for Senior Citizens
155 East 22nd Street

Educational Alliance
197 East Broadway

Good Companion Senior Citizen
334 Madison Street

Grand Coalition Senior Center
80 Pitt Street

Greenwich Center
27 Barrow Street

Hamilton Madison Houses
50 Madison Street

Jacob Riis Houses
15-17 Bialystoker Place

John Paul II Friendship Center
101 East 7th Street

Laguardia Houses Center
280 Cherry Street

Lillian Wald Houses
12 Avenue D

Lira-Mott Street Senior Center
180 Mott Street

Lower East Side
P.S. 134~293 East Broadway

Our Lady of Pompeii
25 Carmine Street

NY Chinatown Senior Citizen Center
70 Mulberry Street

Project Open Door
115 Chrystie Street

Sirovich Senior Center
331 East 12th Street

St. Joseph's Nutrition Program
371 Sixth Avenue

St. Lukes in the Field
487 Hudson Street

Stein Senior Citizens Center
301 East 29th Street

UJC Adult Lucheon Club
15-17 Bialystoker Place

University Settlement Nutrition Program
189 Allen Street

Health Clubs

Bally Total Fitness
641 Sixth Ave at 20th Street
1-800-975-0808

Battery Park Swim & Fitness Center
375 South End Avenue at Liberty Street
(212) 321-1117

Better Bodies Inc.
22 West 19th Street
(212) 929-6789

Chelsea Piers Sports Center
Pier 60 West 23rd Street at Hudson River
(212) 336-6000

Crunch
404 Lafayette Street
(212) 614-0120

David Barton Gym
623 Broadway at Houston Street
(212) 420-0507

Dolphin Fitness Clubs
242 East 14th Street at Ave A
(212) 614-0390

New York Health and Raquet Ball Club
39 Whitehall Street
(212) 269-9800

New York Sports Clubs
151 Reade Street
(212) 571-1000

Peter Anthony Fitness
113 Mercer Street
(212) 274-9003

Physiofitness
584 Broadway at Prince Street
(212) 941-0503

Plus One Fitness Clinic
1 World Financial Center
200 Liberty Street at West Street
(212) 945-2525

The Mind Gym
37 West 19th Street
(212) 242-3800

BATTERY PARK CITY

Battery Park City is one of the "newest" neighborhoods in Manhattan, and is fast becoming one of the city's most desirable places to live. Built on a ninety-two acre landfill excavated during the construction of the World Trade Center, Battery Park City's overall design is inspired by New York's best traditional architecture. Many of the buildings are clad in stone and brick, and have varied rooflines and prominent cornice lines which link them visually to older surrounding buildings.

Filling a need for middle class housing in lower Manhattan, Battery Park City is constantly evolving as new buildings go up while others are in the planning stage. Presently, there are eleven condominiums and eight rental buildings. Thirty percent of the ninety-two acre development is set aside for the construction of parks, ornamental gardens, yacht basins, and other recreational areas.

The 1.2 mile long Esplanade which runs alongside the Hudson River is the first river front park built in Manhattan since the 1950's. It features a wrought iron railing similar to one found in Carl Schurtz Park, hexagonal paving blocks, Victorian lights, and long green benches. South of the Esplanade and along the south cove portion is a walkway which was designed to imitate the wooden piers, natural rock outcroppings, and wild plants that dominated the shoreline of 18th and 19th century New York. Both the Esplanade and the walkway are favorites of joggers, strollers, and fishermen.

The streets of Battery Park City are continuations of the city's grid and provide an unobstructed view of the river. They also integrate the community into the rest of the downtown area. Chambers Street, Vesey, and other streets extend from City Hall into the Battery Park community; West Street runs north-south, and borders the area on its eastern perimeter. Wide streets and sidewalks edged in cobblestones are as much a feature of the neighborhood as are the different types of trees that line each street.

Among its major attractions are the views from the Esplanade including the Statue of Liberty, Ellis Island, and the New Jersey shoreline. The World Financial Center, in Battery Park City, is a complex of four office towers designed by Cesar Pelli and Associates, and is located on fourteen acres of land which integrate office, retail, and public spaces. The entire complex can be traversed indoors via covered pedestrian bridges. The Center's public spaces include the dramatic Winter Garden Atrium, the Courtyard (a three story European-style piazza), and a 3.5 acre park with lush landscaping and reflecting pools.

The Winter Garden, a beautifully designed crystal palace, features an ornate marble grand staircase and marble patterned floors. Inside the 125 foot high glass, vaulted structure, you can find upscale shopping and good restaurants as well as varied exhibitions and performances. The only grove of sixteen soaring tropical palm trees in New York can be found here. At fifty feet tall, they are the garden's floral centerpiece.

When weather permits, lunchtime and evening dining is available outside on the plaza overlooking the North Cove Basin. The Plaza, a 3.5 acre landscaped park, is the first such park built on the Hudson River and is a landmark in public space design. Several site sculptures are located here, as well as throughout the residential portion of Battery Park City. Visual and performing arts programs are often held here in summer.

The apartments in Battery Park City are mainly studios and one bedrooms, with prices determined by square footage, and the degree to which a unit faces the Hudson River. Many units face the river while others have views of the downtown skyline. Two and three bedroom apartments are also available. Rector Place, which enjoys the landscaped view of Rector Park, presents a showcase of some of the best new residential architecture in the city. It consists of ten rental and condominium buildings varying in height and size. Most of the buildings are placed along the western edge to provide a transition in scale from larger buildings in the back to lower buildings along the water's edge. Designed to compete with the uptown market, Rector Place features concierges, state of the art security systems, and health clubs. Many of its 2,200 rental, co-op, and condominium units are small, but well laid out, and most come with marble bathrooms.

Gateway Plaza, a 1,712 unit rental complex opened in 1982, was the first original development and is located just south of the Yacht Harbor. The rents at Gateway Plaza and Rector Place are for middle incomes, whereas at Parc Place, located on South End Avenue adjacent to Rector Park, the rents are a little higher. The list of amenities at Parc Place includes a 24 hour doorman/concierge, valet service, pool, health club, and rooftop garden. Apartments are available furnished or unfurnished, and offer views of the river or of the downtown Manhattan skyline.

Hudson Tower, a 133 unit waterfront condominium, consists of two buildings, a fifteen story hi-rise connected to a five story structure which features six duplex maisonette apartments. Most of the apartments are one, two, or three bedrooms and have river views. Penthouses, which have large terraces, also overlook the water. Other buildings include

Battery Point, the Cove Club, Liberty View, the Soundings, and River Rose. All of the buildings are luxury and have concierges and health clubs.

Soon, ground will be broken for two thousand additional apartments in eight new buildings, a Ritz-Carlton and an Embassy suites hotel, an addition to the Museum of Jewish Heritage and a home for the Skyscraper Museum, two public schools, four ferry slips, a 15-screen multiplex movie theatre and stores. In fact, so many new projects are under consruction or being planned, that the 92-acre landfill is fast running out of room. In the north section, new construction will feature family-sized two- and three-bedroom units to encourage more families with children to settle here.

School District 2, which includes Battery Park City, ranks second on city wide standardized reading tests. Many children in Battery Park City attend PS 234 (in Tribeca), a highly rated school with an extensive arts program. Another good school in Tribeca is the Early Childhood Center, a kindergarten through second grade school. Two new schools that have recently opened in Battery Park City are PS 89, for kindergarten through fifth grade, and IS 89, for sixth through eighth grade. Stuyvesant High School, an excellent school which admits students through a rigorous entrance exam, is located at 345 Chambers Street, at Battery Park City's northern border.

Representing urban planning at its best, Battery Park City is at once one of the most upscale neighborhoods in the city and one of its most humane. There is a sense of repose here, and safety, because it has its own security and limited access for cars and pedestrians. Many young professionals who have jobs on Wall Street or in the World Trade Center have settled here, as have young families.

WALL STREET
The City's Oldest Neighborhood Is New Again

One does not normally think of the downtown area—including Wall Street, the Stock Exchange, and the World Trade Center—as a residential neighborhood. However, since the implementation of the mayor's Economic Revitalization Plan for lower Manhattan, approximately 2,000 new residential units have been created and 7,000 more are expected by the year 2002. Although the majority of units are luxury rentals, condominiums are being built as well. While condo prices in the Wall Street area are about $100 a square foot less than in neighboring areas today, prices will rise as the area develops.

The Alliance for Downtown New York has played a major role in this redevelopment. Its goal has been to "create and promote a safe, live-work, totally-wired community, which will showcase the nation's most historic neighborhood and be the financial capital of the world for the 21st century."

In keeping with this ideal, the mayor's office and business leaders have worked together to create the New York Information Technology Center at 55 Broad Street. This center provides modern office space at affordable rents to emerging high-tech and new media companies. It is hoped that with New York's technological boom, the downtown district can turn into "the urban model for the information age," and help shape the post-industrial city to come.

Renovated pre-war buildings and modern downtown office buildings are newly wired for wide-band Internet access. At the same time,

developers are creating large loft-like live/work spaces. With larger spaces, high-tech wiring, luxury amenities, and interesting pre-war details, Wall Street's newest conversions are renting quickly. Most of the luxury rental buildings are already filled and have waiting lists. Studio rents range from approximately $1,400 to $2,000, one-bedrooms from $1,900 to $2,500, and two-bedrooms from $2,700 to $3,700 in this area. Three-bedrooms are rare.

As the neighborhood's popularity grows, local vendors are adjusting to meet resident needs by staying open later and by opening their stores on weekends. Though this emerging neighborhood does not yet have many grocers, coffee shops, pharmacies, dry cleaners or other services, there are enough now to make living here relatively easy. As the neighborhood expands, so too will the retail market.

The Wall Street area is always clean thanks to the Downtown Alliance, which provides crews to clean the streets. The Alliance also provides a 24-hour patrol service whose duties include providing protection for Wall Street employees and residents.

"Fine dining" is only a short walk away in Chinatown, Little Italy, Soho or Tribeca. Carmine's Restaurant, at 144 Beekman Street, is a neighborhood favorite - "the place to go" on Friday night. However, should the neighborhood grow as quickly as Tribeca and Soho did, there will be cafes and restaurants everywhere, and the present "serenity" of the evening may soon become a thing of the past.

DOWNTOWN CHIC WITH UPTOWN CLASS: BEST NEW BUILDINGS

The Wall Street area has always been the city of the future. It was true for the Dutch traders, the English, and for the Americans who formed the New York Stock Exchange in 1792. Once the world's first commercial district to be wired for electricity, it is today, the first to be wired with wide-band ISDN lines for internet traffic. Some of the best new and converted buildings in this new and exciting 24-hour urban "village" are featured below.

71 Broadway

71 Broadway is a landmark neoclassical building, over 100 years old. It has been completely renovated. The apartments have eight to twelve foot windows which view Trinity Church and the Hudson River (to the North and West, respectively). It has all of the features of a luxury building, including a 24-hour concierge, a health club, a laundry room, tenant storage, and even a lounge with a kitchen/wet bar, billiard table, and large-screen TV. The apartments themselves feature GE-equipped kitchens, large walk-in-closets, and fiber optic wiring, ISDN and T1 capabilities, high speed internet access, multiple phone lines, and satellite or cable hook-ups.

Studios, which range from 537 to 650 square feet, rent for approximately $1,600 to $2,200. One bedroom apartments are in the $2,000 to $3,000 range; they run from 600 to 800 square feet. Both of these sizes are available with lofts. A two bedroom apartment with two full baths (1,000 to 1,230 square feet) will cost approximately $2,800 to $3,700 per month. The two bedroom duplex penthouses are $4,400 to $4,700. These may have a roof top terrace, juliet balconies, or winding staircases, and range from 1,275 to 1,309 square feet.

71 Broadway's on-site rental office may be reached at (212) 344-7171.

25 Broad Street: The Exchange

The grand white marble lobby of this building betrays its neoclassical origins. **The Exchange** is over 100 years old, and was once one of the world's largest office buildings. Completely renovated, it offers all luxury building amenities, such as a 24-hour doorman and concierge, valet, dry-cleaning, video rental, and housekeeping services, a staffed health club, business center, roof deck, private storage, and laundry on every floor. The apartments feature a minimum of eight telecommunications lines and GE-furnished kitchens.

This building has one-, two-, and three-bedroom units. The one bedrooms, just over 800 square feet, start at $1,850. The two bedrooms are 1,050+ square feet and start at $2,600. Three bedrooms start at $4,800. They are 2,600+ square feet.

The buildings marketing agent is Crescent Heights. They may be reached at (212) 835-2500.

80 John Street

80 John Street is a 1920's Art Deco building, refurbished and replete with brass chandeliers and elevator doors. It has a 24-hour concierge, and you may take an elevator directly from the building to the attended parking garage. All apartments have designer kitchens and baths and plenty of closet space; any sized apartment may have a terrace.

Studios run from approximately $1,400 to $2,000, one bedrooms are $1,850 to $2,700. Two bedroom apartments rent for approximately $2,500 to $4,000, and three bedrooms for $3,200 to $3,500.

There is an on-site rental office which is open seven days a week. It can be reached at (212) 344-1737.

55 Liberty Street

This thirty three story building is an historical landmark. Built around 1906, it is one of the tallest residential conversions in lower Manhattan and was one of the first buildings downtown to have a doorman. The apartments have high ceilings, and many come with a private washer and dryer.

The apartments in this building range from studios to full-floor lofts. The lofts may run as high as 2,500 square feet, and rent from a little over $2,000 to around $4,000. There are also duplex lofts.

33

114 Liberty Street: The Engineering Building

Built around 1901, this is a brick and granite condominium building that has been recently renovated. The units are all full floor lofts. Some of the three bedroom lofts run approximately 5,500 square feet; the penthouse unit is 7,000 square feet, and has a large terrace. The apartments run largely in the $1 to $3 million range.

117 Beekman Street

Converted to a condominium in 1983, this building was constructed around 1900. It has 26 apartments and offers a 24-hour doorman. The penthouse is 1,800 square feet, has a wrap terrace, fireplace, and 16 large windows. Other units have both terraces and fireplaces, as well.

170 John Street: Ships Chandlery

This historical landmark was a granite-fronted, Greek revival warehouse—one of very few remaining in lower Manhattan. It has been exquisitely restored to maintain its 1840's appearance, and is today a six story residential condominium, a short walk from the Seaport. The units are mostly two- or three-bedroom duplexes. The three-bedroom apartments run to around 1,500 square feet, the two bedroom units closer to 1,200. Some of the apartments have terraces.

3 Hanover Square

This building sits on Hanover Square, one of the city's historic revival areas. The streets in front are to be repaved with granite cobblestones, the sidewalks with blue stone. Historic lampposts are to replace existing lighting. This particular building was built around 1928 and was converted into a residential co-op in 1984. Units range from studios to mini-lofts. The mini-lofts are large (900 square feet) and have twenty foot ceilings. Every unit has its own storage room. Apartments run from around $70,000 to $200,000.

45 Wall Street

The 435 apartments in this building range from studios to three bedroom units. Some of the apartments are designed to be live/work areas, and have two entrances. All of the apartments come with multiple phone lines, ISDN and T1 capabilities, fiber-optic wiring, and high-speed internet access. They are spacious and have high ceilings; many apartments also have terraces.

The building offers all of the usual luxury amenities: a 24-hour doorman, concierge, valet, conference center, outdoor terrace, gym, golf range, and a direct elevator to the attended parking garage. There is also a penthouse lounge, complete with billiard table, large-screen TV, and enormous wrap-around terrace.

The on-site rental office may be reached at (212) 797-7000.

200 Water Street

This very new building (it was completed in 1998) is situated right at the South Street Seaport. It has studio through two bedroom units. Some of the apartments have terraces, and they are all wired for internet access. The building itself offers a rooftop terrace, health club, doorman, concierge, valet, and laundry facility.

The on-site rental office is run by Rockrose Development. Information can be obtained by calling their main number at (212) 697-4422.

56 Beaver Street

A landmark building and one of the first downtown office buildings to be converted to residential use, it has nine stories and thirty seven units. They are all live/work units which range from one- to two-bedrooms. The one-bedrooms are approximately 750 square feet, the two-bedrooms 1,500 square feet. The building has a roof garden and exercise room.

NEIGHBORHOOD BUSINESSES

BANKS

- **Apple Bank For Savings**
Maiden Lane at Water Street, (800) 722-6888

- **Bank Of New York**
45 Wall Street at William Street, 495-1784

- **Chase Manhattan Bank**
331-337 South End Avenue at Gateway Plaza, 935-9935
55 Water Street at Old Slip Street, 935-9935
16 Wall Street at Nassau Street, 935-9935
120 World Trade Center at Liberty Street, 935-9935
110 Maiden Lane at Pearl Street, 935-9935
214 Broadway at Fulton Street, 935-9935

- **Citibank**
1 Broadway at Bowling Green, 627-3999
120 Broadway at Cedar Street, 627-3999
250 Broadway at City Hall, 627-3999
111 Wall Street at South Street, 627-3999
101 World Trade Center at Liberty Street, 627-3999

- **Marine Midland Bank**
110 William Street at John Street, 608-7877

BARS & CLUBS

- **AJ Kelly's**
6 Stone Street at Whitehall Street, 425-1700

- **Beckett's Bar and Grill**
78 Pearl Street at Hanover Square, 269-1001

- **Café Remy**
104 Greenwich Street at Hector Street, 267-4646

- **The Greatest Bar On Earth**
1 World Trade Center, 107th Floor, Liberty Street at Church Street, 524-7000

- **Johnney's Fish Grill**
250 Vesey Street at 4 World Financial Center, 385-0333

- **John Street Bar and Grill**
17 John Street at Broadway, 349-4659

- **Moran's**
103 Washington Street at Rector Street, 732-2020

- **North Star Pub**
93 South Street at Fulton Street, 509-6757

- **Pearl Bar**
79 Pearl Street at Hanover Square, 514-6000

- **Raccoon Lodge**
59 Warren Street at West Broadway, 766-9656

- **Ryan's Sports Bar and Restaurant**
46 Gold Street at Fulton Street, 385-6044

- **St. Charlie's Café**
4 Albany Street at Greenwich Street, 964-6940

- **White Horse Tavern**
25 Bridge Street at Whitehall Street, 668-9046

BOOKSTORES
- **Borders, Books & Music**
5 World Trade Center at Church Street, 839-8049

COFFEE BARS

- **The Country Café**
80 Maiden Lane at Pearl Street, 742-9456

- **New World Coffee**
100 Wall Street at Water Street, 742-8644

- **New York Coffee Station**
70 Pine Street at Water Street, 514-5011

- **Pasqua Coffee Bar**
250 Vesey Street, 3 World Financial Center
at West Street, 587-9512
100 Church Street at Broadway, 513-1006

- **Starbucks**
24 State Street at Battery Park Place,
482-1180

- **Timothy's Coffee Shop**
7 Hanover Square at Water Street, 742-0646

- **Timothy's Espresso**
120 Broadway at Cedar Street, 374-9647

- **Timothy's World Coffees**
40 Broad Street at Exchange Place, 248-0902

HEALTH CLUBS

- **Battery Park Swim and Fitness Center**
375 South End Avenue at Liberty Street,
321-1117

- **Executive Fitness Center**
3 World Trade Center at Liberty Street,
466-9266

- **New York Health and Racquet Club**
39 Whitehall Street at Water Street,
269-9800
Pier 13-14, Wall Street at South Street,
422-9300

- **New York Sports Club**
30 Wall Street at Nassau Street, 482-4800

- **Plus One Fitness Clinic**
1 World Financial Center, 200 Liberty Street
at West Street, 945-2525

PHARMACIES

- **Battery Park Pharmacy Inc**.
327 South End Avenue at Albany Street,
912-0555

- **Duane Reade**
80 Maiden Lane at William Street, 509-8890
37 Broadway at Exchange Place, 425-8460
50 Pine Street at William Street, 425-3720
67 Broad Street at Beaver Street, 943-3690
1 Whitehall Street at Stone Street, 509-9020
95 Wall Street at Water Street, 363-5830
5 World Trade Center at Vesey Street,
912-0998

TRIBECA

Tribeca is one of the most historic areas of the city, yet its name is almost brand new. An acronym for "TRIangle BElow CAnal Street," Tribeca includes the area that is west of Broadway and south of Canal Street.

Before the 1970's, this area, which had previously been called Washington Market, was a manufacturing center and the city's leading wholesale produce center. Recently, though, it has been transformed into a vibrant and growing residential community.

Artists were the pioneers who led the way. They first discovered Tribeca's abandoned cast-iron warehouses, where rents were low, light was good, and space was abundant. Unfazed by the desolate streets, they were willing to invest their money and sweat into installing kitchens and bathrooms in the raw warehouse spaces. By the mid 1980's, property values began to rise as professionals and developers sought out these huge lofts that were within reach of Wall Street. Many apartments had views of the Hudson River and midtown skyline.

Some of the existing buildings were converted to co-ops and condominiums, and by 1988, Independence Plaza, a three building, 1,330 unit rental complex was built. Young professionals began to move into the new plaza complex and into the surrounding neighborhood. Soon, Tribeca's real estate began to approach that of SoHo's in desirability and price.

In 1970, Tribeca had a population of 273 people; by 1998 there were more than 10,000. Among the most notable residents are Robert DeNiro, Brian DePalma, Harvey Keitel and Martin Scorsese. David Letterman owns a loft here and John Kennedy Jr. sold his when he married Carolyn Bessette-Kennedy.

A rich selection of galleries, nightclubs, and restaurants have opened to accommodate Tribeca's new residents. Some of the city's finest restaurants are located here: Chanterelle, Bouley, Montrachet, Nobu, and the Tribeca Grill, to name a few. A great number of bars and cafes can also be found along Hudson and Greenwich Streets.

Community efforts, in the last 10 years, have brought a new public library and a new public school building (PS 234) to the district. The Washington Market school, a non-profit, Montessori-influenced, early childhood center, is located on Hudson Street, and a combined elementary and middle school is scheduled to open soon.

On warm days, families head toward Washington Market Park, a small green oasis, or to pier 25, a public recreation area built atop 540 cubic yards of sand, which has three beach volleyball courts and a miniature golf course.

LOFT LIVING IN TRIBECA

Hi-ceilinged, cavernous spaces, huge windows and good light are the draw that brings people from all walks of life to Tribeca. Originally, the last bastion of struggling artists who converted illegal commercial spaces into live/work areas, lofts are the darlings of real estate today and Tribeca is the fashionable place to be.

Newer lofts are typically finished with luxurious materials; kitchens have granite countertops and sub-zero refrigerators, bathrooms are complete with vanities, marble and tile, and there is central air-conditioning and architectural details. The end result is often beautiful, functional and highly desirable.

Because they are such a booming market, lofts are often unaffordable for many people. The average price per square foot of a loft in Tribeca (in mid-1998) was $418; in Soho $361; in Flatiron/Gramercy $322 and in Chelsea/Greenwich Village $306. Ranging from approximately $400,000 to well over $1 million, downtown lofts attract a new kind of upscale buyer - typically professionals; lawyers, Wall Streeters, investment bankers, and owners of large corporations.

Regardless of location, the loft market is growing. New areas in the city are opening up with loft conversions now taking place in the far west midtown area and in Brooklyn. These areas may offer better opportunities for grand space at more affordable prices to most buyers.

TRIBECA AND SOHO NEIGHBORHOOD BUSINESSES

BANKS

- **Republic National Bank of New York**
207 Varick Street at Houston Street,
718- 488-4050

- **Citibank**
415 Broadway at Canal Street, 627-3999
108 Hudson Street at North Moore Street,
627-3999

- **Chase Manhattan Bank**
423 Canal Street at Varick Street, 935-9935
345 Hudson Street at King Street, 935-9935

BARS & CLUBS

- **Bubble Lounge**
228 West Broadway at White Street,
431-3433

- **City Wine & Cigar Co.**
62 Laight Street at Greenwich Street,
334-2274

- **The Knitting Factory**
74 Leonard Street at Church Street, 219-3006

- **Liquor Store Bar**
235 West Broadway at White Street,
226-7121

- **Lush**
110 Duane Street at Church Street, 766-1275

- **Milady's Bar and Restaurant**
162 Prince Street at Thompson Street,
226-9069

- **Mitch's Place**
134 Reade Street at Hudson Street, 226-8928

- **Naked Lunch**
17 Thompson Street at Grand Street,
343-0828

- **Nancy Whiskey Pub**
1 Lispenard Street at West Broadway,
226-9943

- **Pravda**
281 Lafayette Street at Prince Street,
226-4696

- **Puffy's Tavern**
81 Hudson Street at Harrison Street,
766-9159

- **S.O.B.'s**
204 Varick Street at West Hudson Street,
243-4940

- **Vinyl**
6 Hubert Street at Hudson Street, 343-1379

- **Wetlands**
161 Hudson Street at Laight Street, 966-4225

- **Yoffa's**
353 Greenwich Street at 19 Harrison Street,
274-9403

BOOKSTORES

- **Oscar Wilde Memorial Bookshop**
15 Christopher Street at Sixth Avenue,
255-8097

COFFEE BARS

- **Café Borgia II**
161 Prince Street at Thompson Street, 677-1850

- **Café Gitane**
242 Mott Street at Prince Street, 334-9552

- **Café Le Gamin**
50 MacDougal Street at Houston Street, 254-4678

- **Café Mona Lisa**
282 Bleecker Street at Seventh Avenue South, 929-1262

- **Café Palermo**
148 Mulberry Street at Grand Street, 431-4205

- **Dean & Deluca Café**
560 Broadway at Prince Street, 226-6800

- **In the Black Espresso Bar**
180 Varick Street at King Street, 807-8322

- **New World Coffee**
412 West Broadway at Prince Street, 431-1015

- **Sosa Borella**
460 Greenwich Street at Watts Street, 431-5093

- **Starbucks**
78 Spring Street at Crosby Street, 219-2961

HEALTH CLUBS

- **Hanson Fitness**
63 Greene Street at Spring Street, 431-7682

- **New York Sports Club**
151 Reade Street at Hudson Street, 571-1000

- **Peter Anthony Fitness**
113 Mercer Street at Spring Street, 274-9003

- **Plus One Fitness**
106 Crosby Street at Prince Street, 334-1116

- **Physiofitness**
584 Broadway at Prince Street, 941-0503

MOVIE THEATERS

- **Angellica Film Center**
18 W. Houston at Mercer Street, 777-FILM #531

- **Film Forum**
Houston Street at Sixth Avenue, 727-8110

- **Anthology Film Archives**
Second Avenue and Second Street, 505-5110

- **Screening Room**
Varick Street at Canal Street, 334-2100

PHARMACIES

- **Citizen Health & Beauty Aids**
541 Broadway at Spring Street, 219-3467

- **Duane Reade**
305 Broadway at Duane Street, 227-6168
598 Broadway at west Houston Street, 343-2567

- **Independence Pharmacy**
352 ½ Greenwich Street at Franklin Street, 406-3700

Community District 2
Canal Street to East 14th Street
Bowery to the Hudson River

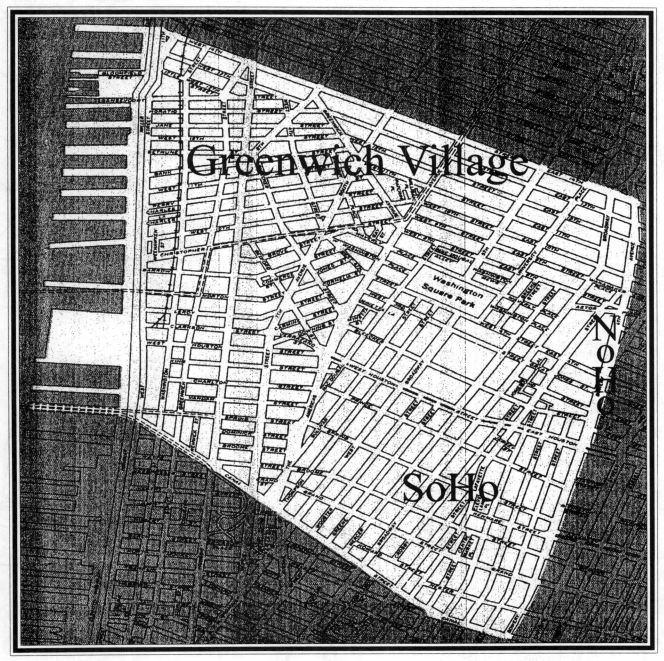

Includes: SoHo, NoHo, Greenwich Village

Manhattan Community District 2
Canal Street to East 14th Street ~ Bowery to the Hudson River

DEMOGRAPHICS

Data presented here is taken from the 1990 Decennial Census

	Number	Percent
POPULATION		
Children (under age 10)	*4,863*	*5.2*
10-19 years	5,854	6.2
20-29 years	20,014	21.3
30-39 years	22,163	23.6
40-49 years	16,157	17.2
50-59 years	9,327	9.9
60+ years	15,727	16.7
TOTAL	94,105	100%
Male	47,273	50.2
Female	46,832	49.8
Median Age	*37.3*	
MARITAL STATUS		
Age 15 & Over		
Never married	44,811	51.2
Married	28,260	32.3
Separated, widowed, divorced	14,386	16.4
EDUCATION		
Less than 9 years	6,265	8.3
High school graduate	64,542	85.8
College graduate	44,471	59.1
Graduate Degree	21,582	28.7
INCOME		
Family	$54,590	
Per Capita	$37,228	
HOUSING UNITS		
TOTAL	56,053	100%
Vacant - for rent or sale	*2,430*	*4.4*
*Renter occupied	40,189	77.1
*Owner occupied	11,914	22.9

**Renter & owner occupied figures add up to the total <u>occupied</u> units,
therefore they do not equal the figure for total housing units.*

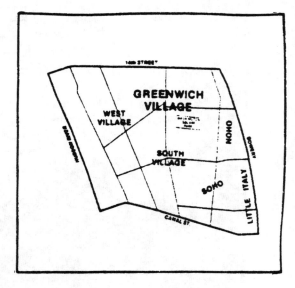

Neighborhood Amenities

Manhattan Community District 2

Parks and Playgrounds

Coporal John A. Seravalli Playground
Hudson, Gansevoort & Horatio Streets

Downing Street Playground
Downing to Carmine Streets,
6th Avenue

James J. Walker Park
Hudson, Leroy, Clarkson Streets, Seventh Avenue

Playground
Minetta Lane,
West 3rd Street & 6th Avenue

Playground
Spring & Mulberry Streets

Playground (New Abingdon)
Hudson, Bleecker & West 11th Streets

Thompson Street Playground
Thompson Street, Spring-Prince Street

Washington Square Park
Fifth Avenue, Waverly Place,
West 4th & MacDougal Streets

Triangles, Malls, Strips and Sitting Areas

Abingdon Square (T)
Ht Wadsworth, Miller Field

Christopher Park
Christopher, Grove & West 4th Streets

Duarte Square Public Place
6th Avenue, Canal & Grand Streets

Father Demo Square
6th Avenue, Bleecker & Carmine Streets

Father Fagan Park
E/S 6th Avenue, Prince & Spring Streets

Grass Strip
S/E/C Minetta Lane & 6th Avenue

Jackson Square (T)
8th Street, Greenwich Avenue, Horatio Street

Kenmare Square
Kenmare & Lafayette Street, Cleveland Place

McCarthy Square
7th Avenue, Charles Street & Waverly Place

Park Strips
Bleecker & Mercer Streets, West Broadway

Sitting Area
N/E/C 6th Avenue & Minetta Lane

Siting Area
S/S West Houston Streeet, 6th Avenue

Sitting Area
6th Avenue, King & Charlton Street

Athletic Facilities

Gymnasium & Public Bath
Carmine & Leroy Streets,
7th Avenue

Recreation Area
Thompson & Canal Streets,
6th Avenue

Recreation Area
West Houston & MacDougal Streets, Sixth Avenue

Recreation
6th Avenue, West 3rd & West 4th Streets

Natural Areas & Others

Greenwich Village Community Garden
West 9th Street,
Ave of Americas

Public Theatre
Lafayette & East 4th Streets, Astor Place

Sheridan Square Viewing Garden
Washington Place, Grove, West 4th & Barrow Streets

IF YOU'RE THINKING OF LIVING IN SOHO

SoHo, the forty block area bounded by Broadway, Canal Street, Sixth Avenue, and Houston Street, is Manhattan's resident art community. It is where most of New York's visual arts and much of its new dance are created.

An acronym for it's location, <u>So</u>uth of <u>Ho</u>uston Street, SoHo has been transformed from a bleak industrial area into a busy marketplace within the last thirty years. It is renowned for its many fine art galleries, restaurants, antique furniture stores and one-of-a-kind boutiques.

On weekdays, its cobblestoned streets are alive with pedestrian and vehicular traffic, while on weekends, flea markets, street vendors, and musicians line the sidewalks. The streets are named rather than numbered, thereby adding to the charm of the neighborhood.

In keeping with it's nineteenth century industrial history, the highest concentration of cast-iron architecture in the country is found in SoHo. The cast-iron technique uses iron beams rather than heavy walls to carry the weight of the floors, thereby allowing the building facade to be opened up with large windows. Rich detail and ornamentation are often found on the buildings' cast-iron facade.

Throughout the nineteenth century, SoHo was a center of light industry. The district was known for its clothing manufacturers, furriers, and doll and box makers. During this time, SoHo acquired its nickname "Hell's Hundred Acres" for the many fires that raged through its overcrowded and cramped streets. The most infamous of these fires was known as the Triangle Shirt-waist Factory Fire of 1911 where an immigrant workforce of young girls died because they had no means of escaping the fire.

By the end of World War II, most of these companies moved north, leaving behind empty warehouses that only poor artists were willing to rent. The artists installed bathrooms and kitchens thereby converting the abandoned factories into living lofts and studios. In 1973, the twenty-six block area from Crosby Street to West Broadway, and from Canal Street to Houston Street, was designated a historic zone. This led to the transformation of SoHo into an upscale and lively artistic community.

Gentrification soon followed as several major uptown art galleries moved to the area. When the Guggenheim Museum opened a SoHo branch on Broadway, money and prestige arrived as well. By the 1980's SoHo had become a fashionable community. It was rich with upscale shopping, fine dining, some of the most impressive architecture in the city, and was also home to many small theatres, visual art, dance and musical performances.

SoHo real estate is dominated by the large lofts and studios that were once workshops and warehouses. Today, a loft in SoHo means money; what used to be a bargain residence may now cost upwards of half a million dollars. Prices are based on the amount of functional space, ceiling height, and the overall condition of the building and apartment.

One drawback to family life in SoHo is that the community has few schools, churches and movie theatres, and many of it's stores are pricey boutiques and art galleries. There are also a lot of tourists, noise, and traffic. For these reasons, if you are not qualified to live in an Artist-in-Residence loft or are unable to afford a market-price apartment in SoHo, you might do better to consider buying in neighborhoods adjacent to SoHo where spaces may be cheaper.

ART GALLERIES IN SOHO

Amos Eno
594 Broadway
226-5342

Anne Phenab
81 Greene Street
219-2007

Artists Space
38 Greene Street
226-3970

Atlantic
475 Broome Street
219-3183

Barbara Gladstone
99 Greene Street
431-3334

Bess Cutler
379 West Broadway
219-1577

Blum Helman Warehouse
80 Greene Street
226-8770

Brooke Alexander
59 Wooster Street
925-4338

Bruce R. Lewin
136 Prince Street
431-4750

Charles Cowles
420 West Broadway
925-3500

Condeso/Lawler
524 Broadway
219-1283

Curt Marcus
578 Broadway
226-3200

Dia Center for the Arts
393 West Broadway
925-9397

DCA
420 West Broadway
334-3331

Dyansen of SoHo
462 West Broadway
982-3638

Edward Thorp
103 Prince Street
431-6880

EM Donahue
560 Broadway
226-1111

Exit Art
548 Broadway
966-7745

Fawbush
76 Grand Street
274-0660

Feature
76 Grand Street
941-7077

55 Mercer
55 Mercer Street
226-8513

First St
560 Broadway
226-9127

Franklin Parrasch
588 Broadway
925-7090

Gagosian
136 Wooster Street
228-2878

Gallery Henoch
80 Wooster Street
966-0303

Harvey
537 Broadway
925-7651

Heller
71 Greene Street
966-5948

Holly Solomon
172 Mercer Street
941-5777

Interart Center
167 Spring Street
431-7500

Jay Gorney
100 Greene Street
966-4480

John Gibson
568 Broadway
925-1192

June Kelly
591 Broadway
226-1660

Klarfeld Perry
472 Broome Street
941-0303

Leo Castelli
420 West Broadway
431-5160

Leo Castelli
578 Broadway
431-6279

Mary Boone
417 West Broadway
431-1818

45

Max Protetch
560 Broadway
966-5454

Meisel
141 Prince Street
677-1340

Metro Pictures
150 Greene Street
925-8335

Nahan Contempory
381 West Broadway
966-9313

Nancy Hoffman
429 West Broadway
966-6676

**New Museum of
Contempory Art**
583 Broadway
219-1355

Nosei
100 Prince Street
431-9253

OK Harris
383 West Broadway
431-3600

Pace
142 Greene Street
431-9224

Pamela Auchincloss
558 Broadway
966-7753

Paul Kasmin
74 Grand Street
219-3219

Paula Cooper
155 Wooster Street
674-0766

Penine Hart
457 Broome Street
226-2761

Phoenix
568 Broadway
226-8711

Phyllis Kind
136 Greene Street
925-1200

Postmasters
80 Greene Street
941-5711

PPOW
532 Broadway
941-8642

Ronald Feldman
31 Mercer Street
226-3232

Reusch
134 Spring Street
925-1137

Sally Hawkins
448 West Broadway
477-5699

Sigma
379 West Broadway
941-0014

SoHo 20
469 Broome Street
226-4167

Solo Impression
520 Broadway
925-3599

Sonnabend
420 West Broadway
966-6160

Sperone Westwater
142 Greene Street
431-3685

Sragow
73 Spring Street
219-1793

Stark
560 Broadway
925-4484

Steinbaum Krauss
132 Greene Street
431-4224

Stephen Haller
560 Broadway
219-2500

Stux
163 Mercer Street
219-0010

Susan Teller
568 Broadway
941-7335

Tenri
575 Broadway
925-8500

Tony Shafrazi
119 Wooster Street
274-9300

Vorpal
459 West Broadway
334-3939

Ward-Nasse
178 Prince Street
925-6951

Wessel O'Connor
60 Thomas Street
406-0040

Witkin
415 Broadway
925-5510

Zarre
48 Greene Street
966-2222

GREENWICH VILLAGE

The area now called Greenwich Village, originally a settlement of the Algonquin Indian tribe, was later a Dutch tobacco plantation, and finally a small British town called Greenwich. It remained an isolated country village when New York's center was located at the island's southern tip until the Yellow Fever epidemic of 1822 ravaged the downtown population. Although the idea of moving the entire city center was abandoned after the plague died down, Greenwich Village soon became a retreat of the rich and famous, and it was for them that the beautiful brownstone rowhouses and townhouses were built. As time passed, the wealthy chose to move uptown and the Village became sought after by artists for its large spaces at cheap rents.

Greenwich Village became home to the avant-garde. It attracted political activists and intellectuals, actors, artists, musicians, dancers, and writers. The gay and women's liberation movements were born here, as was Allen Ginsburg's Beat Generation. Many famous writers lived here; the list reads like a Who's Who of American Art and Letters. Among them were Edgar Allen Poe, Eugene O'Neill, Upton Sinclair, Walt Whitman, Mark Twain, Edna St. Vincent Millay, Herman Melville, O'Henry and F. Scott Fitzgerald.

The era of cheap rents did not last long, however, as it was soon recognized that Greenwich Village was a special part of the city, with it's own history and distinct character. Because of this, much of the area was landmarked, thus preserving forever its low-rise buildings and special features.

Because this part of town was established before the uptown grid was laid out, there are meandering streets and tiny alleys like Washington Mews or MacDougal Alley that remind one of European towns. It is here that the familiar gridwork of city streets lose their regularity and transform into a tangled mess of sidestreets, many of them following what were once cow paths, brooks and grazing trails.

Greenwich Village encompasses a large area, spanning the island from river to river between 14th and Houston (pronounced "Howston") Streets. Its elegant historic buildings form a natural valley which divides midtown from downtown Manhattan. Greenwich Village neatly divides into two separate neighborhoods - the East and West Village. While the East Village is home to the counter culture, there is more of a feeling of the old city in the West Village.

The West Village, with it's 19th century row houses and tree lined streets, has a small town feel; its open air cafes and Jazz clubs add to its easygoing lifestyle. There is a thriving jazz scene here. Clubs, such as

The Village Vanguard, The Blue Note, and Sweet Basil host the greatest names in jazz music, and all-night jam sessions lead to musical innovation.

There are also numerous galleries, little craft and curio shops and "Off-Broadway" theaters, which stay open later than the rest of the city and provide some of the best nighttime entertainment available. Also, with its innumerable bars, cafes and clubs to choose from, and more restaurants per person than anywhere else, the streets are alive night and day.

Washington Square Park is the heart of the Village. It provides a natural amphitheater for human activity, with the central fountain acting as stage for a variety of comedians, jugglers, and performers. It is where everyone, young and old meet, play games and make dates. Open daily until 12 a.m., it is a fun place to relax or to stroll through.

Facing the park on it's northern border, is a beautiful row of Ionic Greek revival houses. These were home to Henry James, Edith Wharton, Edward Hopper and John Dos Passos. While writers and artists still inhabit many of these and other homes in the Village, so do actors, playwrights, rock stars, models, young professionals and older residents who have lived here for many years. A tolerant and pleasant community spirit prevails.

Students have also been a part of the Village scene by attending the many colleges in the area. New York University, in particular, has played a dominant role in Village life, as it is a major land owner here.

Two of the best public schools in the city are located in Greenwich Village - P.S. 3 and P.S. 41 - as well as such excellent private schools as the Little Red Schoolhouse and the Greenwich Village Neighborhood School. Because it has always been a stable, safe community, the Village is an excellent place to raise children.

Many working artists - painters, writers, actors, musicians, or anyone in the arts - live in the Westbeth complex (the rent stabilized, subsidized compound of artists located at Bank and West Streets). Once an isolated area of warehouses and meat markets, this far west community has increasingly been redeveloped and gentrified throughout the 1980's and '90's. Apartments in this community, today, are rarely a bargain. Co-ops typically range in price from $200,000 to more than $500,000 and lofts from $400,000 to more than $600,000 depending on size, light, condition, etc.

An increasing number of new galleries, restaurants, shops, and swinging bars such as Hogs and Heifers, help make this once-barren district the newest trendy nexus of New York nightlife.

THE VILLAGES
NEIGHBORHOOD BUSINESSES

BANKS

- **Chase Manhattan Bank**
158 West 14th Street Seventh Avenue,
935-9935

- **Citibank**
72 Fifth Avenue at West 13th Street,
627-3999
555 LaGuardia Place at West Third Street,
627-3999

BARS & CLUBS

WEST VILLAGE

- **Art Bar**
52 Eighth Avenue at Jane Street, 727-0244

- **Automatic Slims**
733 Washington Avenue at Bank Street,
645-8660

- **Blue Note**
131 West Third Street, 475-8592

- **Bottom Line**
15 West Fourth Street, 228-6300

- **Boxers**
190 West Fourth Street, 633-2275

- **Chumley's**
86 Bedford Street at Barrow Street, 675-4449

- **Elbow Room**
144 Bleecker Street at Thompson Street,
979-8434

- **55 Bar and Grill**
55 Christopher Street at Seventh Avenue
South, 929-9883

- **Mother**
432 West 14th Street, 366-5680

- **The Slaughtered Lamb**
184 West Fourth Street, 627-lamb (5262)

- **White House Tavern**
567 Hudson Street at 11th Street, 243-9260

EAST VILLAGE

- **Beauty Bar**
231 East 14th Street, 539-1389

- **Brownies**
169 Avenue A at 11th Street, 420-8392

- **CBGB**
315 Bowery at Bleecker Street, 982-4052

- **Continental**
25 Third Avenue at Street Marks, 529-6924

- **Coyote Ugly Saloon**
153 First Avenue at Ninth Street, 477-4431

- **Dick's Bar**
192 Second Avenue at 12th Street, 475-2071

- **Fez Under Time Café**
380 Lafayette Street at Great Jones Street,
533-2680

- **Holiday Cocktail Lounge**
75 Street Mark's Place at First Avenue,
777-9637

- **Izzy Bar**
166 First Avenue at Tenth Street, 228-0444

- **KGB**
85 East Fourth Street, 460-0982

- **Max Fish**
178 Ludlow Street at Houston Street,
529-3959

- **McOrley's Old Ale House**
15 East Seventh Street, 473-9148

- **The Mercury Lounge**
217 East Houston Street at Essex Street,
260-4700

- **Opium Den**
29 East Third Street, 505-7344

- **Street Mark's Bar and Grill**
132 First Avenue at Street Mark's Place,
505-0290

- **Sidewalk Café**
94 Avenue A. at Sixth Street, 473-7373

- **Swift's**
34 East Fourth Street, 260-3600

BOOK STORES

- **Shakespeare & Co.**
716 Broadway at Astor Place, 529-1330

- **St. Mark's Bookshop**
31 Third Avenue at St. Mark's Place,
260-7853

- **Three Lives & Co.**
154 West 10th Street @ Waverly Place,
741-2069

COFFEE BARS

- **Brewbar Coffee**
327 West 11th at Washington Street,
807-7471

- **McNulty's Tea and Coffee**
109 Christopher Street, at Hudson Street,
242-5351

- **Oren's Daily Roast**
31 Waverly Place at Washington Square
East, 420-5958

- **Rocco's Pastry Shop**
243 Bleecker Street at Carmine Street,
242-6031

- **Alt.Coffee**
139 Avenue A at 9th Street, 529-2233

- **Café Gigi**
417 East 9th Street, 505-3341

- **Café Orlin**
41 Street Marks Place at Second Avenue,
777-1447

- **Caffe della Pace**
48 East Seventh Street, 529-8024

- **Internet Café**
82 East Third Street, 614-0747

HEALTH CLUBS

- **Crunch**
152 Christopher Street at Greenwich Street,
366-3725

- **David Barton Gym**
623 Broadway at Houston Street, 420-0507

- **Crunch**
54 East 13th Street, 475-2018

- **Dolphin Fitness Clubs**
242 East 14th Street, 614-0390
155 East Third Street, 533-0090

- **Hanson Fitness Center**
826 Broadway at 12th., 982-2233

- **New York Health and Racquet Club**
24 East 13th Street, 924-4600
110 University Place at 13th Street, 989-2300

MOVIE THEATERS

- **Cineplex Odeon Art Greenwich**
Greenwich Avenue at 12th Street, 505-CINE #616

- **Clearview Waverly Twin**
Sixth Avenue at Third Street, 777-FILM #603

- **UA Union Square 14**
13th Street at Broadway, 253-2225

- **CC Village East Cinemas**
12th Street at Second Avenue, 777-FILM #922

- **Cinema Classics**
332 East 11th Street, 675-6692

- **Cinema Village**
22 East 12th Street at Fifth Avenue, 924-3363

- **Quad Cinema**
13th Street at Fifth Avenue, 255-8800

- **Sony Village**
Third Avenue at 11th Street, 982-0400

PHARMACIES

- **Bigelow Apothecaries**
414 Sixth Avenue at Eighth Street, 533-2700

- **Polypharm Drug Co.**
208 Mott Street, 226-1415

- **Village Apothecary**
346 Bleecker Street at West 10th Street, 807-7566

- **Biomed Drugs and Surgical Supply Inc.**
50 Third Avenue at 10th Street, 505-3724

- **Block Drug Store**
101 Second Avenue at Sixth Street, 473-1587

- **East Village Prescription Center**
72 Avenue A at Fifth Street, 260-4878

Community District 3
South Street to East 14th Street ~ East River to Bowery

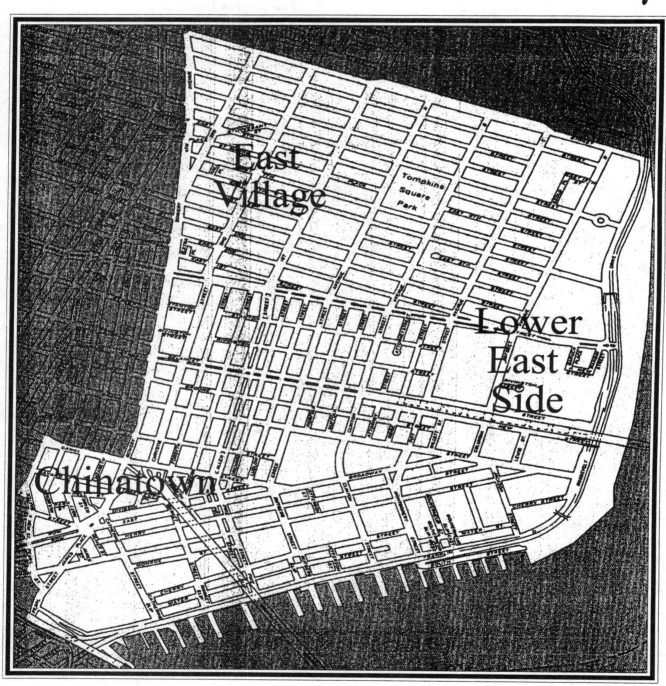

Includes: Chinatown, East Village, Lower East Side

Manhattan Community District 3
South Street to East 14th Street ~ East River to Bowery

DEMOGRAPHICS

Data presented here is taken from the 1990 Decennial Census

	Number	Percent
POPULATION		
Children (under age 10)	*16,808*	*10.2*
10-19 years	20,222	12.5
20-29 years	30,254	18.7
30-39 years	30,294	18.7
40-49 years	20,200	12.5
50-59 years	14,668	9.1
60+ years	29,171	18.1
TOTAL	161,617	100%
Male	80,457	49.8
Female	81,160	50.2
Median Age	*34.2*	
MARITAL STATUS		
Age 15 & Over		
Never married	57,496	42.5
Married	50,669	37.5
Separated, widowed, divorced	27,075	20.0
EDUCATION		
Less than 9 years	31,487	28.3
High school graduate	60,012	53.9
College graduate	23,981	21.6
Graduate Degree	8,562	7.7
INCOME		
Family	$21,345	
Per Capita	$11,309	
HOUSING UNITS		
TOTAL	68,849	100%
Vacant - for rent or sale	*2,304*	*3.4*
*Renter occupied	60,454	92.1
*Owner occupied	5,175	7.9

*Renter & owner occupied figures add up to the total <u>occupied</u> units,
therefore they do not equal the figure for total housing units.*

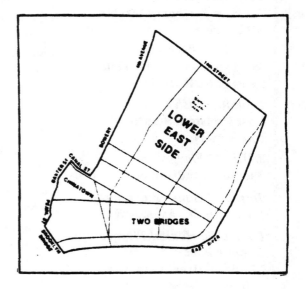

Neighborhood Services

Manhattan Community District 3

Parks and Playgrounds

Alfred E. Smith Park
Catherine Slip, Madison &
South Streets

Bernard Downing Playground
Columbia, Delancey &
Willett Streets

Capt. Jacob Joseph Playground
Rutgers & Henry Streets

Coleman Square Playground
Cherry, Pike & Monroe Sts.

Columbus Park
Baxter, Mulberry, Bayard
& Park Streets

Corlears Hook Park
Jackson & Cherry Streets,
FDR Drive

East River Park
Montgomery to East 12th
Streets, FDR Drive

Hamilton Fish Park
East Houston, Stanton &
Pitt Streets

J.H.S. 82 Playground
Jackson, Madison & Henry Sts.

Jospeh C. Sauer Playground
East 12th St., Aves. A & B

**Laguardia Hopital Playground -
Rutgers Pool**
Madison Street Opposite
Jefferson Street

Lillian D. Wald Playground
Cherry, Montgomery &
Gouverner Street

Martin F. Tanahey Playground
Cherry-water, Cathy-market
Slip

Playground
Clinton, Cherry & Water
Streets

Playground
Essex, Norfolk & Houston Sts.

Playground (Lillian Wald Hses)
East Houston St. West of
FDR Drive

Playground & Pool
Szold Place, East 10th Street

**P.S. 1 Playground ~ Alfred
Smith Houses**
Madison, Catherine-Oliver
Streets

**P.S. 110 Playground ~
Hillman Houses**
Lewis & Delancey Streets

P.S. 134 Playground
Broadway, Henry &
Gouverneur Streets

P.S. 140 Playground
N/S Rivington & Attorney
Streets

P.S. 63 Playground
Ave. A, East 3rd & 4th Sts.

P.S. 97 Baruch Houses Plgd.
Rivington, Mangin Street &
Baruch Place

Sara D. Roosevelt Parkway
East Houston to Canal Streets

Sophie Irene Loeb Playground
Henry & Market Street,
East Broadway

Tompkins Square Park
Aves. A to B, East 7th to 10th
Streets

Vladek Park
Madison-Water Streets,
Jackson-Gouverneur Streets

William H. Seward Park
Canal, Hester, Essex &
Jefferson Streets

Triangles, Malls, Strips and Sitting Areas

Ahearn Park
Grand Street, East Broadway
& Willet

Allen Street Center Plots
East Houston Street, East
Broadway

Catherine Slip Malls
Cherry, South Streets &
Catherine Slip

Cooper Park
3rd to 4th Avenues,
East 6th to East 7th Streets

Gustave Hartman Square
East Houston Street, Avenue C
& East 2nd Street

I L Peretz Square
East 1st, East Houston & Allen
Streets, First Avenue

Kimlau Square
Chatham Square, Oliver Street
& East Broadway

Park
St. James Place & Oliver Street

Schiff Pkwy Center Plots
Delancey Street, Bowery to
Essex Streets

Sitting Area
Pearl & Madison Streets,
St. James Place

St. Marks Place
East 10th Street & 2nd Avenue

Straus Square
Canal & Rutgers Streets &
East Broadway

Triangle
East 10th St., Stuyvesant Pl.

Vest Pocket Park
5th Street, Avenues C & D

THE LOWER EAST SIDE, CHINATOWN AND LITTLE ITALY

The Lower East Side, which has Houston Street, the Bowery, and the East River as its boundaries, was home to Jewish immigrants from Eastern Europe in the late 19th Century. They settled into this working-class, tenement house community with other immigrant populations who had come before. The Irish, who fled the 1848 potato famine, preceded a large exodus of German immigrants. Among the ethnic Germans was a small community of German-born Jews.

By 1880, however, political unrest in Europe brought a massive immigration of over two million Jews to America, many of them arriving on the Lower East Side. In 1905, there were 60 synogogues and 350 active congregations, most of which operated out of storefront shuls. Yiddish was the predominant language spoken in the streets.

Life was hard for each of these diverse groups; there were problems in adjusting to this new country and to one another. The films "Hester Street" and "Crossing Delancy" depict historical and contemporary views of this area's immigrant population.

By the mid-century many hard-working families were able to move out, over the bridges to Brooklyn and Queens and North to Westchester. They were replaced by a flow of new immigrants - mostly Hispanic, Haitian, and Chinese. A sizeable Polish and Ukranian community developed as well.

As a result, the Lower East Side today is an ethnic mix. Remnants of Jewish culture survive in the synagogues, delicatessens, and discount clothing stores on Orchard Street. So, too, remain the Kosher pickle stands on Hester Street and dairy restaurants on Delancy Street. Ratner's, at 138 Delancy Street, is as famous for its meatless cuisine as for its rude waiters. Houston Street still has a number of deli restaurants; the largest of which are Katz's at 205 East Houston Street, and Yonah Schimmel's Knishes at 137 Houston.

Examples of the old tenement houses, where people once lived ten or more to a room, are still to be found. The Lower East Side Tenement Museum at 90 Orchard Street is a partially restored 1863 tenement, now a National Historic Landmark. Available in the Gallery are guided tours, videos and slide shows, art and photographic displays, dramatic readings, and plays.

The tenement buildings and restaurants are not the only remnants; the jewelry shops along Bowery and Canal Street are left over from an old, informal diamond market that once existed there.

The very reputation of the place as being a home for bargain hunters stems partly from the old pushcart trade along Orchard Street, though the pushcarts themselves were banned in the late 1930's.

CHINATOWN AND LITTLE ITALY

Chinatown, a web of narrow streets west of Chatham Square, has been a center of New York's large Chinese community for more than 100 years. With approximately 150,000 residents, it is Manhattan's largest ethnically distinctive neighborhood. Its street and building signs are written in Chinese characters and many of its structures are topped with pagodas. There are seven

Chinese newspapers, 12 Buddhist temples, over 150 Chinese restaurants and about 300 garment factories — all packed into a relatively small district. Recently, Chinatown has expanded north across Canal Street into Little Italy and eastward into the Lower East Side.

All of Chinatown's streets are crowded and every shop does a brisk business. Restaurants are filled with locals and tourists alike. Street markets offer displays of exotic green vegetables, seafood, meat, and poultry. Chinatown has the look and feel of a bountiful and prosperous community. It has the lowest crime rate, highest employment, and least juvenile delinquency of any neighborhood in the city.

However, there are some serious problems here. Non-Union sweatshops reportedly continue to exist with workers being paid below minimum wage. Living conditions are also terrible for these and other poor workers; many of whom live in small rooms in run down tenement buildings.

Because this community is still very much an insular culture, it is hard for Westerners to know much about its interior life. The one time of year when Chinatown opens up to outsiders is during the Chinese New Year Festival, held each year on the first full moon after January 19th. A famous celebration; the streets ring with the sound of firecrackers (although the city recently banned their use) and the dragon dancers wind around Mott Street.

Although Chinatown has almost completely enveloped Little Italy, some parts of Little Italy remain strong. On Mulberry Street the street signs are in Roman letters only, and some of the finest Italian restaurants, featuring the food of every Italian region, can be found here.

Crowds come out for Little Italy's festivals, as well: the Feast of St. Anthony of Padua, which is held on the first two weeks of June, and the even more famous Feast of San Gennaro on the week of September 19th. Images of the Saints are carried through the streets as spectators watch, eat ethnic treats, and play games of chance.

⋆⋆THE⋆EAST⋆VILLAGE⋆⋆

The East Village, between 14th Street and Houston, and Broadway and the FDR Drive, is funkier and more lively than the West Village. Each block has its own character, with Eighth Street, east of Sixth Avenue, being the most commercial block. Many a good buy can be found in its stores, which sell everything from boots and clothes to Novelty Items.

At Third Avenue, Eighth Street turns into St. Mark's Place. This is the heart of one of the most interesting and colorful neighborhoods in all of New York. Along this stretch can be found some of the most exciting nighttime activities, including avant-garde clubs and experimental theatres.

Walking through the East Village, one finds an eclectic blend of cultures; Indian, African-American, Ukrainian, Russian, Jewish, Puerto Rican, Italian and Polish among others - giving an international feel to the neighborhood. Bleeker Street, once known as "The French Quarter," is rich with ethnic restaurants and cafes, live entertainment and fine dining.

Always a center for bohemian counter-culture, the East Village still retains its political anti-establishment edge. The film "Desperately Seeking Susan" typifies the present fashion and music scenes of the punk population, and politically conscious murals and street artist paintings decorate sidewalks and buildings.

In the 1950's, the poet Allen Ginsberg had an apartment that became a gathering spot for the Beat Generation; Frank O'Hara lived on East 9th Street, and Jack Kerouac stayed briefly. In the 1960's, this area became the province of hippies and folk singers like Bob Dylan, who lived on McDougal Street. Madonna also lived here before she became a star. The Village Voice, founded in part by Norman Mailer, became the advocate of radical politics and social commentary; more recently, the prize-winning Broadway musical "Rent" was set here.

Contradictions abound in the housing market as well, as rows of tenements stand cheek to jowl with new luxury hi-rise co-ops and converted factory buildings. Ukrainian and Hispanic immigrants, starving artists and investment bankers rub shoulders on the street, and purple-haired rockers sit down to breakfast in Polish coffee shops.

Always a diverse population, these disparate groups seem to keep an easy peace amongst themselves. Their common enemy is the developers who spell displacement for long time residents and for some beloved neighborhood institutions. This is an activist community composed of strong block associations that will fight to keep their neighborhood's diversity intact. Though gentrification most likely will occur, it will do so slowly and over the objections of these groups. Because the East Village is a special place, its very success at luring wealthier, mainstream residents might be its undoing. Yet, it's precisely the outlaw/outcast nature of the East Village that is its greatest draw.

Neighborhood Enclaves: Peter Cooper Village And Stuyvesant Town

Peter Cooper Village and Stuyvesant Town, built in the mid-1940's between East 14th and East 23rd Streets, from First Avenue to Avenue C, are two adjoining communities that were created for middle-class families.

While First Avenue bustles with shopping and traffic, residents can enjoy a peaceful existence within these gated enclaves. They can walk along paths by neatly trimmed lawns and near children's playgrounds and feel insulated from the hustle and bustle.

Built after World War II by the Metropolitan Life Insurance Company, married veterans were given preference among the applicants. Singles and unmarried couples were ineligible. While the communities are more diverse today--there are single people, married and unmarried couples, young and old, and people of all races and religions--the enclaves still embody the quiet, sheltered retreats their planners intended.

Peter Cooper Village, completed in 1947, between 20th and 23rd Streets, contains 2,495 rental apartments in 21 buildings. Stuyvesant Town, from 14th to 20th Streets, has 8,756 slightly less expensive apartments. Because of their below market rents, there are long waiting lists for both complexes.

Community District 4
West 14th Street to West 57th Street
Eighth Avenue to the Hudson River

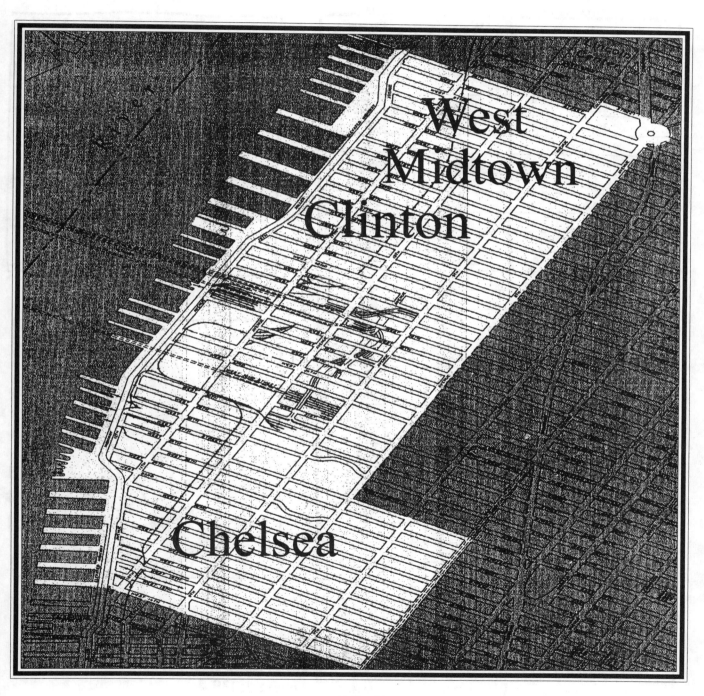

Includes: Chelsea, Clinton

Manhattan Community District 4
West 14th Street to West 59th Street ~ Eighth Avenue to Hudson River

DEMOGRAPHICS
Data presented here is taken from the 1990 Decennial Census

	Number	Percent
POPULATION		
Children (under age 10)	4,823	5.8
10-19 years	4,765	5.6
20-29 years	17,120	20.3
30-39 years	21,082	25.0
40-49 years	13,226	15.7
50-59 years	8,262	9.8
60+ years	15,153	17.9
TOTAL	84,431	100%
Male	43,578	51.6
Female	40,853	48.4
Median Age	37.2	
MARITAL STATUS		
Age 15 & Over		
Never married	41,438	53.4
Married	20,599	26.6
Separated, widowed, divorced	15,525	20.0
EDUCATION		
Less than 9 years	6,444	9.3
High school graduate	56,410	81.3
College graduate	19.388	27.9
Graduate Degree	12,830	18.5
INCOME		
Family	$36,427	
Per Capita	$24,957	
HOUSING UNITS		
TOTAL	53,759	100%
Vacant - for rent or sale	3,652	6.8
*Renter occupied	41,781	85.4
*Owner occupied	7,134	14.6

*Renter & owner occupied figures add up to the total occupied units,
therefore they do not equal the figure for total housing units.*

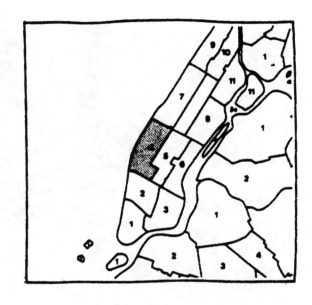

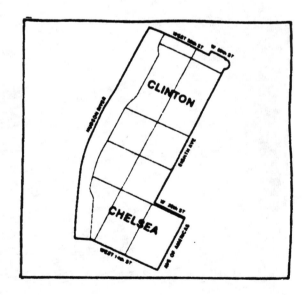

TOTAL LAND AREA
Acres: 1,339.4
Sq. Miles: 2.1

Neighborhood Services

Manhattan Community District 4

Parks and Playgrounds

Chelsea Park
9th to 10th Avenues,
West 27th to 28th Streets

Clement Clarke Moore Park
West 22nd Street, 10th Avenue

De Witt Clinton Park
West 52nd to West 54th Streets,
11th to 12th Avenues

Dr. Gertude B. Kelly Playground
West 17th Street, 8th to 9th
Avenues

May Matthews Playground
45th Street between 9th and
10th Avenues

McCaffrey Playground
West 43rd Street, 8th and 9th
Avenues

47th Street Playground
Eastside of 10th Avenue,
West 47th to 48th Streets

Penn Station South Hses Plgd
West 26th Street,
8th to 9th Avenues

Athletic Facilities

Chelsea Recreation Center
S/Side of West 25th Street,
9th o 10th Avenues

NY School of Printing Rec Area
N/Side of West 49th Street,
9th & 10th Avenues

Natural Areas

Clinton Community Garden
West 47th to 48th Streets,
9th and 10th Avenues

Manhattan Community District 5

Parks and Playgrounds

Bryant Park
Between 5th and 6th Avenues,
West 40th to 42nd Streets

Madison Square Park
Broadway to Madison Avenue,
East 23rd to 26th Streets

Union Square
Broadway to 4th Avenue,
East 14th to 17th Streets
This Park has been newly
renovated and now hosts
open-air farmers markets
on Mondays, Wednesdays,
Fridays and Saturdays. Locally grown
produce, fruit, flowers and baked goods,
cheeses, wines and ciders are sold here.

Triangles, Malls, Strips and Sitting Areas

Greeley Square
Broadway, Sixth Avenue,
West 32nd and 33rd Streets

Herald Square
Broadway, Sixth Avenue,
West 34th to 36th Streets

Park Ave Center Plots
East 17th to 32nd Streets,
Park Avenue South

Park Avenue Center Plots
East 34th to 40th Streets,
Park Avenue

Worth Square
Broadway to Fifth Avenue,
West 24th to 25th Streets

CHELSEA
14TH STREET TO 30TH STREET
SIXTH AVENUE TO THE HUDSON RIVER

In 1750, all that is Chelsea today was rural farmland. Purchased by Capt. Thomas Clarke for his retirement, Chelsea was named after the Chelsea Royal Hospital, an old soldiers' home in London. In the 1830's, Clarke's grandson, Clement Clarke Moore (author of "A Visit From St. Nicholas"), decided to develop the area, and by the turn of the century, Chelsea had become an upper-class enclave. 23rd Street became a millionaires' row of elegant brownstones, and "Ladies' Mile", a shopping district on Sixth Avenue, became a mecca for wealthy women. The Chelsea opera house, Tin Pan Alley theatres, nightclubs, and other local attractions drew the rich and famous. It was here that Diamond Jim Brady sipped champagne from Lillian Russell's slipper, and here where movie production got its start in New York in 1905.

By the 1940's, however, all this had changed. A wave of immigrant workers to the piers and factories built along the river had a drastic impact on the very nature of Chelsea. The rich fled, and their elegant brownstones were subdivided and converted into rooming houses. Chelsea began to deteriorate into a low-income area, with declining homes, piers, and factories.

In the late 1960's, though, a revitalization began which changed the neighborhood once again and still continues to this day. Signs of renewal are everywhere. Few stores are vacant; restaurants, art galleries, espresso bars, bookstores, and bistros are all around. The area has become a sizzling night spot with trendy bars and discos sprouting up overnight. Barnes and Noble, Filenes Basement, and Burlington Coat Factory are among the large chain stores revitalizing the

retail district on Sixth Avenue, and Macy's (the world's largest department store) still hugs the corner of 34th Street. On Seventh Avenue, between 15th and 17th Street, such stores as Williams-Sonoma, Pottery Barn, and Jensen-Lewis offer a wide range of home furnishings, while the area's restaurant row, Eighth Avenue between 14th and 23rd Street, doubles as Chelsea's bustling Main Street.

Chelsea's population wears many faces. There is an artistic community of photographers, models, and designers, who mix easily with a large gay community and with an older population who live primarily in the middle-income Penn Station South co-ops. Two subsidized housing developments, the Robert Fulton Houses and the Elliot-Chelsea Houses, provide apartments for low-income families.

While lofts are the dominant residences, "Brownstoning" seems to be the lifestyle of choice for many of those drawn to this area. Because only a few hi-rise buildings have been built here, the population is low. In fact, Chelsea is one of the least densely populated areas in the city, and future guidelines for residential construction seek to preserve the neighborhood's scale.

The Historic District is Chelsea's centerpiece. It encompasses parts of West 20th, 21st, and 22nd Streets, and Ninth and Tenth Avenues. This is prime Chelsea real estate and vacant brownstones are difficult to find. Townhouses, here, typically sell for over one million dollars.

There are few quality prewar doormen buildings other than the London Terrace apartments. This complex of rental and co-op units was built in the 1930's, and features an Olympic sized indoor swimming pool and a gym. Prices for one-bedrooms typically begin at $150,000; two-bedrooms at $300,000 and go to more than $600,000. Rentals are hard to get and have long waiting lists.

Family life in Chelsea is good. There are many schools, parks, and several different houses of worship. A selection of nursery schools and public schools include P.S. 11, P.S. 33, I.S. 70, the Bayard Rustin High School for the Humanities, and the Fashion Industries High School. The McBurney Y.M.C.A. on 23rd Street offers day care among other programs for children and adults. Two Roman-Catholic elementary schools, St. Columbia and Guardian Angel, offer private school religious education.

The Chelsea Piers Sports and Entertainment Complex on the Hudson River, from 17th to 23rd Streets, offers a variety of activities for adults and young people, including two outdoor rollerblade and roller-skating rinks, running tracks, an ice-skating rink, driving range, health spa, swimming pool, and a rock-climbing wall.

Chelsea is a wonderful microcosm of all that is diverse and rich about New York City, and it has one additional advantage over its kindred neighbors SoHo and Tribeca; it is closer to midtown — the heart of Manhattan.

CHELSEA
NEIGHBORHOOD BUSINESSES

BANKS

- **Carver Federal Savings Bank**
261 Eighth Avenue at 23rd Street, 989-4000

- **Chase Manhattan Bank**
238 Eighth Avenue at 23rd Street, 935-9935

- **Citibank**
322 West 23rd Street, 627-3999

- **Union Chelsea National bank**
250 Ninth Avenue at 25th Street, 989-3700

BARS & CLUBS

- **Hynes Bros.**
219 Ninth Avenue at 23rd Street, 727-2616

- **Hackers, Hitters and Hoops**
123 West 18th Street, 929-7482

- **Ohm**
16 West 22nd Street, 229-2000

- **Rear**
127 Ninth Avenue at 16th Street, 627-1680

- **Ta Room**
3 West 8th Street, 691-7666

- **Heartland Brewery**
35 Union Square at 17th Street, 645-3400

COFFEE BARS

- **Chelsea Coffee Co.**
140 Ninth Avenue at 19th Street, 206-7325

- **Newsbar**
2 West 19th Street at Sixth Avenue,
255-3996

- **Paradise Muffin Café**
139 Eighth Avenue at 17th Street, 647-0066

HEALTH CLUBS

- **Bally Total Fitness**
641 Sixth Avenue at 20th Street, 645-4565

- **Chelsea Piers Sports Center**
Pier 60, West 23rd Street at Hudson River, 336-6000

MOVIE THEATERS

- **Clearview Chelsea**
23rd Street at Seventh Avenue, 777-FILM #597

- **Clearview Chelsea West**
333 West 23rd Street at Eighth Avenue, 777-FILM #614

- **Sony 19th Street East**
19th Street at Broadway, 260-8000

PHARMACIES

- **New London Pharmacy**
246 Eighth Avenue at 23rd Street, 243-4987

- **Stadlanders Pharmacy Wellness Center**
126 Eighth Avenue at 16th Street, 807-8798

Community District 5

East 14th Street to Central Park South
Lexington Avenue to Eighth Avenue

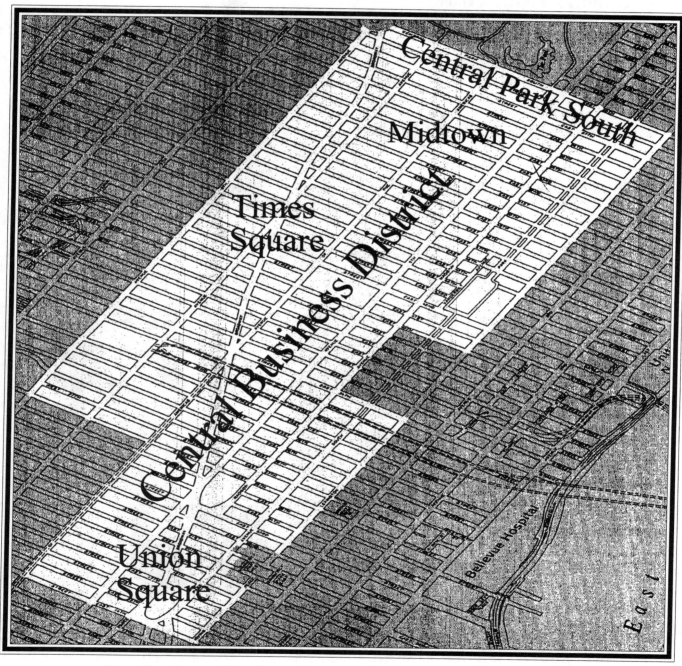

Includes: Union Square, Times Square,
Central Park South (59th St.), Central Business District

Manhattan Community District 5

East 14th Street to Central Park South (59th Street) ~ Lexington Avenue to Eighth Avenue

DEMOGRAPHICS

Data presented here is taken from the 1990 Decennial Census

	Number	Percent
POPULATION		
Children (under age 10)	*1,757*	*4.1*
10-19 years	1,923	4.4
20-29 years	10,435	24.0
30-39 years	10,231	23.5
40-49 years	7,253	16.7
50-59 years	4,321	9.9
60+ years	7,587	17.5
TOTAL	43,507	100%
Male	21,841	50.2
Female	21,666	49.7
Median Age	*37.2*	
MARITAL STATUS		
Age 15 & Over		
Never married	21,480	52.1
Married	11,867	28.8
Separated, widowed, divorced	7,917	19.2
EDUCATION		
Less than 9 years	1,059	3.0
High school graduate	32,011	89.6
College graduate	19,655	55.1
Graduate Degree	8,896	24.9
INCOME		
Family	$72,735	
Per Capita	$39,058	
HOUSING UNITS		
TOTAL	30,436	100%
Vacant - for rent or sale	*6,653*	*10.4*
*Renter occupied	17,771	74.7
*Owner occupied	6,012	25.3

*Renter & owner occupied figures add up to the total <u>occupied</u> units, therefore they do not equal the figure for total housing units.

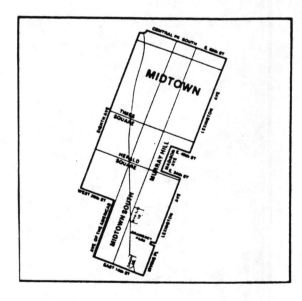

TOTAL LAND AREA
Acres: 1,046.4
Sq. Miles: 1.6

Community District 6
East 14th Street to East 59th Street
East River to Lexington Avenue

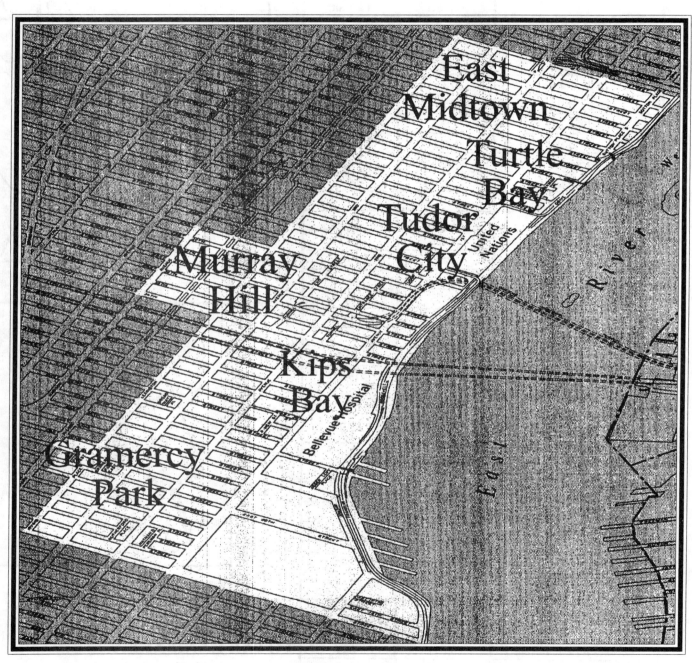

Includes: Gramercy Park, Kips Bay, Murray Hill, Tudor City, Turtle Bay

Manhattan Community District 6

East 14th Street to East 59th Street ~ East River to Lexington Avenue

DEMOGRAPHICS

Data presented here is taken from the 1990 Decennial Census

	Number	Percent
POPULATION		
Children (under age 10)	*6,185*	*4.6*
10-19 years	5,645	4.3
20-29 years	23,992	17.9
30-39 years	28,855	21.6
40-49 years	22,966	17.2
50-59 years	16,452	12.3
60+ years	29,654	22.2
TOTAL	133,748	100%
Male	60,526	45.3
Female	73,222	54.7
Median Age	*40.9*	
MARITAL STATUS		
Age 15 & Over		
Never married	56,645	45.2
Married	45,371	36.2
Separated, widowed, divorced	23,323	18.6
EDUCATION		
Less than 9 years	3,308	2.9
High school graduate	105,845	92.6
College graduate	67,397	59.0
Graduate Degree	30,425	26.6
INCOME		
Family	$75,250	
Per Capita	$45,110	
HOUSING UNITS		
TOTAL	92,829	100%
Vacant - for rent or sale	*5,679*	*6.1*
***Renter occupied**	62,842	75.6
***Owner occupied**	20,309	24.4

**Renter & owner occupied figures add up to the total <u>occupied</u> units,
therefore they do not equal the figure for total housing units.*

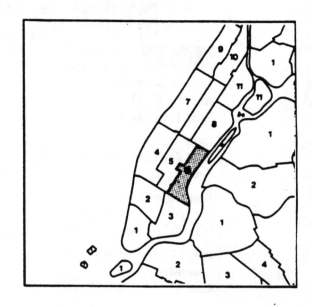

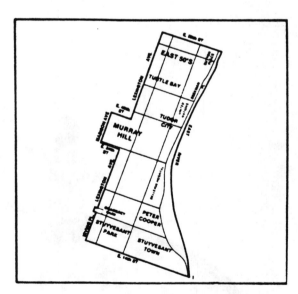

TOTAL LAND AREA
Acres: 875.2
Sq. Miles: 1.4

Neighborhood Services

Manhattan Community District 6

Parks and Playgrounds

John J. Murphy Park
Avenue C, FDR Drive,
East 17th Street

Park
East 26th and 28th Streets,
Second Avenue

Playground
N/Side of East 29th Street,
W/Side of Second Avenue

P.S. 40 Playground
Second Avenue,
East 19th to East 20th Streets

St. Vartan Park
First to Second Avenues,
East 35th to East 36th Streets

Stuyvesant Square
Rutherford-Livingston Place,
East 15th to 17th Streets

Athletic Facilities

J.H.S. 104 Recreation Area
East 20th to East 21st Streets,
First to Second Avenues

Public Bath (Asser Levy)
East 23rd to East 25th Streets,
FDR Drive

GRAMERCY PARK: THIRD AVENUE TO PARK AVENUE SOUTH 18TH STREET TO 23RD STREET

In the midst of New York's famously frenetic streets, Gramercy residents may have found the golden key to peace and the slower-paced, genteel charm of old. From its very beginning, the Gramercy Park area was meant to be a place cut off from the rest of the city: an exclusive area for the wealthy to stroll leisurely among their own kind. Samuel B. Ruggles developed the area by guaranteeing the sole use of the park to his wealthy buyers. That privilege remains to this day. Gramercy is the last surviving private park in New York City.

The keys, needed to enter through the park's eight foot iron gates are no longer made of gold. However, they are still given only to the owners of the lots immediately surrounding the park and to a few qualified residents. The park is open to the public, however, on three-occasions: Gramercy Park Day, Christmas Day, and on Yom Kippur when fasting worshippers from a nearby synagogue are permitted to rest between services. The only other time the park has been opened was during the Draft Riots of 1863 when troops camped inside.

The streets surrounding the park are just as unchanged as the park itself - and so are the people. Affluent, conservative professionals still live in the landmark brownstones which once housed Samuel Tilden, Edwin Booth, and Ida Tarbell. Around the park are several examples of Greek Revival townhouses from the early 1800's, with the lacy iron ornamentation built to create a charmingly rustic touch. On the East side of the park is a building noted as possibly being the city's first co-op. The more extravagant Gothic Revival of the Victorian period is exemplified in Samuel Tilden's house, which is presently being restored by the National Arts Club.

Indeed, many residents have recently banded together to restore the neighborhood blocks to their original splendor. A part of 29th Street, between Irving Place and Third Avenue, has become once again the "block beautiful" that *American Homes and Gardens* named it in 1914.

Gramercy Park has never taken well to change. Even as early as the 1890's, residents resisted a proposed cable car line. In 1912, the resistance continued with residents halting a proposed extension of Lexington Avenue that would have gone through the park, and continues into the present day, as once again residents are banding together to stop McDonald's from settling into the area.

However, growth and modernization seem to be unstoppable in New York City. The area just off the park contains many large apartment buildings which are somewhat more affordably priced, and new buildings continue to go up at the fringes of the neighborhood.

The location is excellent for Midtown office workers, who can enjoy being just a few steps away from work, yet still luxuriate in the peaceful residential feel that surrounds the park.

Lured by the influx of new residents, a number of new restaurants and cafes have sprung up in the area. It is possible to sample almost any type of cuisine here today. Yet even in their eateries, Gramercy residents still cling to relics of another age. Many residents can be found in a place once frequented by O. Henry - Pete's Tavern on 18th Street. The tavern survived Prohibition as a speakeasy; and has remained a local favorite.

Like Pete's Tavern, the Gramercy Park area is a remnant of another time, excellently preserved, however closely the bustling modern streets of the city surround it. So little has changed in this neighborhood, that to this day, the phrase "a key to the park" is used in ads to entice possible buyers into the area.

Aa Bb Cc Dd Ee Ff Gg Hh Ii Jj

SCHOOLS

PUBLIC AND PRIVATE SCHOOLS

Some of the City's best public and private schools are located Downtown. Among these, P.S. 234 in Tribeca is so popular among neighborhood families that children from outside its catchment area cannot get in. Another elementary school, P.S. 11 at 320 West 21st Street, is also popular with neighborhood families for its mix of progressive and traditional methods in teaching reading and writing skills. It's curriculum is based on literature, instead of textbooks, with all subjects taught around a central theme.

Other special programs include swimming lessons in P.S. 11's indoor pool and ballroom dancing. Children who score in the 90th percentile on the IQ test are eligible for admission to the school's gifted program.

The Salk School of Science, at 320 East 20th Street, attracts students with a special interest in science and medicine. Students are encouraged to work with doctors and medical-school faculty at nearby NYU medical center on science projects and also to explore the practical and ethical questions of science with staff members.

Baruch College Campus High School, at East 18th Street, was founded in 1997 with only 100 students and a faculty of five. It is a school so small that the principal sometimes substitutes for its teachers. Located on the sixteenth-floor of Baruch College, classrooms have panoramic city views. Students have access to Baruch's library, cafeteria and gym.

NYC Lab School for Collaborative Studies, at 333 West 17th Street, is another tiny, alternative high school with an individual approach to learning. Though academic standards are high, students can choose their electives and pursue independent studies.

Every senior must choose a research project and enlist a teacher to "mentor" a yearlong research project; every eighth-through-tenth grader must join a book discussion group. Lab's middle school ranked Number One in city-wide reading scores this year.

There are a number of high quality schools in the city, ranging from general public schools and special "Gifted and Talented" public schools to various private schools. Since there are many good schools to choose from, the hardest part for parents will be deciding which school is right for their child and whether or not to send their child to a neighborhood school or to a school outside of their district.

Parents can gather information on the schools they are considering by talking to school principals, teachers and other parents. They can ask for such information as school test scores, average class sizes, and a school's educational philosophy. While touring prospective schools, its students should appear excited to be learning. If they are not excited, then the school is failing to meet their needs. A valuable and telling statistic to know is how many of the school's students go on to college after graduation. Also, one might inquire which colleges or universities graduates attend, to get a sense of the caliber of education students receive.

If you are considering a public school, it's a good idea to begin searching for a suitable one at least one year in advance. Parents have the option to enroll their child in any public school **only so long as there are available seats**. You can begin by calling the school district office. They will be able to supply you with a list of schools within the district and answer your questions about any special programs they offer. Also, many elementary schools hold open houses for parents.

School districts may offer seminars to explain the options, present informational programs, and guide the application process.

Other sources of public school information are:

- The 92nd Street Y, (212) 996-1100, which offers an annual seminar on school choice.
- The Public School Association, (212) 868-1640, which offers seminars for parents.
- "The Parents Guide to Choosing a Public Elementary School in New York City" is available from the office of the Manhattan Borough President, (212) 669-8300.
- The "New York City Government Offices" section of the Manhattan telephone book lists public schools by district heading.
- For any further information on parochial elementary schools, contact the Archdiocese of New York at (212) 691-3381; for high schools, at (212) 371-1000.

Many New Yorkers are unaware of the excellent "Gifted and Talented" programs offered within the public school system. These fine programs feature accelerated classes for academically advanced students as well as for those who have special interests in the arts and sciences.

While there is no comprehensive list of special programs that is easily available, you can find information about these programs in any of the public schools you visit. Ask for the phone number of the Gifted and Talented Coordinator for the Downtown school district and contact the coordinator for details about available programs.

To find out the district number of other special schools you may be interested in and for other information, the Board of Education's Zoning and Integration Unit can be reached at (718) 935-3566.

A list of public and private schools located between Battery Park City and 29th Street and from River to River follows. All of the private schools are considered good, and some are the finest in the country. These schools may differ from one another in educational philosophy, but not in standards of excellence. Some are more traditional and require uniform dress and strict attention to a given curriculum. Others are more liberal, and allow greater personal choice in what children may wear and study. Some are boys schools; some girls schools; and some are co-ed. Some schools go only up to the sixth grade while others continue up through high school.

A service that can be helpful in checking out private schools is The Parents League of New York, located at 115 East 82nd Street, (212) 737-7385. In addition to the excellent information they have, they offer counseling sessions with a specialist from their School Advisory Service. This is a non-profit organization, and for an annual $35 membership, they will help you choose a school or find a tutor.

Another source to check for private schools is the "New York Independent Schools Directory." (This can be obtained at the Parents League's office). It is published by The Independent Schools Admissions Association of Greater New York, which is a non-profit organization formed to promote the educational purposes of their member schools. The publication contains descriptions of some 120 private schools that enroll children from pre-school through high school. More generally, "The Manhattan Family Guide to Private Schools," by Catherine Hausman and Victoria Goldman, describes 57 elementary and high schools in the Greater New York Area and gives practical advice to parents seeking to place their children in private schools. Also, "The Parents' Guide to New York City's Best Public Elementary Schools" is a comprehensive guide to the 100 best elementary schools in New York City.

*NOTE: A listing of private and parochial schools is provided under each community district on the pages that follow.

School District Two   (212) 337-8700
330 West 18th Street
New York, NY 10011

COMMUNITY DISTRICT ONE

PUBLIC SCHOOLS

GROUP DAY CARE

Finest Care Child Care   1 Police Plaza

BMCC Early Childhood Center   199 Chambers Street

DAYCARE (VOUCHER)

FED Kids, Inc.   26 Federal Plaza

Washington Street Market School   55 Hudson Street

ELEMENTARY SCHOOLS

PS 234 - Independence School   300 Greenwich Street

HIGH SCHOOLS

Satellite Academy High School   51 Chambers Street

High School for Leadership & Public Service   100 Trinity Place

Stuyvesant High School   345 Chambers Street

High School for Economic & Finance   100 Trinity Place

Murry Bergtraum High School   411 Pearl Street

PUBLIC COLLEGE - CUNY

Borough of Manhattan Comunity College   199 Chambers Street
(CUNY)

INDEPENDENT - DEGREE GRANTING INSTITUTION

College of Insurance   101 Murray Street

New York Law School   57 Worth Street

NYU School of Business Administration   100 Trinity Place

Pace University   1 Pace Plaza

PROPRIETARY - DEGREE GRANTING INSTITUTION

Stenotype Academy Inc.   15 Park Row

School District Two
330 West 18th Street
New York, NY 10011

(212) 337-8700

COMMUNITY DISTRICT TWO

PUBLIC SCHOOLS

GROUP DAY CARE

Greenwich House Pre-school	27 Barrow Street
Baxter Street DCC	143 Baxter Street
The House of Little People	165 West 12th Street

HEADSTART CENTER

Chinese Headstart	180 Mott Street

ELEMENTARY SCHOOLS

PS 3 - The Charette	490 Hudson Street
PS 41 - Greenwich Village School	116 West 11th Street
PS 130 - The DeSoto School	143 Baxter Street

HIGH SCHOOLS

Unity High School/Project Door	121 Sixth Avenue
Lower Manhattan Outreach Center	16 Clarkson Street
City-AS-School High School	16 Clarkson Street
The Legacy School (Alternative)	33 West 13th Street
Chelsea Vocational High School	131 Avenue of Americas

SPECIAL/OTHER SCHOOLS

PS 721 - Manhattan Occupational Training Center	250 West Houston Street

PRIVATE AND PAROCHIAL SCHOOLS

ELEMENTARY SCHOOLS

St. Anthony School	60 Macdougal Street
St. Jospeh School	111 Washington Place
Our Lady of Pompeii School	240 Bleecker Street
St. Patrick's School	233 Mott Street
St. Bernard - St. Francis Xavier School	327 West 13th Street
Grace Church School	86 Fourth Avenue
St. Luke's School	487 Hudson Street

COMMUNITY DISTRICT TWO

PRIVATE AND PAROCHIAL SCHOOLS

ELEMENTARY SCHOOLS

City & Country School	146 West 13th Street
Little Red School House	196 Bleecker Street
Village Community School	272 West 10th Street

SENIOR HIGH SCHOOL

Elisabeth Irwin High School	40 Charlton Street

INDEPENDENT - DEGREE GRANTING INSTITUTIONS

College for Human Services	345 Hudson Street
Graduate School of Figurative Art	419 Lafayette Street
Hebrew Union College	1 West 4th Street
New School for Social Research	66 West 12th Street
New York University	70 Washington Square
Parsons School of Design	66 Fifth Avenue
Pratt Institute - Pratt Manhattan	295 Lafayette Street
Yeshiva University Cardozo Law School	55 Fifth Avenue

PROPRIETARY - DEGREE GRANTING INSTITUTIONS

Tobe-Coburn School for Fashion Careers	686 Broadway

COMMUNITY DISTRICT THREE

PUBLIC SCHOOLS

HEAD START CENTERS

Cardinal Spellman HS Center	137 East 2nd Street
Family Head Start	383 Grand Street
University Settlement HS Program	184 Eldridge Street
Escuela Hispana Montessori Inc	12 Avenue D
Escuela Hispana Montessori Inc	18 Avenue D
DeWitt Reformed Church	280 Rivington Street
DeWitt Reformed Church	123 Ridge Street
Educational Alliance HS Center	197 East Broadway
Grand Street Head Start	294 Delancey Street
Hamilton Madison Head Start	50 Madison Street
Hamilton Madison Head Start	80 Catherine Street

ELEMENTARY SCHOOLS

PS 15 - Roberto Clemente School	333 East Fourth Street
PS 19 - Asher Levy School	185 First Avenue
PS 20 - Anna Silver School	166 Essex Street
PS 34 - Franklin D. Roosevelt School	730 East 12th Street
PS 61 - Anna Howard Shaw School	610 East 12th Street
PS 63 - William McKinley School	121 East Third Street
PS 64 - Robert Simon School	600 East Sixth Street
PS 97 - Mangin School	525 East Houston Street
PS 110 Florence Nightingale School	285 Delancey Street South
PS 134 - Henrietta Szold School	293 East Brodway
PS 137 - John L. Bernstein School	327 Cherry Street
PS 140 - Nathan Straus School	123 Ridge Street
PS 142 - Amalia Castro School	100 Attorney Street
PS 188 - John Burroughs School	442 East Houston Street
PS 1 - Alfred E. Smith School	8 Henry Street
PS 2 - Meyer London School	122 Henry Street
PS 42 - Benjamin Altman School	71 Hester Street
PS 124 - Yung Wing School	40 Division Street
PS 126 Jacob Riis School	80 Catherine Street

COMMUNITY DISTRICT THREE

PUBLIC SCHOOLS

GROUP DAY CARE

Educational Alliance DCC	197 East Broadway
Grand Street CCC	300 Delancey Street
Hamilton-Madison House CCC	60 Catherine Street
Henry Street Settlement DCC	301 Henry Street
MFY Group CCC	108 Avenue D
League for Child Care	184 Eldridge Street
Virginia Day Nursery	464 East 10th Street
Confucius Plaza School-Age	40 Division Street
Emmanuel DCC	737 East 6th Street
Hester Street School Age DCC	115 Chrystie Street
Pike Street School Age DCC	112 Henry Street
Educational Alliance CCC	34 Avenue D
East Third Street After School	121 East 3rd Street
Oliver Street School Age DCC	8th Henry Street
First Avenue After School - Age DCC	185 1st Ave - PS 19
Puerto Rican Council DCC	180 Suffolk Street
Association DC Program	710-712 East 9th Street
Little Star of Broome DCC	131 Broome Street
Coalition for Hum Hsg	60 Essex Street
Childrens Liberation DCC	150 First Avenue
Action for Progress DCC	255 East Houston Street
Grmnt Ind DCC of Chinatown	115 Chrystie Street

DAYCARE (VOUCHER)

Chinatown YMCA	100 Hester Street

FAMILY DAY CARE OFFICE

University Settlement FDC	184 Eldridge Street

COMMUNITY DISTRICT THREE

PUBLIC SCHOOLS

INTERMEDIATE/JUNIOR HIGH SCHOOLS

JHS 22 - G. Straubenmuller JHS	111 Columbia Street
JHS 25 - Marta Valle JHS	145 Stanton Street
JHS 56 - Corlears JHS	220 Henry Street
JHS 60 - O.M. Beha JHS	420 East 12th Street
IS 131 - Dr. Sun Yat Sen School	100 Hester Street

HIGH SCHOOLS

Manhattan International High School	80 Catherine Street
Auxiliary Services	198 Forsythe Street
Lower East Side Prepatory School	145 Stanton Street
Seward Park High School	350 Grand Street
East Side Community High School	420 East 12th Street
Chancellor's Model School Project	145 Stanton Street
Leadership Secondary School	111 Columbia Street

SPECIAL/OTHER SCHOOL

P.S. 94	442 East Houston Street
P.S. 751 - School For Career Development	113 East 4th Street

PRIVATE AND PAROCHIAL SCHOOLS

ELEMENTARY SCHOOLS

St. Brigid School	185 East Seventh Street
St. George Elementary School	215 East Sixth Street
Immaculate Conception School	419 East 13th Street
Mary Help of Christians School	435 East 11th Street
Our Lady of Sorrows School	219 Stanton Street
Connelly Center Education Holy Child M	220 East 4th Street
Beth Jacob Elementary School	142 Broome Street
St. James School	37 St. James Place
Transfiguration School	29 Mott Street
The Transfiguration Kindergarten School	10 Confucius Plaza

COMMUNITY DISTRICT THREE

PRIVATE AND PAROCHIAL SCHOOLS

MIDDLE/JUNIOR HIGH SCHOOL

Nativity Mission School   204 Forsyth Street

SENIOR HIGH SCHOOL

LaSalle Academy   44 East Second Street

Notre Dame School   104 Saint Mark's Place

St. George Academy   215 East Sixth Street

K-12 SCHOOLS

Mesivta Tifereth Jerusalem   141-147 East Broadway

INDEPENDENT - DEGREE GRANTING INSTITUTION

Cooper Union   41 Cooper Square

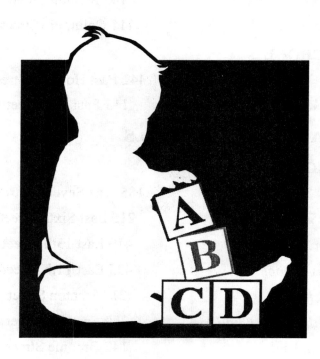

School District Two   (212) 337-8700
330 West 18th Street
New York, NY 10011

COMMUNITY DISTRICT FOUR

PUBLIC SCHOOLS: SCHOOL DISTRICT TWO

GROUP DAY CARE

Hudson Guild CCC   459 West 26th Street

McBurney Early Childhood   215 West 23rd Street

HEAD START CENTERS

Hudson Guild Head Start   459 West 26th Street

Hudson Guild Head Start   441 West 26th Street

ELEMENTARY SCHOOLS

PS 11 - William T. Harris School   320 West 21st Street

PS 33 - Chelsea School   281 Ninth Avenue

INTERMEDIATE/JUNIOR HIGH SCHOOLS

IS 70 - O. Henry School   333 West 17th Street

HIGH SCHOOLS

Legacy School For Intergrated Studies   125 West 14th Street - 4th Flr.

Vanguard High School   125 West 14th Street - 3rd Flr.

Project Blend   351 West 18th Street

Liberty High School   250 West 18th Street

Career Educational Center High School 250 West 18th Street

School - Physical City   333 West 17th Street

High School - Humanities   351 West 18th Street

Fashion Industries High School   225 West 24th Street

PRIVATE AND PAROCHIAL SCHOOLS

ELEMENTARY SCHOOL

St. Columba School   331 West 25th Street

Guardian Angel High School   193 Tenth Avenue

Corlears School   324 West 15th Street

SPECIAL/OTHER SCHOOLS

Bayview Correction Facilitiy   550 West 20th Street

The Lorge School   353 West 17th Street

INDEPENDENT - DEGREE GRANTING INSTITUTIONS

General Theological Seminary PE   175 Ninth Avenue

Technical Careers Institute   320 West 31st Street

School District Two
330 West 18th Street
New York, NY 10011

(212) 337-8700

COMMUNITY DISTRICT FIVE

PUBLIC SCHOOLS

GROUP DAY CARE

UCP NYC Manhattan Day Care   122 East 23rd Street

Graham Windham CCC   33 Irving Place

PRIVATE AND PAROCHIAL SCHOOLS

SENIOR HIGH SCHOOL

Xavier High School   30 West 16th Street

K-12 SCHOOL

U.C.P. - NYC   122 East 23rd Street

SPECIAL /OTHER SCHOOL

John A. Coleman School   590 Avenue of Americas

POST SECONDARY DEGREE GRANTING INSITUTIONS

Fashion Institute of Technology (SUNY)   227 West 27th Street

NYS College of Optometry (SUNY)   100 East 24th Street

INDEPENDENT - DEGREE GRANTING INSITUTIONS

American Academy of Dramatic Arts   120 Madison Avenue

College of New Rochelle -
Theological Seminary   5 West 29th Street

New York Theological Seminary   5 West 29th Street

COMMUNITY DISTRICT SIX

PUBLIC SCHOOLS

GROUP DAY CARE

Educare Early Childhood Center   484 Second Avenue

DAYCARE (VOUCHER)

McBurney - PS 40   320 East 20th Street

East Manhattan School   208-210 East 18th Street

Epiphany School   234 East 22nd Street

FAMILY DAY CARE OFFICE

Jewish Child Care Office- Public   575 Lexington Avenue

ELEMENTARY SCHOOLS

PS 40 - August Goudens   319 East 21st Street

PS 116 - Mary L. Murray School   210 East 33rd Street

INTERMEDIATE/JUNIOR HIGH SCHOOLS

JHS 104 - Simon Baruch JHS   330 East 21st Street

HIGH SCHOOLS

East Manhattan Outreach Center   240 Second Avenue

High School for Environmental Studies   345 East 15th Street

Health Prof & Human Services High School   345 East 15th Street

Washington Irving High School   40 Irving Place

Manhattan Comp Night High School   240 Second Avenue

SPECIAL/OTHER SCHOOLS

PS/JHS 47 School - Deaf   225 East 23rd Street

PS 106 Bellevue Psychiatric Hospital   East 27th Street & 1st Ave

PS 226   345 East 15th Street

PRIVATE AND PAROCHIAL SCHOOLS

ELEMENTARY SCHOOLS

Jack & Jill School of St. George Str   209 East 16th Street

The Epiphany School   234 East 22nd Street

Acorn School   330 East 26th Street

East Manhattan School   208 East 18th Street

COMMUNITY DISTRICT SIX

PRIVATE AND PAROCHIAL SCHOOLS
K-12 SCHOOL

Friends Seminary   222 East 16th Street

PUBLIC COLLEGE - CUNY

Bernard M. Baruch College   155 East 24th Street

Graduate School of Political Management   17 Lexington Avenue

INDEPENDENT - DEGREE GRANTING INSTITUTION

NYU Collge of Dentistry   345 East 24th Street

NYU College of Medicine   550 First Avenue

Phillips Beth Israel School of Nursing   310 East 22nd Street

PROPRIETARY - DEGREE GRANTING INSTITUTION

School of Visual Arts   209 East 23rd Street

HOUSES OF WORSHIP

HOUSES OF WORSHIP

There are many churches and synagogues of all denominations in Downtown. Many of these have special historical or architectural significance and most reach out to help serve their local communities.

Here are some of the most historic and architecturally interesting houses of worship:

* **Brotherhood Synagogue** (Conservative), at 28 Gramercy Park South, was built in 1859 and is a landmark. Starkly simple in design, the building was originally one of two Quaker meeting houses overlooking lovely Gramercy Park. It was renovated and turned into a synagogue in 1975. Services to the community include a shelter for the homeless, a religious school and facilities to aid Jewish immigrants.

* **Church Of The Ascension** (Episcopal), at 36 Fifth Avenue in the heart of Greenwich Village is New York's first Gothic Revival church. Built in 1841, its tasteful interior features a beautiful John La Farge altar mural and an illuminated stained-glass window. An exceptional choir performs liturgical music on Sundays and at special evening concerts.

* **Eldridge Street Synagogue** (Orthodox), at 12 Eldridge Street on the Lower East Side, was the most luxurious of the many Synagogues that once thrived in this area. Currently under renovation, services, weddings and bar mitvahs are still held downstairs; (the main sanctuary was abandoned in the 1950's). Tours of the synagogue, and the history of the Lower East Side, are given by the Eldridge Street Project.

* **Grace Church** (Episcopal), at 802 Broadway in Greenwich Village, was built in 1846 and is one of the most magnificent examples of Gothic Revival architecture in the nation. Worship is traditional, however, with wonderful music. Community services include adult classes on a variety of topics and outreach programs to youth, seniors and AIDS victims.

* **John Street United Methodist Church,** at 44 John Street, is the home of America's oldest Methodist congregation. Built in 1841, the present building is the third Methodist church on this site; the first was built in 1768. Dwarfed by Wall Street's high-rise buildings, this landmarked church seems out of place and time, harkening back to an earlier era in New York's history.

* **Marble Collegiate Church** (Dutch reformed), at 272 Fifth Avenue in Murray Hill, traces its roots back to the city's first Dutch congregation organized by Peter Minuit in 1628. Dr. Norman Vincent Peale was its pastor from 1932 to 1984.

* **St. Joseph's Roman Catholic Church,** at 365 Sixth Avenue, is Manhattan's oldest surviving Roman Catholic Church. At Washington Place, in the heart of Greenwich Village, it is a bustling family church. It was also the first Catholic church to open a shelter for homeless men in the city.

* **St. Paul's Chapel** (Episcopal), at Broadway and Fulton St., in lower Manhattan is Manhattan's oldest surviving building. Built in 1764-66, the Georgian-style church, with its distinctive spire was designed primarily by architect Pierre L'Enfant, who later laid out the city plan for Washington D.C.

George Washington, the Marquis de Lafayette and General Cornwallis were among it's early worshippers.

* **Trinity Church** (Episcopal), at Broadway and Wall Street, in lower Manhattan was founded in 1697 and was the city's first Episcopal congregation. The present Gothic Revival edifice is the third on this site and is one of New York's best known landmarks. Once New York's tallest building, because of its 280 foot spire, it is still sometimes referred to as New York's first skyscraper.

OTHER SIGNIFICANT HOUSES OF WORSHIP INCLUDE:

* **Bialystoker Synagogue** 713 Bialystoker Place, Lower East Side
* **Church of the Epiphany** (Roman Catholic) Second Avenue at 22nd Street
* **Civic Center Synagogue** (Orthodox) 49 White Street, West of Broadway
* **First Presbyterian Church** 48 Fifth Avenue, between 11th and 12th Streets
* **Holy Trinity Chapel** 58 Washington Square South, Greenwich Village
* **Judson Memorial** (Baptist-United Church of Christ)
  55 Washington Square South, Greenwich Village
* **The Little Church Around The Corner** (Episcopal) 1 East 29th Street
* **St. George's Ukranian Catholic Church** 30 East 7th Street, East Village
* **St. James Church** (Roman Catholic) 32 James Street, Chinatown
* **St. Luke-In-The-Fields Church** (Episcopal) 485 Hudson Street, West Village
* **St. Peter's Church** (Roman Catholic) 22 Barclay Street, Lower Manhattan
* **St. Mark's Church In-The-Bowery** (Episcopal) 2nd Avenue and 10th Street, East Village
* **Tiffereth Israel Synagogue** (Conservative) 334 East 14th Street, East Village

NOTES

real estate

Rentals

UNFURNISHED APARTMENTS

Real Estate

Real Estate

furnished

apts

Real

state

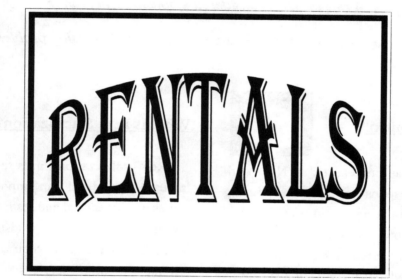

RENTALS

Unfurnished
Apartments

Real Estate

Rentals

unfurnished apts

Chapter 2

Rentals

Manhattan's Rental Market:
An Overview

The complex story of New York City's rent-regulated housing market is a tale of good intentions gone wrong - - of laws designed to protect the poor ultimately benefitting the well-to-do and the lucky, and of everyone, landlord and tenant alike, squeezed between the two jaws of a vise.

Here are some facts:

- *The constant shortage of apartments in New York City has created arguably the worst housing crisis in the country.*

- *New York's vacancy rate is approximately 3.4 percent and dropping. In Manhattan, the rate is less than 2%. A rate of 5% is considered a housing emergency.*

- *Rent regulation may or may not be the cause of New York's housing problems.*

What is Rent Control?

Rent control was first enacted in New York City in 1943 in response to a serious housing shortage that began during World War II. Laws were written to protect tenants from landlords who unscrupulously raised rents to exorbitant levels or who evicted tenants without just cause.

About 70,000 apartments in New York City today are covered by rent control. Rent-controlled tenants are called "Statutory tenants" and do not need a lease. Typically these tenants are elderly (the median age is 70), and have lived in their apartments continuously since before July 1st 1971. A rent controlled apartment rarely comes back on the market; it is usually passed along to family members when it does. Should such an apartment become vacant, it could then be decontrolled in which case the rent would rise to fair-market value.

What is Rent Stabilization?

Rent stabilization limits the amount of rent increase a landlord can impose when a lease comes up for renewal and restricts the right of the owner to evict tenants. It also legally requires landlords to maintain their buildings and to provide essential services. Maximum rent increases for renewal leases are calculated each year in July, by the State's Rent Guidelines Board, and put into effect in October. The Board listens to both landlord and tenant advocates and determines the fairest percentage increase that a landlord can have. In 1995, rent increases were 2% on one-year lease renewals, and 4% on two-year renewals. Current rent increases are 5% for one-year and 7% for two-year leases; the largest rent increase in seven years.

In addition to lease renewal increases, land-lords may also be permitted to increase rents when an apartment is vacated (even if it's only for one day), when apartments are renovated or when major capital improvements are made.

• Note: Most apartments built in the post-war period from 1947 to 1974 in buildings containing six or more units are rent stabilized. Under the 421-A Tax Abatement, apartments built or extensively renovated after 1974 are partly stabilized. Initial tenants receive a rent increase of 2.2% annually, after the first lease date for a period of nine years in addition to the increases voted by the Rent Guidelines Board. After 10 years, this 2.2% increase is abated and the apartment becomes fully stabilized. Should this type of unit be vacated by the original tenant, however, then it would be deregulated.

What are Fair-Market Rents?

Currently, under the amended 1997 luxury vacancy decontrol law, apartments that would rent for $2,000 or more a month, when vacated, can be decontrolled, as would occupied apartments with rents of $2,000 or more where the household income exceeds $175,000 for two years. In many cases, landlords are able to push their rents up to the $2,000 minimum by combining the vacancy allowance, plus lease increases, with the pass-along-cost of improvements made to the apartment. In this way, thousands of apartments have been deregulated with the State's blessing, and landlords have found a way to get around rent regulation restrictions.

In addition to luxury decontrolled units, rental apartments in co-op and condo buildings are also exempt from rent regulations, as are rental units built after 1973 without tax incentives and units in buildings with less than six apartments.

What is the Promise of Deregulation?

The promise of luxury and other decontrol laws is the renovation of apartments, and buildings, that have not had substantial improvements in years. The long term benefits may include a greater incentive for developers to build rental housing in New York City again. The goal is that with an increase of rental units, rents which are currently rising to new heights will begin to fall and those tenants who are paying the highest rents will have the option of moving out of their apartments or renegotiating their leases. Tenants who now pay below market prices for their apartments, would find their rents going up to a price somewhere between the highest and the lowest rent paid for their unit in their building. A leveling effect would be created, as all apartment rents came into line with one another.

What is the Immediate Result of Deregulation?

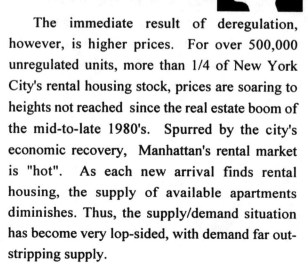

The immediate result of deregulation, however, is higher prices. For over 500,000 unregulated units, more than 1/4 of New York City's rental housing stock, prices are soaring to heights not reached since the real estate boom of the mid-to-late 1980's. Spurred by the city's economic recovery, Manhattan's rental market is "hot". As each new arrival finds rental housing, the supply of available apartments diminishes. Thus, the supply/demand situation has become very lop-sided, with demand far outstripping supply.

Rents have risen approximately 30% to 40% since 1993. Yet even at such highly inflated prices, landlords have several hopeful applicants for every available apartment. One thing is for certain: vacant apartments do not stay on the market very long ; they are usually rented in no more than a few days.

In both Greenwich Village (West of Fifth Avenue) and the Upper Westside (West 60th to West 96th Street) vacant apartments are particularly scarce. When an apartment does become available, it usually is rented within twenty-four hours.

There is no immediate end in sight to the tight rental market. Co-ops or condos that were once rented (because their owners were unable to sell them) are now being sold in an increasingly hot sales market. These apartments, which make up about one-half the rental supply, are no longer available to prospective renters who must now look elsewhere. But where?

Tenants in landlord-owned buildings with stabilized leases will not move because they cannot find anything cheaper or better. There are few new high-rise buildings being constructed in the city today. (Developers will eventually put up new construction again to cash in on high rental prices, but that may not happen for a few years.) Meanwhile, rents will continue to skyrocket.

What are Current Rents in Manhattan?

It's hard to pin down exact rents for comparable units throughout Manhattan, because no such data exists in any database. Brokers, however, keep track of the market by doing their own surveys. According to recent reports, studio apartments in high rise buildings throughout Manhattan rent for about $1,000 to $1,500 a month; one-bedroom units, for about $1,500 to $3,000; two-bedroom units for about $2,500 to $4,500; and three-bedrooms for $3,500+.

Similar units in walk-up buildings will cost somewhat less.

NOTE:
- *A new 90-page booklet titled "What Every Landlord and Tenant Should Know" put out by the Citizens Housing and Planning Council gives good advice to both groups about their respective rights and obligations.*
Single copies of the handbook cost $5 and are available from the city council at 50 East 42nd Street, Suite 407, New York, NY 10017. Telephone: (212) 286-9211.

- *A recent survey of prices in __new__ luxury and loft buildings is given on the following pages. These rents do not reflect apartment prices in older rent-stabilized buildings whose rents would be less.*

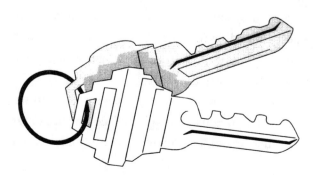

Rental Building Guide

$ $ $ $ $ $

The Villager 194 East 2nd Street New York, NY 10009	Shaya B. Development Broker: Ardor Realty *Fee: 15% (212) 794-1330	One-bedrooms - $1,750+ Two-bedrooms - $2,200+ Three-bedrooms - $3,900+
280 East 2nd Street New York, NY 10009	Manhattan Skyline Mgt. (212) 889-1850	Studios - $1,400+ One-bedrooms - $1,900+
70 East 3rd Street New York, NY 10003	Park Square Assoc. *Brokerage Fee: 1 Month Rent (212) 529-9595	Studios - $900+ One-bedrooms - $1,200+
94 East 4th Street New York, NY 10003	Bettina Equities Co. (212) 744-3330	Studios - $1,400+ One-bedrooms - $1,900+ Two-bedrooms - $2,200+
527 East 6th Street New York, NY 10009	Park Square Assoc. *Brokerage Fee: 1 Month Rent (212) 529-9595	Studios - $1,200+ One-bedrooms - $1,500+
32-34 East 7th Street New York, NY 10009	Jakobson Properties (212) 533-1300	Studios - $1,000+ One-bedrooms - $1,400+ Two-bedrooms - $2,000+
299 East 8th Street New York, NY 10009	Park Square Assoc. *Brokerage Fee: 1 Month Rent (212) 529-9595	Studios - $900+ One-bedrooms - $1,400+ Two-bedrooms - $1,600+
315-317 East 9th Street New York, NY 10003	Park Square Assoc. *Brokerage Fee: 1 Month Rent (212) 529-9595	Studios - $1,000+ One-bedrooms - $1,100+
320 East 9th Street New York, NY 10003	Bettina Equities (212) 744-3300	Studios - $1,000+ One-bedrooms - $1,500+
Devonshire House 28 East 10th Street New York, NY 10003	Felder Mgt. Assoc. (212) 685-5250	Studios - $1,500 One-bedrooms - $2,500 Two-bedrooms - $3,500
254 East 10th Street New York, NY 10003	Bettina Equities (212) 744-3330	Studios - $1,000+

*Note: • See Building Directory, Part III, for a complete description of building amenities.
• Prices continue to rise and may be higher at the time that you call.

245 East 11th Street New York, NY 10003	Jakobson Properties (212) 533-1300	Studios - $1,500+ One-bedrooms - $1,900+ Two-bedrooms - $2,200+
70 East 12th Street New York, NY 10003	Bettina Equities (212) 744-3330	Studios - $1,300+ One-bedrooms - $1,800+ Two-bedrooms - $2,500+
150 East 18th Street New York, NY 10010	American SIBA corp. (212) 764-0700	Studios - $1,750+ One-bedrooms - $2,300+ Two-bedrooms - $3,200+
Gramercy 22 12 East 22nd Street New York, NY 10010	Abington Holdings (212) 759-5000	Studios - $1,600+ One-bedrooms - $2,500+
131 East 23rd Street New York, NY 10010	Zucker Organization/Developer Manhattan Skyline Mgt. (212) 889-1850 or 997-4813	Studios - $1,600+ One-bedrooms - $1,800+ Two-bedrooms - $2,300+
Gramercy Court 214 East 24th Street New York, NY	Abington Holdings (212) 759-5000	Studios - $1,600+ One-bedrooms - $1,800+ Two-bedrooms - $2,500+
The Stanford 45 East 25th Street New York, NY 10010	Exclusive Rental Broker: Citi Habitats - *Fee: 15% (212) 685-7300	Studios - $1,100+ One-bedrooms - $1,800+ Two-bedrooms - $2,600+
The Townsway 145 East 27th Street New York, NY 10016	Algin Mgt. (212) 725-0566 or (718) 896-9600	Studios - $1,200+ One-bedrooms - $1,600+ Two-bedrooms - $2,500+
207 East 27th Strret New York, NY 10016	Abington Holdings (212) 759-5000	Studios - $1,400+ One-bedrooms - $1,800+
The Habitat 154 East 29th Street New York, NY 10016	Manhattan Skyline Mgt. On-site Agent: (212) 889-1850 or (212) 977-4813	Studios - $1,700+ One-bedrooms - $2,500+
The Biltmore Plaza 155 East 29th Street New York, NY 10016	Milford Mgt. (212) 684-5900	One-bedrooms - $2,300+ Two-bedrooms - $3,300+
210 East 29th Street New York, NY 10016	Abington Trust (212) 759-5000	Studios - $1,200+ One-bedrooms - $1,900+ Two-bedrooms - $3,400+

Rental Building Guide

$ $ $ $ $ $ $

Left Bank 77 West 15th Street New York, NY 10003	Manhattan Skyline Mgt. (212) 889-1850 or (212) 977-4813	Studios - $1,200+ One-bedrooms - $1,400+
Chelsea Court 250 West 19th Street New York, NY 10011	B&L Mgt. Co. (212) 980-0980	Studios - $1,600+ One-bedrooms - $1,900+ Two-bedrooms - $2,600+
434 West 19th Street New York, NY 10011	B&L Mgt. Co. (212) 980-0980	Studios - $1,100+ One-bedrooms - $1,600+
The Carteret 208 West 23rd Street New York, NY 10011	Jakobson Properties (212) 929-7060 or (212) 533-1300	Studios - $1,500+ One-bedrooms - $2,100+ Two-bedrooms - $2,300+
412 West 25th Street New York, NY 10011	Abington Holdings (212) 759-5000	Studios - $1,100+ One-bedrooms - $1,500+ Two-bedrooms - $1,900+

*Note: • See Building Directory, Part III, for a complete description of building amenities.
         • Prices continue to rise and may be higher at the time that you call.

Rental Building Guide
$ $ $ $ $ $ $

85 Avenue A New York, NY 10009	Park Square Assoc. *Brokerage Fee: 1 Month Rent (212) 529-9595	Studios - $1,400+ One-bedrooms - $1,600+ Two-bedrooms - $2,300+
105 Avenue B New York, NY 10009	Park Square Assoc. *Brokerage Fee: 1 Month Rent (212) 529-9595	One-bedrooms - $1,100+ Two-bedrooms - $2,000+
Liberty View 99 Battery Place New York, NY 10280	Milford Mgt. On-site Agent (212) 898-4800	Studios - $1,800+ One-bedrooms - $2,000+ Two-bedrooms - $3,400+
Delmonico's Building 56 Beaver Street New York, NY 10004	Time Equities On-site Agent (212) 206-6044	Studios - $1,400+ One-bedrooms - $1,900+ Two-bedrooms - $2,800+
The Exchange 25 Broad Street New York, NY 10004	Insignia Mgt. On-site Agent (212) 217-2901	Studios - $2,000+ One-bedrooms - $2,100+ Two-bedrooms - $2,700+
71 Broadway New York, NY 10006	NRK Mgt. (212) 344-7171	Studios - $1,600+ One-bedrooms - $2,000+ Two-bedrooms - $2,800+
18-20 Cornelia Street New York, NY 10014	Jakobson Properties (212) 533-1300	Studios - $1,300+ One-bedrooms - $1,600+ Two-bedrooms - $1,800+
Tribeca Tower 105 Duane Street New York, NY 10007	Related Companies On-site Agent (212) 346-7900	Studios - $1,900+ One-bedrooms - $2,500+ Two-bedrooms - $3,800+
Soho Court 301 Elizabeth Street New York, NY 10012	Owner: Zucker Organization (212) 889-1850	Studios - $1,600+ One-bedrooms - $2,200+ Two-bedrooms - $3,000+
77 Fifth Avenue New York, NY 10003	Bettina Equities (212) 744-3330	Studios - $1,400+ One-bedrooms - $1,600+ Two-bedrooms - $2,600+

*Note: • See Building Directory, Part III, for a complete description of building amenities.
• Prices continue to rise and may be higher at the time that you call.

26, 28 & 30 Greenwich Avenue New York, NY 10011	Jakobson Properties (212) 533-1300	Studios - $1,400+ One-bedrooms - $1,900+ Two-bedrooms - $2,200+
110 Greenwich Street New York, NY 10006	Jakobson Properties (212) 533-1300	Studios - $1,500+ One-bedrooms - $2,000+ Two-bedrooms - $2,500+
The Archive 666 Greenwich Street New York, NY 10014	Rockrose Development Co. On-site Agent (212) 691-9800	One-bedrooms - $2,800+ Two-bedrooms - $3,400+
92 Grove Street New York, NY 10014	Eberhart Bros. (212) 570-2400	Studios - $1,300+ One-bedrooms - $1,700+ Two-bedrooms - $2,600+
The West Coast Apts. 95-97 & 110-114 Horatio St. New York, NY 10014	Rockrose Development On-site Agent (212) 727-3500	Studios - $1,600+ One-bedrooms - $2,300+ Two-bedrooms - $3,300+
Red Square 250 East Houston Street New York, NY 10002	Park Square Assoc. On-site Agent *Brokerage Fee: 1 Month Rent (212) 529-9595	Studios - $1,500+ One-bedrooms - $2,000+ Two-bedrooms - $2,500+
Printing House 421 Hudson Street New York, NY 10014	Orb Mgt. Ltd. On-site Agent (212) 243-1320 x222	One-bedrooms - $2,800+ Two-bedrooms - $3,800+ Three-bedrooms - $4,600+
519-525 Hudson Street New York, NY 10014	Time Equities (212) 206-6044	Studios - $1,000+ One-bedrooms - $1,300+
Zeckendorf Towers 1 Irving Place New York, NY 10003	Maxwell Kates Rlty. (212) 674-9150	Studios - $1,800+ One-bedrooms - $2,300+ Two-bedrooms - $3,600+
100 Jane Street New York, NY 10014	Rockrose Development (212) 727-3500	Studios - $1,600+ One-bedrooms - $2,300+ Two-bedrooms - $3,000+
41 John Street New York, NY 10038	Time Equities (212) 206-6044	One-bedrooms - $2,500+ Two-bedrooms - $3,800+
Renaissance 100 John Street New York, NY 10038	Insignia Mgt. On-site Broker: City Habitats (212) 489-6666	Studios - $1,500+ One-bedrooms - $2,000+ Two-bedrooms - $2,900+
10 Jones Street New York, NY 10014	Abington Holdings (212) 759-5000	One-bedrooms - $2,100+
22 Jones Street New York, NY 10014	Abington Holdings (212) 759-5000	Studios - $1,500+ One-bedrooms - $1,800+

105 Lexington Avenue New York, NY 10016	Bettina Equities (212) 744-3330	Studios - $1,100+ One-bedrooms - $1,600+ Two-bedrooms - $2,300+
Beta South 151 Lexington Avenue New York, NY 10016	Bettina Equities (212) 744-3330	Studios - $1,100+ One-bedrooms - $1,500+
124 MacDougal Street New York, NY 10012	Jakobson Properties (212) 533-1300	Studios - $1,200+ One-bedrooms - $1,600+ Two-bedrooms - $1,800+
The Soho Abbey 284 Mott Street New York, NY 10012	Abington Holdings (212) 759-5000	Studios - $1,500+ One-bedrooms - $1,900+ Two-bedrooms - $2,500+
80 Nassau Street West New York, NY 10038	Time Equities (212) 206-6044	One-bedrooms - $1,900+ Two-bedrooms - $3,500+ Three-bedrooms - $4,500+
166, 178 Norfolk Street New York, NY 10002	Park Square Associates *Brokerage Fee: 1 Month Rent (212) 529-9595	Studios - $900+ One-bedrooms - $1,300+
Tribeca Bridge Tower 450 North End Avenue New York, NY 10280	Manager: Brown, Harris, Stevens On-site Broker: Feathered Nest, Inc. (212) 217-6001	One-bedrooms - $2,300+ Two-bedrooms - $3,400+ Three-bedrooms - $4,700+
19 Gramery 239 Park Avenue South New York, NY 10003	Abington Holdings (212) 759-5000	One-bedrooms - $2,700+
Gramercy Place 280 Park Avenue South New York, NY 10010	Insignia Residential Broker: Citi Habitats *Fee: 15% (212) 529-8888	One-bedrooms - $2,900+ Two-bedrooms - $4,300+
Park 23 295 Park Avenue South New York, NY 10010	Abington Holdings (212) 759-5000	Studios - $1,500+ One-bedrooms - $2,200+ Two-bedrooms - $3,300+
Coenties Slip Apts. 66 Pearl Street New York, NY 10004	Orb Mgt. (212) 734-2464	Studios - $1,100+ One-bedrooms - $1,200+ Two-bedrooms - $2,000+
50 Prince Street New York, NY 10012	Linmar L.P. (212) 759-5000	Studios - $1,500+ One-bedrooms - $2,100+
Tribeca Abbey 121 Reade Street New York, NY 10013	Abington Holdings (212) 759-5000	Studios - $1,500+ One-bedrooms - $2,100+ Two-bedrooms - $3,200+

Liberty Court 200 Rector Place New York, NY 10280	Milford Mgt. On-site Agent (212) 898-4800	Studios - $1,800+ One-bedrooms - $2,000+ Two-bedrooms - $3,000+
Parc Place 225 Rector Place New York, NY 10280	Related Companies On-site Agent (212) 945-0500	Studios - $2,000+ One-bedrooms - $2,200+ Two-bedrooms - $3,400+
River Rose 333 Rector Place New York, NY 10280	Rockrose Development On-site Agent (212) 786-0537	Studios - $1,600+ One-bedrooms - $2,000+ Two-bedrooms - $3,000+
Liberty House 377 Rector Place New York, NY 10280	Milford Mgt. On-site Agent (212) 898-4800	Studios - $2,000+ One-bedrooms - $2,100+ Two-bedrooms - $3,500+
Liberty Terrace 380 Rector Place New York, NY 10280	Milford Mgt. On-site Agent (212) 898-4800	Studios - $2,000+ One-bedrooms - $2,100+ Two-bedrooms - $3,500+
Tribeca Pointe 41 River Terrace New York, NY 10282	Rockrose Development On-site Agent (212) 370-4141	Studios - $1,800+ One-bedrooms - $2,200+ Two-bedrooms - $3,900+
Rutherford Place 305 Second Avenue New York, NY 10003	Orb Mgt. Corp. On-site Agent (212) 473-9066	Studios - $2,200+ One-bedrooms - $3,400+ Two-bedrooms - $4,500+
450 Sixth Avenue New York, NY 10011	Manhattan Skyline (212) 889-1850	Studios - $2,100+ One-bedrooms - $3,200+ Two-bedrooms - $3,900+
Gateway Plaza 375 South End Avenue New York, NY 10280	Lefrak Org./ Gateway Plaza Mgt. On-site Agent (212) 488-9456	Studios - $1,600+ One-bedrooms - $2,000+ Two-bedrooms - $2,500+
172-176 Spring St. New York, NY 10012	Time Equities (212) 206-6044	Studios - $1,000+ One-bedrooms - $1,200+ Two-bedrooms - $1,500+
102, 128 St. Mark's Place New York, NY 10009	Jakobson Properties (212) 533-1300	Studios - $1,000+ One-bedrooms - $1,200+ Two-bedrooms - $1,500+
97-119 Sullivan Street New York, NY 10012	Manhattan Skyline (212) 889-1850	Studios - $1,200+ One-bedrooms - $1,700+
240 Sullivan Street New York, NY 10012	Time Equities (212) 206-6044	One-bedrooms - $1,300+
64 Third Avenue New York, NY 10003	Jakobson Properties (212) 533-1300	Lofts: 400-2,000 sq. ft. $1,500-$5,000

Manhattan Promenade 344 Third Avenue New York, NY 10003	ATA Enterprises On-site Agent (212) 684-1130	Studios - $1,700+ One-bedrooms - $2,400+ Two-bedrooms - $3,400+
Eastview Tower 382 Third Avenue New York, NY 10016	Abington Holdings (212) 759-5000	Studios - $1,400+ One-bedrooms - $2,200+ Two-bedrooms - $2,500+
230-234 Thompson Street New York, NY 10012	Time Equities (212) 206-6044	Studios - $1,100+ One-bedrooms - $1,300+ Two-bedrooms - $1,500+
1 Union Square South New York, NY 10003	The Related Companies On-site Agent (212) 253-1400	Studios - $2,500+ One-bedrooms - $3,000+ Two-bedrooms - $4,300+
45 Wall Street New York, NY 10005	Rockrose Development On-site Agent (212) 797-7000	Studios - $1,500+ or $1,800+ One-bedrooms - $2,000+ Two-bedrooms - $3,300+
11 Waverly Place New York, NY 10003	Jakobson Properties On-site Agent: (212) 533-1300	Studios - $1,200+ One-bedrooms - $1,900+ Two-bedrooms - $2,200+
189 Waverly Place New York, NY 10011	Jakobson Properties (212) 533-1300	Studios - $1,300+ One-bedrooms - $1,600+ Two-bedrooms - $1800+
Le Rivage 21 West Street New York, NY 10006	Rose Associates On-site Agent (212) 509-2121	Studios - $1,600+ One-bedrooms - $2,300+ Two-bedrooms - $3,100+
47 West Street New York, NY	Time Equities (212) 206-6173	Lofts: 2,000-6,000+ sq. ft. $3,000-$12,000

real estate

Rentals

UNFURNISHED APARTMENTS

Real Estate

Real Estate

Unfurnished Apartments

furnished

apts

Real

estate

SHORT-TERM
FURNISHED RENTALS

Real Estate

Rentals

unfurnished apts

Rentals

Chapter 3

SHORT TERM FURNISHED

For executives who need to be in town for an extended period, new arrivals who have not yet found an apartment while relocating, and many visitors who come to New York on a regular basis, short-term furnished rentals have provided an easy solution. These short-term, extended stay rentals provide the same comforts as residential living without the obligation of a long-term lease. They are also suitable for people who cannot tolerate the noise of renovations, and need a temporary residence where they can continue their daily routine without interruption.

Many of these apartments come with fully equipped kitchens, cable TV/VCR, personal phone lines, fax/modem connections, and business centers. They may also include maid and laundry service, concierge, health club, and other luxuries. Some short-term furnished rentals require only a minimum one month stay, but for many, a three month lease is required. Occupancy taxes apply for some, and may vary depending on the status of the building. The tax scale is 13.25% for stays of up to 30 days; 9% after that. Should you stay for 180 days or longer, no taxes apply. Furnished rentals within residential apartment buildings are usually not taxed.

For those who prefer hotel accommodations, Manhattan offers more than 200 hotel listings, with area shops, restaurants, and theatres all conveniently located nearby. Prices vary greatly among hotels. If you are on a budget and looking for a hotel room with rates starting under $150 a night, a list of safe, clean, and comfortable budget hotels follows. Also listed are some residence/hotels, for women only, in secure residential neighborhoods.

Whether your stay is for one month, six months or longer, New York has a short term furnished rental or budget hotel to suit your needs.

FURNISHED RENTALS

BRISTOL PLAZA
210 EAST 65TH STREET (BETWEEN SECOND & THIRD AVENUES)
212-826-9000

- ❑ Located in the heart of the Upper East Side
- ❑ Ten-year old building with garage
- ❑ Luxury condominium suites
- ❑ Studios, one and two bedroom apartments
- ❑ Furnished with daily maid & linen service
- ❑ Complimentary membership for Pool & Health Club
- ❑ Available on long or short term leases
- ❑ Lease rates from $5,200 for studios, $5,400 for one-bedrooms, $8,100 for two-bedrooms
- ❑ Average stay – three months
- ❑ Studios, one and two-bedroom apartments range in price from $4,000 to $ 11,000 per month
- ❑ Short-term and extended stays are available

CHURCHILL CORPORATE SERVICES
6 EAST 32ND STREET (BETWEEN FIFTH & MADISON AVENUES)
212-686-0444

- Manages over 250 turnkey furnished apartments in 26 residential buildings throughout New York City
- Included are studios, one-, two-bedroom apartments, with monthly prices ranging from $2,200 for studios, $2,900 for one-bedrooms, and $4,500 for two-bedrooms
- Local phone calls, cable and utilities up to $100 are included in the rent
- Optional services include business equipment, rental and maid service
- Renters receive special discounts at the New York Health & Racquet Club in their area

THE ENVOY CLUB AT EASTBRIDGE LANDING
377 EAST 33RD STREET (AT FIRST AVENUE)
212-481-4600

- Upscale furnished apartments with hotel services occupy the 3rd and 7th floors of this residential apartment building

THE PHILLIPS CLUB AT THE GRAND MILLENNIUM
1965 Broadway (between 66th & 67th Streets)
212-835-8800

- Residential condominium apartment building, built in 1996
- One, two and three-bedroom suites range in size from 650 to 2,000 square feet
- Prices range from $5,500 to $16,000 per month depending on size
- Average stays of 115 days

PIERRE DEUX
369 BLEECKER STREET (AT THE CORNER OF CHARLES STREET)
212-691-1400 EXT. 212 - MARY BETRI, RENTAL AGENT

- Four small and intimate apartments above a French antique store
- Two duplexes, one simplex, and one two-bedroom unit beautifully furnished with antiques and Ralph Lauren linens
- Very private
- Concierge service and cleaning service provided by antique shop personnel
- Rentals available on a three month minimum basis
- Prices range from $4,000 to $8,000 per month

HEMSLEY CARLTON HOUSE
680 MADISON AVENUE (BETWEEN 61ST & 62ND STREETS)
212-838-3000

- ❑ Located on chic Madison Avenue; Maxim's Restaurant is on the premises
- ❑ 160 Junior suites (studios), plus one and two-bedroom suites
- ❑ Lease rates from $6,500 for studios, $9,000 for one-bedrooms and $12,000 for two-bedrooms
- ❑ Manned elevators
- ❑ Room service

THE MANHATTAN CLUB IN THE PARK CENTRAL HOTEL
200 WEST 56TH STREET (BETWEEN SEVENTH AVENUE & BROADWAY)
212-707-5000

- ❑ Time share with weekly or nightly use throughout the year
- ❑ 252 Suites; including junior one-bedrooms and two bedrooms ranging in size from 400 to 1,100 square feet
- ❑ All the amenities of a luxury hotel, including a health club, two conference rooms and a lounge area where breakfast and cocktails are served

THE MARMARA MANHATTAN
310 EAST 94TH STREET (AT THE CORNER OF SECOND AVENUE)
212-427-3100

- ❑ Located in Yorkville
- ❑ Eight year old 32 story building with 108 suites
- ❑ Condominium apartments converted to short-term rentals
- ❑ Spacious and elegantly furnished apartments, all with river or city views
- ❑ Studios, one, two & three-bedroom suites ranging in size from 360 to 1,450 square feet
- ❑ Lease rates from $3,750 for studios, $4,500 for one-bedrooms, $7,750 for two-bedrooms, and $12,000 for three-bedrooms
- ❑ Building offers cordless phones, fax, stereo w/CD, WEB TV & VCR

RESIDENTIAL SUITE HOTELS

BEEKMAN TOWER
3 MITCHELL PLACE (AT 49TH STREET & FIRST AVENUE)
212-355-7300

- ❑ The 26 story Beekman Tower is considered an art deco landmark
- ❑ Recently renovated, each of its suites reflect traditional styling; some have terraces and river views
- ❑ Facilities include a fitness center, restaurant and roof-top cocktail lounge, guest laundry and full kitchens
- ❑ Business services include secretarial services, dataport, fax service and meeting/banquet rooms
- ❑ Monthly rates range from $6,270 for studios, $6,870 for one-bedrooms and $12,570 for two-bedrooms

DUMONT PLAZA
150 EAST 34TH STREET (BETWEEN THIRD & LEXINGTON AVENUES)
212-481-7600

- ❑ Built in 1986, and renovated in 1993, this hotel has modern facilities: a fitness center with sauna, full kitchens, restaurant, guest laundry, and valet parking
- ❑ Business services include dataports and fax service, secretarial services, voicemail, and meeting/banquet rooms
- ❑ Monthly rates range from $5,820 for studios, $6,570 for one-bedrooms and $12,150 for two-bedrooms

EASTGATE TOWER
222 EAST 39TH STREET (BETWEEN SECOND & THIRD AVENUES)
212-687-8000

- ❑ Renovated in 1994, this midtown hotel boasts a fitness center, restaurant, guest laundry and valet parking
- ❑ Spacious suites include full kitchens
- ❑ Business services include dataports, faxes, secretarial services and a meeting/banquet room
- ❑ Monthly rates range from $5,820 for studios, $6,570 for one-bedrooms, and $12,150 for two-bedrooms

LYDEN GARDENS
215 EAST 64TH STREET (BETWEEN SECOND & THIRD AVENUE)
212-355-1230

- ❑ Renovated in 1994, this 13 story building near New York's finest medical institutions offers valet service, full kitchens and a guest laundry
- ❑ Business services include dataports and fax service
- ❑ Monthly rates range from $5,970 for alcove studios/junior one-bedrooms, $6,570 for full one-bedroom suites

LYDEN HOUSE
320 EAST 53RD STREET (BETWEEN FIRST & SECOND AVENUES)
212-888-6070

- ❑ Renovated in 1994, this 11 story building on a quiet midtown street, offers 80 suites with full kitchens; many have terraces. Guest laundry is also available.
- ❑ Business services include secretarial services, dataports and fax service
- ❑ Monthly rates range from $5,820 for studios, and $6,720 for one-bedrooms

PLAZA FIFTY
155 EAST 50TH STREET (CORNER OF THIRD AVENUE)
212-751-5710

- ❑ Renovated in 1993, this 22 story building offers valet parking, a fitness center, guest laundry, full kitchens and terrace suites
- ❑ Business services include secretarial services, dataports, fax service and voicemail
- ❑ Monthly rates range from $3,600 for guest rooms, $5,970 for studios, $7,020 for one-bedrooms, and $11,970 for two-bedrooms

SHELBURNE MURRAY HILL
303 LEXINGTON AVENUE (CORNER OF 37TH STREET)
212-689-5200

- ❑ Renovated in 1992, this 16 story building near the United Nations and midtown, offers valet parking, full kitchens, a restaurant, fitness center and guest laundry. Many of its suites have terraces.
- ❑ Business services include dataports, fax service, secretarial services, voicemail, and a meeting/banquet room
- ❑ Monthly rates range from $5,820 for studios, $6,570 for one-bedrooms and $12,150 for two-bedrooms

SOUTHGATE TOWER
371 SEVENTH AVENUE (CORNER OF 31ST STREET)
212-563-1800

❑ Built in 1929, and recently renovated, this 28 story building offers valet parking, a fitness center, full kitchens, restaurant, and guest laundry. Many of its suites have terraces.
❑ Business services include dataports and fax service, secretarial services and meeting/banquet rooms
❑ Monthly rates range from $3,750 for guest rooms, $4,950 for studios, $6,570 for one-bedrooms and $10,500 for two-bedrooms

SURREY HOTEL
20 EAST 76TH STREET (BETWEEN FIFTH AND MADISON AVENUES)
212-288-3700

❑ Renovated in 1992, this, European-style hotel is a tranquil retreat. The four-star restaurant "Daniel" is on the premises.
❑ Hotel facilities include a fitness center, full kitchens and kitchenettes, and guest laundry
❑ Business services include dataports and fax service, secretarial services, voicemail and meeting/banquet rooms
❑ Monthly rates range from $6,900 for studios, $8,100 for one-bedrooms and, $15,000 for two-bedrooms

*Note:
   These nine all-suite hotels, located in prime New York neighborhoods, are part of the Manhattan East Suite Hotel chain. Reservations and information may be obtained by calling each hotel separately or by calling (212) 465-3600 or (800) 637-8483.

Budget Hotels:
Under $150 Per Night

A number of hotels, particularly smaller properties in residential neighborhoods, quote weekly and monthly, as well as daily rates. Hotels that charge less than $150 a night (for a double room, not including tax) are considered inexpensive in Manhattan. You can expect to be accommodated with clean rooms, tight security, and decent service. Several of these hotels are listed below.

- **Bellclaire Hotel**
  250 West 77th Street
  (212) 362-7700
  Rates: Starts at $119 per day.

- **Best Western President**
  234 West 48th Street
  (212) 246-8800
  Rates: $99+ for a single, $109+ for doubles.

- **Carlton Arms**
  160 East 25th Street
  (212) 684-8337
  Rates: Starting at $52 for a single, and $66 for a double.

- **Chelsea Inn**
  46 West 17th Street
  New York, NY 10011
  (212) 645-8989
  Reminiscent of many a small European hotel, of the 27 rooms on the first two floors of converted brownstones, eight share a bath with one other room. All rooms are clean and simple, have kitchenettes, and guest have their own front door key for evening hours when the desk is untended.
  Rates: single with a shared bath, $119; studio, $149; suite for two, $179; two-room suite for up to four, $219.

- **Excelsior**
  45 West 81st Street
  New York, NY 10024
  (212) 362-9200
  This hotel, in a great location, faces the Museum of Natural History and Central Park.
  Rates: $149 single, $149 double, $199 for a one-bedroom suite.

- **Habitat Hotel**
  130 East 57th Street
  New York, NY 10022
  (212) 753-8841
  This hotel offers weekly, as well as daily, rates. It has an excellent location, and is usually full to overflowing, though the rooms are small and spartan.
  Rates: $115 for a single and $130 for a double with private bath.

- **Hotel on the Avenue**
  2178 Broadway, at 77th Street
  (212) 362-1100
  Rates: Begin at $125 to $145 for a double.

- **Iroquois**
  49 West 44th Street
  (212) 840-3080
  Rates are $199 for a single or double.

- **Lexington**
  511 Lexington Avenue, at 48th Street
  (212) 755-6963
  Rates: Start at $165 per day for a single and $185 for a double.

- **Malibu Studios**
  2688 Broadway, at 102nd Street
  (212) 222-2954
  Rates: Begin at $49 for a single, $69 for a double.

- **The Manhattan**
  17 West 32nd Street
  (212) 736-1600
  Rates begin at $149 for a single, and $169 for a double.

- **Off SoHo Suites**
  11 Rivington Street, at Second Avenue
  (212) 979-9808
  Rates begin at $97 per day for a single or a double.

- **Penn Plaza Howard Johnson**
  215 West 34th Street
  (212)947-5050
  Rates are $99 per day for a single and $129 for a double.

- **Pickwick Arms**
  230 East 51st Street
  New York, NY 10022
  (212) 355-0300.
  Randomly-sized rooms, some without baths, don't deter fans from this older hotel with its East 50s location.
  Rates: Singles are $95, doubles are $120.

- **Portland Square**
  132 West 47th Street
  (212) 382-0600
  Rates: $95 for a single, $109 for a double.

- **Riverside Tower**
  80 Riverside Drive (80th St.)
  (212) 877-5200
  Rates are $85 for a single and $90 for a double.

- **The Comfort Hotel**
  129 West 46th Street
  (212) 221-2600
  Rates: $149 per day for a single or a double.

- **Westpark Hotel**
  308 West 58th Street
  New York, NY 10019
  (212) 246-6440
  With a grand location facing Columbus Circle and Central Park and coordinated, tidily-renovated rooms—those 16 (out of 99) with park views are especially nice.
  Rates: $95 for a single or double.

- **Wolcott**
  4 West 31st Street
  (212) 268-2900
  Rates are $120 for a single or double.

BED AND BREAKFAST

It is a well kept secret that may surprise many visitors: there really is a selection of bed and breakfasts in Manhattan. Sometimes it's a resourceful New Yorker letting out an extra room; at other times visitors may have an entire apartment to themselves. There are many advantages to staying at a bed and breakfast. To begin with, they are cheaper than comparable hotel rooms, and may include breakfast. However, they may offer less privacy, service, or convenience than a hotel.

Bed and breakfast owners prefer to have a measure of anonymity. Rather than advertise, they use agencies as intermediaries. Although this is an unregulated industry, reputable agencies monitor the quality of service and accommodation of the bed and breakfasts they represent. It is a good idea to shop around by phone first, and be as specific as possible about location, likes and dislikes. Bed and breakfasts usually require at least a two night stay, although there may be exceptions for off seasons. Most also require a 25% deposit or more, which includes the agency's commission. Book well in advance for the best choice.

- **ABODE BED AND BREAKFAST**
  P.O. BOX 20022
  NEW YORK, NY 10028
  (212) 472-2000

This agency represents about 200 unhosted apartments, most of which are in Manhattan. They request business references from guests. There is a two night minimum. Rates start at $135 per night for a studio.

- **BED, BREAKFAST, AND BOOKS**
  35 WEST 92ND STREET
  NEW YORK, NY 10025
  (212) 865-8740

Named for the book business which the owners also operate, this agency tends to attract a rather bookish clientele. It is one of the more established agencies, handling about 35 apartments all over Manhattan, most of which are hosted. The prices range from $80 to $100 for a hosted single, $100 to $110 for a double, and $110 to $150 for a studio. They have a two night minimum requirement.

- **NEW WORLD BED AND BREAKFAST**
  150 FIFTH AVENUE, SUITE 711
  NEW YORK, NY 10011
  (212) 675-5600
  OR, (800) 443-3800

This agency handles about 120 apartments, all of which are in Manhattan. Unhosted apartments range from $85 for a single; $90 for a double. There is a two night minimum.

- **URBAN VENTURES, INC.**
  P.O. BOX 426
  NEW YORK, NY 10024
  (212) 594-5650

This was the first agency of this type, and offers over 500 rooms. Most of them are in Manhattan. The daily rates vary with location and degree of luxury. They range approximately from $75 to $80 for hosted singles, $90 to $120 for doubles, and $110 to $350 for unhosted apartments. There is a two night minimum for the hosted rooms, three nights for the apartments.

Women's Residences

KATHERINE HOUSE   (212) 242-6566
(LADIES CHRISTIAN UNION)
118 West 13th Street
$150+ Weekly (3 month minimum)
*Includes breakfast & dinner
*Requires a three month minimum stay

THE MARKIE RESIDENCE   (212) 242-2400
(SALVATION ARMY)
123 West 13th Street
$220+ Weekly for a private room and bath
*Includes two meals a day
*Requires a one month minimum stay

PARKSIDE EVANGELINE RESIDENCE   (212) 677-6200
(SALVATION ARMY)
18 Gramercy Park South
(Corner of Irving Place)
$184+ Weekly (3 month minimum)
*Includes breakfast & dinner
*Requires $500 refundable security deposit

ROBERTS HOUSE   (212) 683-6865
(LADIES CHRISTIAN UNION)
151 East 36th Street
$150+ Weekly
*Includes breakfast & dinner
*Requires a three-month minimum stay and
guest must be 18-25 years old

WEBSTER APARTMENTS   (212) 967-9000
419 West 34th Street
$162-199 Inc. tax Weekly
(3 month minimum)
*Includes breakfast & dinner

 Whether you are a member of the YMCA or not, anyone wishing to rent a room at one of the three Y's in Manhattan can do so. All of the Y's rent rooms on a daily basis, and two of the Y's house both men and women. Additionally, renting a room includes the use of all athletic facilities on the premises. A list of YMCA's with single or shared rooms follows.

McBurney YMCA
206 West 24th Street
(212) 741-9226

For men and women
Rates are $55 per day for single rooms

West Side YMCA
5 West 63rd Street
(212) 875-4100

For men and women
Rates are: $65 a day (single)
                    $75 a day (double)
Health club and pool included

The Vanderbilt YMCA
224 East 47th Street
(212) 756-9600

Men only
Rates are: $65 a day (single)
                    $78 a day (double)
Health club and pool included

De Hirsch Residence
92nd Street YM-YWHA
1395 Lexington Avenue
(212) 415-5650

For men and women ages 18 to 26 only
Rates are: $69 a day (single)
                    $45 a day (double)
with a three night minimum
Monthly rate: $695 to $795 (single/double)

Other Temporary Lodgings

Accomodations in university dorms and B & Bs also provide temporary shelter while one is seeking permanent housing. Some university dormitories are open only to those carrying current student ID cards; others are open to everyone. Please ask when you call.

University Dorms : Summer Only

Barnard College
2009 Broadway
(212) 854-8021

Ask for director, Summer Program 1998 rates: an air conditioned room is $122 per person per week, two-week minimum. Meal plans are extra.

Columbia University's Intern Housing
c/o Conference Housing Office
116 Wallach Hall
(212) 854-2946

Rates run about $100 a week. There is a one-month minimum stay payable in advance.

New York University Dormitories
c/o NYU Housing Office
14 Washington Place
(212) 998-4620

Check website: www.NYU.Edu/housing/summer for rates and availibility. There is a three-week minimum stay requirement.

APARTMENT FOR RENT
THE URBAN HUNTER

Chapter 4

APARTMENT FOR RENT
THE URBAN HUNTER

REQUIREMENTS:
IMAGINATION, ASSERTIVENESS, AND A LOT OF SHOELEATHER

Finding an apartment in a tight market takes imagination, assertiveness and unrelenting pursuit. If you seriously want to find an apartment, you cannot be quiet or shy about telling everyone you know, and everyone you meet, about your search. Talk to store owners, people standing in front of their buildings and mail carriers. Let everyone at work know; let your friends and business acquaintances know; let your clergyman and fellow parishioners know.

If you are a college student or a college graduate, check your college's bulletin board, where postings of apartment sublets or shares may be placed. Also, your alumni association may be able to assist you with information and advice. Other places to look may be super-markets and other stores where notices are placed by tenants who want to sublet or break their leases. A "furniture for sale" sign may also be tip-off to a possible future vacancy.

By networking and checking out all leads, you are more likely to find a <u>good</u> apartment at a <u>reasonable</u> rent, than by any other means. Most reasonably priced apartments are never given out to rental agencies nor are they advertised in the paper. They are rented to a landlord's friends, family members and business acquaintances; and to those who are referred by them.

The following pages describe four different strategies for capturing the elusive "no-fee" apartment.

1. TALK TO DOORMEN

Doormen and superintendents of rental buildings often know if any apartments are available, or will be coming available, in their buildings. Offer to compensate them (generously) for their effort, should you find an apartment through them. Be sure to ask for their telephone number and call them every few weeks.

2. INQUIRE AT CO-OP AND CONDO BUILDINGS

Ask at co-op and condo buildings if you are considering a sublet for one or two years. Sometimes sublets, particularly in condo buildings, can be extended for indefinite periods of time. Many renters perceive these buildings to be safer, better maintained, and better staffed than rental buildings. What's more, they have a certain stability afforded by buildings with more permanent residents. Buildings built as condos may have better construction, greater quality, and more amenities than similar rental buildings. Another potential plus is that owners may have redecorated or even rebuilt their units to maximize their investments, and you may find an absolutely beautiful apartment in one of these buildings.

Since there are no controls on what an owner can ask for a co-op or condo sublet, asking prices tend to reflect market conditions, and prices may be similar to units in luxury rental buildings. Owners may be willing to negotiate, however, especially if they think you would be an excellent tenant and, in the case of a co-op, be easily approved of by the board.

In addition to owner sublets, some new condo buildings, unable to sell all their apartments, may also rent out some of their remaining units. These will be advertised in the newspapers and there will be an on-site agent to assist you.

Many of these new buildings have pools and full service health clubs, saunas and steam rooms. In addition, there may be other amenities such as recreation rooms, barbecue facilities and landscaped rooftop sun decks. Independent managers usually run these facilities and organize social events. Many upwardly mobile single people are attracted to the club-like atmosphere of these facilities, and find them to be a good way to meet new people.

Whether renting in a new condo building, or subletting through an owner, a potential tenant's references and financial statements must be excellent. One week's salary should equal a month's rent. A rule of thumb used by landlords is to require that your annual salary be at least 40 to 50 times greater than one month's rent. The most accurate way for you to see what you can afford is to use the worksheet on page 145. List all of your monthly expenses and compare that total to your monthly net income.

If a prospective tenant has just started a new job, or his income or credit history is not quite good enough, he may need to have a guarantor. A guarantor is someone who guarantees the rent if the tenant fails to pay. That person must have an excellent credit history and an income that is at least 75 times the rent he is guaranteeing. He must also reside in the United States.

The building's management company will provide the application forms to the applicant. They should be filled out completely and honestly. The information is treated discreetly and is never revealed to any public or private agency (including federal or state tax authorities.)

In the case of a co-op sublet, the owner will review the application and then pass it along to the managing agent for processing. It will then be sent to the co-op's Board of Directors for a final review. Sometimes a personal interview is required with one or more board members. However, some co-op units do not require board approval. These are sponsor apartments, or apartments that were bought by owners or investors when the buildings were converted. Their leases gave them the right to sublet without requiring board approval.

Unlike co-op owners (who own shares in a corporation, rather than real property), condo owners do hold real property, and their management cannot deny them permission to sublet. However, management may review the potential tenant's application and charge the owner a rental fee.

Co-op and condo sublets are usually for one year, with a possible option for a second. In the case of a co-op, the board may retain the full right to evict, and the owner is held responsible for the conduct of the rental tenant.

3. CHECK NEWSPAPER ADS

The most common approach taken by apartment hunters is to check the classified ads in the Sunday edition of The New York Times. If you are a Times subscriber, or get your paper delivered by a service, you may get the Sunday Real Estate section early on Saturday morning. You can also get early access to this section on the Internet, where you can also view Sunday's ads on Saturday.

Although the Sunday edition of the New York Times has the most classified ads, the Wednesday Times, The Village Voice and the Upper East Side Resident are also worth checking. The Voice generally has lower priced apartment ads and specializes in the Greenwich Village and Soho areas. The Wall Street Journal's Friday edition lists apartments for rent in Manhattan. The Post and The Daily News primarily carry classified listings for Brooklyn, The Bronx, and Queens.

The Apartment Rental section of the New York Times follows the Co-op and Condo Sales section and is divided into two main categories: Furnished and Unfurnished Apartments. These are further divided by numbers of rooms - with Studios (1 and 2 rooms) being listed first, by One-bedrooms (3 rooms) second, and then by Two-or-more bedrooms (4 to 6 rooms and over). Houses, Professional Spaces, Lofts and apartment shares are also listed.

FURNISHED SUBLETS: Furnished sublets may be offered for short-term housing. Some are advertised for periods of as little as one week. Most are for periods of one month or longer, with leases ranging up to one or two years. A furnished sublet may be a useful temporary measure, until you find a more permanent apartment. A number of brokers specializing in these apartments advertise in the New York Times and The Voice. Broker commissions range between 1/2 and 1 month's rent for periods of up to one year.

*NOTE: See Chapter 3 for additonal information regarding short-term furnished rentals.

LARGE DISPLAY ADS: Large display ads are usually for new luxury buildings, which have many apartments available. These will be among the most expensive apartments on the market. The starting price listed for each size unit usually refers to the least desirable apartment of it's type on the lowest floor. To view these apartments, you can either call ahead to make an appointment with the on-site agent, or go directly to the building. The landlord's representative will show you whatever is available in the building, and you can negotiate the best deal for yourself. Always carry a check and I.D. with you, and be ready to give a "good-faith" deposit when you see an apartment you want. (Be sure to write "good faith deposit" on the check. This will help you to get your money back, should you decide not to take the apartment, or should a problem arise.)

Other large ads that list several apartments in different locations are broker ads. A broker must identify himself by stating his name, or the name of his company. Should you find an apartment through a broker you will have to pay a fee for his service. Fees can range up to 15% of one year's rent, for a lease of one year or longer.

"NO FEE" ADS: Smaller ads are usually placed directly by landlords, managing agents, or co-op or condo owners. These ads may say "owner" or may say "No fee" and give a telephone number that can be called over the weekend. Occasionally, an ad is placed by a rental tenant who wants to sublet his apartment. In the case of a tenant sublet, the landlord has the right to approve a prospective subtenant. Should a tenant obtain the landlord's permission to sublet a rent-stabilized apartment, the rent stabilization laws will protect the sublettee.

117

A sublet tenant may pay only the same rent as the prime tenant, unless the prime tenant includes his own furniture. In that case, he may charge the sublettee 10% more rent than he is paying. Taking a sublet apartment can turn out to be a good deal, especially if you get to take over the lease. However, the tenant cannot promise you takeover rights. Taking an illegal sublet, one without the landlord's knowledge or permission, is not advised. You would not be able to put your name on the mailbox, put a phone in your name, or come and go openly; and you could be evicted at any moment.

ROOMMATE SHARES: Other ads will be for roommate shares. About half of all recent college graduates share apartments in Manhattan. Individuals who are looking for someone to share their rent with may advertise directly. There are several roommate agencies that also advertise. Under rent stabilization guidelines, any sole tenant of a rent stabilized apartment has the legal right to share his or her space with a roommate. The person whose name is on the lease retains the rights to the apartment. There is no legal restriction on the rent that a prime tenant may ask of the roommate. It will reflect the market rate and should be negotiated between the two parties.

One-bedroom apartments are often shared by roommates who subdivide the living room to create a second bedroom. A company called The Livingspace Company leases a pressurized room divider system for $595 plus a refundable $200 materials deposit. The divider looks like a permanent wall, and can be installed within three hours. It can be painted; pictures can be hung on it; and when you move, it can be dismantled in less than an hour. For more information, call (201) 824-0636.

Note : *The New York State Tenant and Neighborhood Coalition at 198 Broadway, N.Y.C. N.Y. (Room 1000) publishes a 22 page booklet called "A Tenant's Guide to Subletting and Apartment Sharing". It details the practical and legal ramifications of each.*

4. CHECK LANDLORDS AND MANAGEMENT COMPANIES

You should begin your search about 45 days before your intended move-in date. If you want to familiarize yourself with the market prior to this, you can go to "open houses" advertised by owners and landlords, or call the management companies listed in Part III of this book. During this preview period, you should try to see as many apartments as possible; check your credit, and get your references and other documentation together. Having a good credit rating is essential to renting an apartment. Landlords, and co-op or condo owners, will do a credit check prior to lease signing. Therefore, it might be a be a good idea to check, and if need be repair, your credit history in advance of your search. The three national credit bureaus are:

TRW: 800-392-1122
Trans Union: 800-851-2674
Equifax: 800-685-1111

All three bureaus track individual credit histories and will give you a copy of your credit report. You can get a complimentary copy, once a year, from TRW, by writing to them at: TRW Credit Information, Consumer Assistance, PO Box 2350, Chatsworth, CA 91313-2350. Include your name, address, social security number, date of birth and proof of residence in your letter.

When you call landlords' offices to inquire about available apartments, you will be asked how much you can afford to pay in rent. It's best to be honest and to give a real maximum figure, otherwise you may not see an apartment that suits you. You will also be asked about your space requirements, desired location, and when you will want to move.

By understanding your needs and expectations, the person you are speaking to may be able to help you. He or she may know of something coming up that might be right for you. Be courteous when dealing with landlords and managing agents. Showing them that you are pleasant and realistic will help you find the apartment you seek.

Four *TIPS* to be Successful

Since you will be one of many people to call on almost any rental ad, there are some strategies that should be followed if you are to be successful.

1. Get a jump on your competition by reading and calling the ads as early as possible.

2. Try to make yours the first appointment of the day, and arrive on time. If it is an open house that you are responding to , you should arrive a little early.

3. Always carry your checkbook, photo I.D., references and $50 in cash or your ATM card with you. Have enough money in your checking account to cover the security deposit and the first month's rent.

4. Be prepared to make a decision quickly

APPLYING FOR THE APARTMENT YOU WANT

Should you see an apartment you like through a landlord or management company, go back to their office immediately and fill out their application. They will require a check to process your application; it should not exceed $100. You will need to give them information regarding your finances and show references and other documentation to back up your statements.

This is also the best time for you to ask any questions you may have, and to negotiate the rent and/or lease start dates. If you noticed that the apartment needed painting or repairs, this is the time to address these concerns. If you have a pet, you should let the landlord know; many do not allow dogs in their buildings, though cats are usually accepted.

Landlords require certified checks for the first month's rent and for the security deposit. Personal checks are usually not accepted. If you do not have the money available at the time of your application, the landlord may give you 24 hours to secure it. If you have just moved to New York, and your bank is out of town, you can have the money wired to a Western Union outlet or directly into the landlord's account. A sample form of a lease application, is shown on page 127.

REFERENCES AND DOCUMENTS YOU WILL NEED

1. You will need a letter of employment from your supervisor or personnel department, written on company letterhead, stating your job description, length of employment and total income including salary, bonuses and commissions. Try to get a

personal reference from a superior. You also might consider having a guarantor's letter and information available, should you need it, as well as a personal letter of reference.

If you are self-employed, you will need a letter from your accountant, written on his letterhead, verifying your relationship with him and stating the total amount of your combined assets. This should be accompanied by your last two years tax returns, plus investment statement, net worth statements, etc.

2. You will need to show a recent bank statement and a current pay stub (with year to date information).

3. You will need to have information regarding:
• your present and previous landlords, including their address and telephone numbers
• business and personal references, including names, and telephone numbers
• bank account numbers, including branch contact persons and their telephone numbers

4. You will need identification such as a driver's license, birth certificate, or social security card.

SIGNING THE LEASE

A lease is a contract between the owner of an apartment and a tenant. It guarantees the right of the tenant to occupy the unit for a specific amount of time in exchange for a sum of money called a rent payment. Most leases are standard forms and can be bought in commercial stationary stores. As you look over the lease, you will notice that most of its provisions are written to protect the landlord. But tenants' rights, and obligations, are also clearly spelled out. (See the Tenants' Rights Section which follows).

Every lease must have certain minimal information in order to be valid. This information must include your and your landlord's name and address, the building address and apartment number, the amount of rent and when the rent is due. The lease dates — beginning and ending— should also be included. After the lease is signed by you and your landlord, you will each retain a copy for your records.

In rent-stabilized apartments, landlords must attach the previous rent paid so that the tenant can calculate the increase and thus know if he is paying the legal rent. If you are not given this information, and you suspect that you are being overcharged, you can call (718) 563-5789 or write to the State Division of Housing and Community Renewal district office and request the status of your apartment.

Any separate agreements that you make, such as his promise to paint the apartment, should be written as a separate rider and made part of the lease agreement. Do not rely on oral promises, which will usually not be enforceable. Both the landlord and the tenant should initial any changes made to the lease, and any repairs should be made before you move in. Be aware that any structural improvements you are allowed to make, such as track lighting, built-ins, or immovable walls, may become the landlord's property when you move out. His right to this property will depend on how much damage would be caused by removing these new structures. For this reason, you should not put up anything that cannot be easily dismantled with minimum damage to walls, floors and ceilings.

As a rent-stabilized tenant, you are entitled to a one year lease when you move into your apartment, and to an automatic extension of one or two years thereafter (assuming that you have satisfied the terms and conditions of the lease).

Your landlord should send you a renewal lease offer by certified mail four months before your lease expires. You will then have 60 days in which to accept the renewal. Should you decide to stay, sign the renewal lease and mail it back to your landlord. He should then countersign it and mail it back to you within 30 days. Should you prefer not to renew, however, the landlord must be given at least 30 days notice of your intention to vacate the premises.

THE SECURITY DEPOSIT

A security deposit is usually one additional month's rent that you pay upon lease signing. It should be put into an escrow account and given back to you, with interest, at the end of your lease term. If you have caused any damage to the apartment, other than normal wear and tear, the cost of repairing the damage will be taken out of your security deposit. Cigarette burns on counter tops or torn draperies are not considered ordinary wear and tear; nor are large nail holes left from removing bookshelves or heavy pictures. These have to be filled in and smoothed out, or they are considered to be structural damage. It might be a good idea to take a careful inventory of the apartment before signing the lease. List any defects you find on walls, floors, furniture, fixtures, appliances, etc., give your landlord a copy and keep one for yourself. Ask him to sign and date both copies. If there is a dispute later about any damage you may or may not have done, your list will protect you.

• Security deposits may also be applied by the landlord against monthly rent payments due under the lease in the event you fail to pay.

WINDOW GUARDS

Landlords of rent-stabilized buildings are required by law to install window guards in all windows, except those leading to a fire escape, for tenants who have children under 10 years of age. Tenants who do not have children may also request window guards, but landlords are not required by law to install them.

A temporary surcharge, not to exceed $10 per installation may be charged. This charge is separate and apart from the base rent and may not be added to the rent. Nor can it be passed along to a new tenant.

For additional information, or to report a landlord's failure to comply with this law, call the NYC Department of Health at (212) 693-4636.

SUBLETTING OR ASSIGNING YOUR LEASE

Should you have to break your lease for any reason, you are liable for all of the unpaid rent through the end of the lease term, unless the landlord relets the apartment, in which case you will only be liable for the time the apartment remained vacant. To limit your liability, you could try to sublet the apartment. Unless your lease says "No subletting," you are permitted to sublet for two years within any four year period of time. You will still be legally responsible for all the rent payments, but your sublettee will be making them to you, or directly to your landlord.

Should you decide to sublet, send a certified or registered letter to your landlord at least thirty days in advance, explaining the reason.

121

A substantial reason, such as a job transfer or family emergency, is best and may help smooth the way. Include information about where you will be, the length of the sublease and the qualifications of your prospective subtenant (to show that he would be an acceptable and financially responsible person). Include your sublettee's name, address, telephone number, place of business, occupation and income. Enclose a copy of your lease and your proposed sublease. Your landlord should respond to your letter within 10 days if he requires additional information, or within 30 days by approving or disapproving your sublet request. A landlord's failure to respond within 30 days is seen as approval. If your landlord unreasonably refuses your request, you may have to take him to court. A court will decide whether or not his grounds for refusal are reasonable.

A better way to divest yourself entirely of all responsibility for the rent is to assign your lease to a new tenant. The landlord would then be entitled to a rent increase and, therefore, be more likely to let you out of your lease willingly. You will need your landlord's written consent. Should the landlord unreasonably refuse to give this consent, you will then be released from your lease obligation after 30 days notice. However, should the landlord reasonably turn down your assignee, you will still be obligated for the remainder of your lease term. Make certain that your replacement tenant has good credit and meets the income requirements for the rent.

TENANTS' RIGHTS

As a rent stabilized tenant, you are entitled to certain services, such as heat and hot water, garbage collection and building maintenance. These, and other services, fall under the law known as a "Warranty Of Habitability." This law requires landlords to provide premises that are fit for habitation, and that meet certain minimum standards of health and safety.

WARRANTY OF HABITABILITY

If the owner is negligent in the upkeep of his building, and there are serious problems that create health risks, these may be in violation of the building code and your landlord may be fined in court. It would be wise to seek a landlord-tenant's attorney's advice in such a situation.

REPAIRS

Your landlord is also responsible for repairs to fixtures, such as plumbing, and to keep in good working order appliances that were installed, such as refrigerators and stoves. You should know the name of the person, or office, to call when things break down. That person (the landlord, managing agent, or super) should address the problem in a timely fashion. If, however, repairs are not made within a few days, follow up in writing, keeping a copy for yourself. You may need a record of your complaints, should you have to take future legal action. It also might be possible, if all efforts fail, to pay for the repairs and to withhold that amount from future rent. A rent reduction may be ordered if a court finds that the landlord violated the law. Again, let a good attorney guide your actions.

WHERE TO COMPLAIN

• Housing Court: Deals with landlord-tenant complaints. Tenants can bring Housing Rent actions against owners for various "Warranty of Habitabilty" violations; landlords can charge tenants with nonpayment of rent. Most tenants appear without attorneys although attorneys may accompany or act for tenants. The court fee is $35.

• Division of Housing and Community Renewal: Tenants can file complaints in any agency office. There are no filing charges.

• Criminal Court: Tenants can file charges for criminal actions such as harassment, assault or theft.

• State Supreme Court: Tenants can file charges accusing a landlord of a pattern of illegal activity and seek an injunction.

EXTERMINATION SERVICES

Your building may have monthly extermination service. This is necessary in every building in New York City. It's almost impossible to keep roaches and other pests under control without a comprehensive and persistent effort. Ask your super when the exterminator is due to arrive and then arrange to let the exterminator into your apartment. If you cannot be home, it would be wise to have the super or one of the buildings' staff accompany him. Let that person know which rooms you want to have sprayed. Using consumer pesticides between exterminator visits can also help to control the problem within your own four walls. Boric acid can be effective, but be careful to keep it out of reach of small children and household pets.

NOISE POLLUTION

Perhaps the most common complaint of renters is that their apartment is noisy. It could be a neighbor who constantly plays music too loudly, a dog barking or a screaming couple in the apartment next door sharing the intimate details of their life. You have the right to "quiet enjoyment of your premises." This is stated in your lease. If you have tried working things out with your neighbors to no avail, then the next step is to inform your landlord of your problem in writing. Again, keep a copy for yourself. If the landlord cares about his building, he will want to be informed.

The landlord should then take steps to let the problem tenant know that he is in violation of his lease and risks eviction. If you get no response from the owner, you should speak to an attorney specializing in landlord-tenant law. The police can also be involved at any point if the disturbance makes your living environment unbearable. It's a good idea to keep a written record of the dates and times of the noise and if you can to tape-record it. Should you need to make a court appearance, this will bolster your case.

Note: *A 37 page booklet called "Rent Smart" is published by the State Consumer Protection Board, 99 Washington Avenue, Albany, N.Y. 12210. It describes tenants' rights in New York State. You can write, or call (518)474-1471, for a free copy.*

EVICTIONS

As a rent-stabilized tenant, you should not have to worry about coming home one day to find your furniture on the street and your apartment door padlocked. Those days are gone. You can be evicted for non-payment of the rent or for other serious violations of the lease, but the eviction process takes time. First you will be given a chance to correct the violation(s) and if you do, the eviction proceeding will stop. If you do not, then the next step for the landlord is to seek an eviction order in court. You have the right to defend yourself. At the very least, this will slow down the eviction process considerably, and hopefully, you can make a case (e.g. breach of the warranty of habitability or right of quiet enjoyment) that will prevent your being evicted.

However, should a landlord obtain a judgment in his favor, then you will be evicted by the sheriff's office. The landlord himself cannot evict you or seize any of your possessions. He could be accused of trespassing or stealing should he do so, and would be subject to both civil and criminal penalties. From the day that you first receive an eviction notice to the day that you may actually be forced to move, a period of several weeks to several months may elapse. Meanwhile, you have time to find another apartment. If you are not able to find something else you can afford, it might still be possible to get a "stay of eviction" — a delay that might last several weeks or longer. Being evicted is certainly serious; you may well wind up homeless. But it will not happen overnight.

USING A REALTOR

If you do not have a lot of time to look on your own, you can enlist the aid of a broker. By working with a broker, a prospective renter taps both the broker's inventory and knowledge of the market. This can save you time and energy. However, it may be the most costly way to lease an apartment, especially if a broker's fee is involved. Sometimes a broker's fee is paid by landlords who are anxious to have their apartments shown and rented quickly. Be aware though, that these apartments are likely to be higher priced because the broker's fee is already factored in.

The current range of fees, for a one year lease or longer, runs from one month's rent to 15% of the first year's rent. (For example: If the monthly rent is $1500, the annual rent would be 12 x $1500 = $18,000 x 15% = $2,700.) Adding this to the monthly rent considerably raises the cost of the apartment. Since there are no city or state regulations that set these fees, they can be negotiated with the broker and possibly even with the owner of the apartment, who may be willing to pay part of the fee.

When looking for an agent, it is best to be as specific as possible about what you want and what you can can afford. If your agent is good, he will listen to you carefully and show you a few of the best apartments he has that comes closest to meeting your needs. It would be wise to contact several rental agencies and look at as many suitable apartments as possible before selecting one. Brokers get listings from neighborhood landlords, and though most of their listings are open-listed with many realtors, some brokers may serve as exclusive agents for one or more landlords. Additionally, each broker may specialize in a certain type of property. Some may handle rent-stabilized walk-up and elevator buildings; others may specialize in luxury buildings.

At each office, you will be asked to sign a "fee Agreement." This obligates you to pay the fee for any apartment you rent which was shown to you by the agent, unless the owner is willing to pay the broker's commission. This protects the broker by eliminating the possibility of a client's "doubling-back" to rent the apartment directly from the owner. It might be possible, especially with higher priced apartments, to negotiate the fee agreement before signing. You should ask the broker to show you "No Fee" apartments in your price range.

Service and expertise will vary from broker to broker. You may enjoy being driven to see apartments by one person, and enjoy the knowledge and low-key approach of another. A good agent will be congenial, easy to work with and sensitive to your needs. You should listen carefully to that person's advice. He or she sees apartments daily, and can help you understand what types of apartments can be found within your budget.

Should you find something though a broker, the rental application and lease will be done in his or her office. The application will have questions regarding employment and income, and ask for landlord, business and personal references. It will also ask about where you bank and what credit cards you have. You may be asked to provide a copy of your W-2 tax form (or 1099 tax return) as well as three most recent pay stubs. One of the services that a broker provides to an owner is to screen potential tenants to see if they meet the reference check. If you are a recent graduate, or new to the city, a lack of job or credit history, may result in your not being accepted by the landlord or co-op board. A guarantor, and/or a letter from your employer, can help. A broker's fee should not be paid until you are offered a lease signed by the landlord.

LISTING SERVICES

One alternative to using a broker, is to subscribe to a listing service. Listing services charge flat fees instead of commissions, and provide a list of available apartments that match the renter's requirements. Many of these listings are obtained from major landlords and managing agents, and are the same ones that brokers get. The renter can then call directly to make his or her own appointment. Updated lists are mailed or faxed regularly until an apartment is found.

A list of these services includes:

- Apartments Illustrated (212) 645-9797
- Homeline (212) 220-HOME x270
- The Apartment Store (212) 545-1996
- The Apartment Source (212) 343-8155

Another service called The Apartment Fone, is free to the apartment seeker. For the cost of a local call, anyone can listen to information on apartment rentals, sales and roommate shares. Callers specify any one of these categories by pressing a button. They can also specify the location, type of apartment, and price. The Apartment Fone can be reached 24 hours a day by dialing (212) APT-FONE.

You should also consider looking for an apartment by checking these sites on the internet:

- GSB Virtual Realty http://www.net realty.com
- Real Estate On-Line http://www.ny realty.com
- Rent Net http://www.rent.net.com

WHERE TO GET HELP

The following is a list of organizations you can turn to for help and advice regarding your rights as a tenant in New York City:

- The Open Housing Center   (212) 941-6101
  594 Broadway   Ste. 608
  NYC NY   10012
  This is a nonprofit agency that provides assistance, both legal and otherwise, to insure that no-one seeking housing is discriminated against because of race, color, creed, sexual orientation, children or marital status. There is no charge for their service. To find out more about your legal rights as a tenant in New York City, you can ask them to send you an excellent free booklet called "The Tenant Fact Book".

- The New York State Division of Housing and Community Renewal   (212) 240-6008
  Rent Hotline# (718) 739-6400
  This agency administers all rent control and rent stabilization programs in the city of New York. Tenant questions and complaints should be addressed here.

- The New York State Tenant and Neighborhood Coalition
  198 Broadway   (212) 695-8922

- The Metropolitan Council on Housing
  198 Broadway   (212) 693-0550

- The Lenox Hill Neighborhood Association
  331 East 70th Street   (212) 744-5022

Some groups that are local to the neighborhoods of the Upper East side, the Upper West side, and Downtown are:

- The Lenox Hill Neighborhood Association
  331 East 70th Street   (212) 744-5022

- The West Side Tenants Union
  200 West 72nd Street   (212) 595-1274

- The Good Old Lower East Side
  525 East 6th Street   (212) 533-2541

126

SAMPLE:
APPLICATION FOR LEASE OF APARTMENT

APARTMENT INFORMATION   Date_____, 19_____

House No. _____ Apartment _____ No. of rooms_____

Term of Lease _____ From _____ To_____

Rent per month $_____ Security_____

PERSONAL INFORMATION

1. Applicant's name _____ Social Security # _____

2. Present address_____ Phone_____

3. Business or employer _____ Phone_____

   Address _____ Length of Emp._____ Type of Business _____

   Position in office_____ Income_____

   Additional source of income_____

4. Present landlord _____Address _____ Phone_____

   How long a tenant_____Reason for moving _____

5. References (personal)

   a.) Name _____ Phone _____ Address_____

6. References (business - to verify employment)

   a.) Name _____ Phone _____ Address_____

7. Credit cards (for charge accounts name only)

8. Name of Bank _____ Checking _____ Savings_____

   Address _____ Account #_____

   Name of Bank_____Checking_____Savings _____

   Address _____ Account #_____

9. Accountant _____ Address _____ Phone _____

10. Attorney _____ Address _____ Phone_____

127

A GLOSSARY OF COMMON REAL ESTATE TERMS

Some real estate terms that are commonly used by brokers (and their definitions) are:

AS IS: A property being rented or sold without any promise to improve its condition.

BOARD OF DIRECTORS: The elected officers of a co-op or condo who run the building.

COOPERATIVE (CO-OP): A residential apartment building whose title is held by a corporation. Tenants own shares in the corporation and hold proprietary leases to their apartments.

CONDOMINIUM: A residential apartment building in which each owner has absolute ownership of his apartment, plus an undivided interest in the common elements of the building.

CREDIT REPORT: Credit companies provide complete reports (for a fee) disclosing a credit holder's past and present residences, the status of his credit accounts, and any judgments or liens against him.

SIMPLEX: An apartment whose floorplan consists of one level.

DUPLEX: An apartment whose floorplan consists of two levels.

TRIPLEX: An apartment whose floorplan consists of three levels.

EXCLUSIVE AGENCY: A contract between an owner of a property and a broker in which only one broker may sell or rent the property.

MANAGEMENT COMPANY: A company hired by a landlord to oversee the operation of his building(s). The company may hire the superintendent and provide other services such as screening tenant applicants, collecting rents, etc.

128

MAKING AD~SENSE OF IT ALL

Because advertising is so expensive, realtors and individual owners frequently abbreviate the words that describe their apartments. This page lists some commonly used abbreviations and their meanings.

A.	A/C	-	Air Conditioning	F.	FDR -	Formal Dining Room
	ASAP	-	As Soon As Possible	G.	Gar -	Garage
B.	BO	-	Best Offer	H.	Hi flr -	High floor
	BRs	-	Bedrooms		Hlth clb -	Health club
	Bth	-	Bath	I.	Imm -	Immediate
C.	C/A/C	-	Central Air Conditioning	L.	Lux -	Luxury
	CC	-	Common Charge	M.	Mds -	Maid's Room
	Conc	-	Concierge		Mnt or Mt -	Maintenance
D.	D/A	-	Dining Area	P.	Princ -	Principal
	DR	-	Dining Room	R.	RET -	Real Estate Tax
	DM or Drmn	-	Doorman	S.	S.F. -	Square foot
	D/W	-	Dishwasher		Stu -	Studio
	Dplx	-	Duplex apartment		Svc -	Service
E.	EIK	-	Eat-In-Kitchen	T.	TD -	Tax Deduction
	Elv	-	Elevator		terr -	terrace
	Exp	-	Exposure(s): North (N) South (S) East (E) West (W)	V.	Vu -	View
				W.	WBF -	Wood-burning fireplace
					W/D -	Washer/Dryer

BEFORE THE HUNT: SOME PRELIMINARY CONSIDERATIONS

Chapter 5

BEFORE THE HUNT:
SOME PRELIMINARY CONSIDERATIONS

The key factors in determining an apartment's value are:

1. Location, location, location
2. The amenities of the apartment
3. The apartment's space and layout
4. The amenities of the building

This chapter is a step-by-step guide to help you determine your preferred location, space requirements, and desired amenities in the apartment and the building.

1. Location: Choosing a Neighborhood

To acquaint yourself with each area you are considering, it's a good idea to walk around the neighborhood during the day; hang out at night. Ask yourself these questions:

• Do I enjoy the general appearance of the area - its look and character?

• Do I feel safe?

• Do the people I see appeal to me: are they the type of people I would want as friends and neighbors?

If you've answered yes to these questions, talk to some of the people you see. Ask them about living in the neighborhood. The New York Police Department's Community Liason Officer can give you information about crime rates in the area, and local Community Boards can provide you with general information about the area — its libraries, schools, houses of worship, social services, and recreational facilities.

2. Apartment Amenities

The location of an apartment within a building affects it's desirability and value. For example: an apartment on a low floor, not getting much light, will be less desirable than a sunny apartment on a high floor; an apartment facing north, or into an inner courtyard, will be less desirable than one facing south, or onto the street. Having a balcony, terrace, or other unique feature will add value to an apartment.

Garden apartments (and other apartments on the ground floor) are more vulnerable to break-ins and are therefore, less desirable. If you are considering living in a ground floor apartment, then investing in good, professionally-installed window gates is essential. A window-gate should open quickly and easily from the inside but be impervious to anyone trying to enter from outside.

3. Space

After choosing your neighborhood, space is the next most important consideration. If you are considering buying a co-op or a condo, you should look at many similar apartments, in approximately the same price range, and use the chart on page 136 to help you make space/price comparisons.

The following list describes various types of apartments ranging from Studios to Two-bedrooms.

STUDIOS: One or two rooms—counting the kitchen, but not the bath. The kitchen may be a part of the living room or a separate room. The size of the studio may vary from a tiny closet-like space (approximately 10 ft. x 12 ft.) to a nice sized living area of 12 or 15 ft. by 20 or 30 ft. Studios may also have a dining or sleeping alcove, in which case they are called "junior one-bedrooms." Typically, these apartments have one or two closets, and may or may not have a dressing area off the bath.

ONE-BEDROOMS: Three rooms; a living room, bedroom, and a separate kitchen. They are typically 650 to 750 square feet. Those with a windowed alcove, that can be converted to another room (a bedroom or den) are called "junior 4's," "junior two-bedrooms," or "convertible two-bedrooms." These apartments are approximately 750 to 900 square feet and have larger rooms and more closets than do straight layouts.

TWO-BEDROOMS: Four rooms; a living room, two bedrooms, and a kitchen. A "convertible-three bedroom" or "junior 5," is a two-bedroom apartment with a windowed alcove, that can be used as an additional room. Two-bedroom apartments typically have about 1000 to 1300 square feet of space.

4. Evaluating the Building

You will find that apartments come in many styles with variations of light, space and configuration, reflecting the variety of buildings in which they are found. It is important to distinguish between those amenities you would like, and those which are essential. Here are a few questions you may ask yourself: Is having a doorman or a garage essential? Is large space or charm preferable? Do newer buildings appeal to me or are prewar buildings more my style? Be specific. The more detailed you are about what you want, and need, the easier your search will be as you narrow your choices.

THE HIGH-RISE BUILDING, with a doorman, affords maximum security to tenants; (security should be everyone's first concern). The doorman's primary job is to make sure that anyone who enters the building identifies himself, and that the tenant is notified whenever someone comes to visit. No one is allowed into the building unless authorized to do so by the tenant. A doorman also holds doors open, directs repairmen, accepts packages, hails taxicabs and generally gives help when help is needed. Doormen are usually trustworthy, discreet, and pleasant and, other than the superintendent, they are the people you are most likely to interact with to get things done.

Every high-rise building has an elevator. In pre-war buildings, security personnel may include an elevator operator in addition to, or instead of, a doorman. Live-in-superintendents are available in many doorman buildings for maintenance and repairs.

Modern luxury high-rise buildings may have in-door garages, roof-top sundecks, health-clubs or swimming pools. Some may have party rooms and children's playrooms. Laundry rooms, bicycle rooms and storage bins are usually found in the basement, and most modern high rises have central air-conditioning and cable T.V. connections. In addition, some luxury buildings may have maid's and/or valet service.

One of the possible drawbacks to high-rise living is that the lifestyle can be cold and impersonal. Tenants usually keep to themselves and maintain their anonymity. If you would prefer a (possibly) friendlier, more homey environment, you may want to consider a brownstone.

BROWNSTONE BUILDINGS, are typically 18 to 20 feet across and 40 to 50 feet in depth. A landlord may divide a floor in half to make two small one-bedroom apartments, or he may rent the whole floor as a "floor-through apartment." If there is a second bedroom, it is usually very small.

Typically, a walk-up building, of any construction, is called a "Brownstone." Apartments in these types of buildings can have nice architectural details, such as high ceilings, moldings, fireplaces, brick walls, and hardwood floors. They can have a cozy sense of living in a home, rather than in an apartment building; and usually people living in small buildings get to know one another. The main drawback to "Brownstone" living is that there may not be a super or landlord on the premises to respond when there is an emergency or when repairs need to be made. There are no services, other than maintenance, and few modern conveniences. The condition of these buildings also varies quite a bit, with some buildings and apartments substantially renovated, and others in close to their original state.

Most importantly, there is less security. Most renovated "Brownstone" buildings have TV or buzzer-intercom systems to let visitors in, and locked front doors. Sometimes, there is a locked inner vestibule door as well. Your first consideration should always be good security. At minimum, there should be good locks on all exterior doors and a good TV or buzzer-intercom system. The entrance hall should be well-lit and safe, with no hidden places for a mugger to lurk.

You should check the mail boxes to see if they have been tampered with, and the stairways to see if they are clean and well lit. The building should have adequate fire safeguards. It should have a fire-escape on the outside or fire-proof stairways. There should be a sprinkler system in public areas, and smoke detectors and alarm systems in place.

Don't hesitate to ask questions about everything that concerns you. Ask if there have been any recent burglaries in the building and then check with the local police department. It's best to be aware of any possible obstacles to your future happiness before you move in.

EVALUATING THE APARTMENT

Here are some things you should check for as you inspect each apartment:

THE KITCHEN

Kitchens are normally equipped with a sink, stove and refrigerator. Luxury units may also have diswashers and microwave ovens. Eat-in kitchens are rare, and usually are found only in pre-war buildings and in larger apartments.

What To Look For

- Is the kitchen adequately equipped?
- Are the age and condition of the appliances good?
- Is there enough counter space and cabinet space?
- Is the water pressure adequate?
- Are there enough electrical outlets for appliances?
- Is there a window for ventilation (or a vent?)

THE BATHROOM

Bathrooms are usually about 5' x 6' in modern buildings, and have fairly standard fixtures. Older buildings may have larger bathrooms with deeper bathtubs and pedestal sinks. Every bathroom should have a medicine cabinet, towel rack, and an electrical outlet. Having a separate linen closet, outside of the bathroom, is a plus.

What To Look For

- Are the sink, tub, toilet, and shower clean and in good working order?
- Is the tile clean?
- Is there a window for ventilation?
- Is the water pressure good?

OTHER APARTMENT FEATURES:
WHAT ELSE TO LOOK FOR

- The floors, walls, and ceilings should be in good condition. The paint job should be fresh and the plaster should not be chipping or cracking. Hardwood floors should be sanded and polyurethaned, and vinyl floors, tile or carpeting should be cleaned.

- The apartment should have a sufficient number of light fixtures, electrical outlets and phone jacks, and they should be conveniently placed.

- Windows should open and close easily, as should cabinets and closet doors.

- There should be adequate closet and storage space for your needs.

- If there is an air-conditioning unit, (either a central air-conditioner or a separate window unit) find out if you, or the building, will pay for the electricity to run the A.C.

- Check out the size and layout of the space. Apartments in newer buildings usually do not have vestibules or hallways. The rooms are rectangular and usually take up every square foot of space. Older buildings frequently have a more gracious flow of space, with foyers leading to the main rooms. Room sizes should be sufficient for you to live comfortably with your furniture and possessions (or you may feel cramped and claustrophobic.) Rooms should be rectangular or it may be difficult to arrange furniture. Finally, the bath should be off the living room so that your guests don't have to go through the bedroom to use it.

- Take notes as you view each apartment. At the end of the day, go over what you've written, especially noting those apartments that meet most of your needs. You should be able to narrow down the one or two most likely prospects. A worksheet that you can use when viewing apartments is provided on the next page.

TIP:
Look at no more than five apartments in any one day; more than that will confuse you. If possible, bring a camera and take pictures so that you will clearly remember the property later on.

Comparing Apartments
for Sale or Rent

	Apt #	Apt #
Address and Apt. No.		
Building Type (Lux, Elev, Twnhs)		
Building Amenities		
Space (Total Square Feet)		
Rent or Sales Price		
Maintenance (if co-op)		
Deductible Portion of Maintenance		
C.C. and R.E. Tax (if condo)		
Building's Financial Condition		
Down Payment Required		
Apartment Condition		
Kitchen		
Bath(s)		
Layout (flow of space)		
Views		
Special Apt. Features		
Average Room Size		
Price Per Square Foot (For co-ops, add your share of the underlying mortgage to the purchase price then divide by square footage.)		

NOTES

THE COMPLETE
HOME BUYER'S GUIDE TO
MANHATTAN
CO~OPS AND CONDOMINIUMS

Chapter 6

MANHATTAN'S CO~OP/ CONDO MARKET: AN OVERVIEW

When considering the purchase of a home, serious decisions must be made based upon where you want to live, how much you can afford, how long you intend to stay, and whether to buy a co-op or condominium. You will need to also determine how and where to obtain a mortgage loan, and how to find professional help.

This chapter will give you the information you need to help you choose a co-op or condominium, negotiate a contract, obtain a mortgage loan and find professional help in closing. Please see Chapter 5 for additional help in choosing a neighborhood, determining space needs, evaluating apartment and building amenities, and calculating an individual apartment's worth.

TO RENT OR TO BUY? THAT IS THE QUESTION.

As Manhattan rents continue to sky-rocket, more and more people in their early to mid-twenties are moving from a rental apartment to a co-op or condo. They are buying approximately 30% of all the studio and small one-bedroom apartments that come on the market: couples and families typically buy the larger units. This surge of interest in buying-versus-renting is primarily due to high rents and to the benefits of property ownership.

One of these benefits is that mortgage interest payments and co-op/condo real estate tax payments, can be deducted from the federal income tax, whereas rents cannot be. Also, by lowering the amount of income on which taxes are paid, a tax payer may be able to shift into a lower tax bracket, thus saving even more money.

Another benefit of ownership is potential investment appreciation of property. The buyer can acquire a growing stake in his home as he pays off his mortgage and as his home appreciates in value. (Under normal circumstances, this will at least keep pace with inflation.) Also, the home can be used as collateral for future loans. Should the property be sold, there is the additional opportunity to roll over the gain into a more expensive home.

Home ownership, however, is not for everyone. Owning makes sense for those who stay in their homes for more than seven years, because during the first few years there is little or no buildup of equity. Most mortgage payments during those years do not substantially reduce the loan principal. Renting makes sense for those who live in a home less than five years, who invest at a rate higher than appreciation and who pay less rent than they would pay to buy, after taxes.

Home ownership in Manhattan usually takes the form of buying an apartment in a high rise building called a Cooperative or a Condominium.

What is a Cooperative?

A Cooperative (Co-op) is a residential apartment building whose title is held by a corporation. Apartment owners hold proprietary leases to their apartments and shares in the corporation that are allocated to a particular unit, thus becoming co-owners of the building with a specific right to occupy their apartment.

Each apartment is given a certain number of shares, according to its size and desirability. Maintenance payments are based on the numbers of shares each unit has, and go toward paying the building's expenses. These expenses include mortgage interest payments, municipal tax payments, insurance, and operating expenses. Tenants have voting rights (commensurate with the number of shares they hold) in electing the building's board of directors. It is the board of directors who oversees the management of the building. This includes making financial decisions, maintenance decisions, and approval decisions as regards prospective new tenants. The co-op board has the right to approve or disapprove of any potential new owner. Approval decisions are normally made based on an applicant's perceived financial stability, as well as his ability to fit peacefully in with his neighbors. However, the board can lawfully reject an applicant for any reason other than a discriminatory one.

Co-op boards can also rule on whether to allow any major renovations to be made in the apartment. Their concern will be for the structural integrity of the building; its pipes, wires, etc. For this reason, alteration plans must be authorized before work may begin.

Because co-op ownership entails joint liability, there is greater financial risk than in a condominium. If a shareholder defaults on his maintenance payments, other tenants can become personally liable. In a worst case scenario, if a co-op's mortgage debt or taxes are not paid, its mortgage can be foreclosed or it can be sold for nonpayment of taxes, in which case the building may revert back to being a rental building and a shareholder's entire investment could be lost. For this and other reasons, the rules of the corporation can be very strict. It's best to be aware of all of a building's rules and restrictions before purchasing, and to carefully study with an accountant, financial advisor and/or lawyer the "Financials" of the building.

What is a Condominium?

A condominium in New York City is a residential apartment building in which each owner has absolute ownership of his apartment, plus an undivided interest in the common elements of the building. Unlike a co-op, in which an owner holds shares in a corporation, a condo owner holds a recorded deed to a particular unit. As in a co-op, a condominium board of directors is elected by the owners. They have the same responsibilities and powers as a co-op board, except that they cannot turn down a potential buyer or sublet tenant. This means that an owner can sell or sublet to whomever he pleases.

As the owner of "real property," the condo resident also has the right to make interior renovations without the board's approval, as long as the renovation work does not affect the buildings common elements. Any damage that may be done to the roof, pipes, or structural walls must be repaired by the owner.

Condos are more expensive to buy than co-ops, but their monthly maintenance fees, called common charges, are generally lower. The monthly common charge pays for property maintenance and repairs, insurance, management fees and utilities. Should a condo owner default on these payments, the building's management could place a lien against the unit.

Deciding to Rent or Buy

To help you make the decision whether to rent or purchase, consider the advantages of each. Compare the costs of buying versus renting, then follow your head and your heart.

Reasons to Rent

- There are no ownership responsibilities - the landlord is responsible for maintenance problems
- Your capital may earn more money invested elsewhere
- You want the freedom to move whenever you wish
- You plan on traveling extensively or living part-time elsewhere
- Your time frame is less than three years and you would need to sell before you moved on

Reasons to Buy

- You can renovate, decorate, and do as you please - you own the property
- Home ownership costs can be budgeted and generally remain stable; rents will increase over time
- Your home will most likely increase in value
- Mortgage interest and real-estate taxes are deductible on your tax-return and lower your overall annual ownership costs

---

HOW THE INTERNET CAN HELP

A variety of calculators are available to help you make your decision to rent or buy. Check out these web sites:

- www.huecu.org - Mortgage Mart, a service of Harvard University Employees Credit Union
- www.aba.com - American Bankers Association
- www.midwisc.com - MidWisconsin Bank
- www.countrywide.com - Countrywide Mortgage Co.

What To Do Before You Buy

- Spend time learning the market in the location you are interested in. Since the current sales market in Manhattan is "hotter" than it's been since 1987, (surpassing 1985-1987 in volume) co-ops, condos, and townhouses sell so quickly that buyers very often don't have time to think. If you wait, you may lose the opportunity to purchase. Therefore it's best to look at a lot of properties first, learn the market, then make an immediate offer on something you like.
- Obtain pre-approval for a mortgage. Sellers prefer buyers who have a pre-approved mortgage through a lending institution. The usual down payment for any co-op or condo is 10 to 25 percent of the purchase price; it may be higher for luxury co-op units.
- Understand initial costs, including the lender, broker, and attorney fees. Your closing costs are likely to be 3 to 5 percent additional.
- Analyze the purchase from an investment perspective, as you would for any other investment, such as a stock purchase.

Financing In A "Hot" Market

In today's overheated sales market, you will have to act quickly to obtain a mortgage loan. A delay in financing could mean losing your desired property to another buyer. Therefore, getting a pre-approved mortgage loan as soon as you start looking makes perfect sense. Reasons to follow this strategy when time is of the essence are listed below.

- Being pre-approved makes you a stronger bidder.
- Pre-approvals are usually good for three or four months and can be updated if you need more time.
- You are not committed to the lending institution that provides your pre-approval. You can still shop around for the best rates and options.

Understanding The Mortgage Process

Mortgage lenders can be banks, savings and loans or credit unions. If you enlist the services of a mortgage broker, however, you may get a better interest rate. Brokers have access to the rates of most lending institutions, and extensive knowledge of the many loan programs available. They are full-time professionals and will tailor your needs to the best loan package available at the time of application.

In order to determine whether you qualify for a loan, and for how much, you will have to provide your loan officer or broker with the following information: your social security number, a list of debt obligations and liabilities, tax returns for the past two years, current income verification and copies of recent bank statements. If your down payment is a gift, you will also need to bring a letter from the gift provider.

The entire loan approval process takes about four to six weeks. Once the loan is approved, the bank issues a commitment letter to the buyer or to the buyer's broker.

HOW MUCH CAN I AFFORD?

The mortgage qualification process involves calculating how much of a loan you can readily afford. Therefore, qualification depends on your adjusted gross income, monthly housing costs, and debts (see tables below). The greater your down payment, the more loan options you will have as you are considered a better loan risk. In general, you should expect to be able to afford two to two-and-a-half times your gross income.

A bank officer will look at your total income, your total debt, and your past credit history. Two criteria banks use to qualify you for a mortgage loan are:

A) Your total annual housing expenses should not exceed 25 to 28 percent of adjusted gross income for FNMA loans, and 28 to 31 percent for jumbo loans. These include mortgage payments, property taxes, home insurance and private mortgage insurance.

B) Your total housing expenses, plus other long-term debt service, should not exceed 33 to 36 percent of adjusted gross income. Long-term debt includes anything that takes at least 10 months to repay.

To Calculate Your <u>Monthly Gross Income</u>, use Table A (below).

Annual Gross Salary	$ _____
Annual Interest	$ _____
Annual Dividends	$ _____
Other Annual Income	$ _____
ANNUAL GROSS INCOME	$ _____
(Divide by 12)	
MONTHLY GROSS INCOME	$ _____

Do include income from all sources that are steady and consistent. Do not include income from occasional jobs, bonuses, or investment gains.

To calculate how much of a loan you may qualify for, use Table B.

Table B:
The Mortgage Worksheet

A. Gross Monthly Income $_____

B. Multiply by 33% $_____

C. Estimated Monthly Maintenance,

    Taxes and Insurance $_____

D. B minus C: Subtotal $_____

E. Monthly Payment for Other Debts $_____

F. D minus E: Remaining Balance

    for Mortgage Payment $_____

G. Divide F by .00665 for

    Estimated Loan Amount $_____

*(This calculation is for a 30 year fixed-rate mortgage at 7% interest in the current market.)

MONTHLY MORTGAGE PAYMENT FOR A $10,000 LOAN						
%	5 Years	10 Years	15 Years	20 Years	25 Years	30 Years
4.0	184.17	101.25	73.97	60.60	52.79	47.75
4.5	186.44	103.64	76.50	63.27	55.59	50.67
5.0	188.72	106.07	79.08	66.00	58.46	53.69
5.5	191.02	108.53	81.71	68.79	61.41	56.78
6.0	193.33	111.03	84.39	71.65	64.44	59.96
6.5	195.67	113.55	87.12	74.56	67.53	63.21
7.0	198.02	116.11	89.89	77.53	70.68	66.54
7.5	200.38	118.71	92.71	80.56	73.90	69.93
8.0	202.77	121.33	95.57	83.65	77.19	73.38
8.5	205.17	123.99	98.48	86.79	80.53	76.90
9.0	207.59	126.68	101.43	89.98	83.92	80.47
9.5	210.02	129.40	104.43	93.22	87.37	84.09
10.0	212.48	132.16	107.47	96.51	90.88	87.76
10.5	214.94	134.94	110.54	99.84	94.42	91.48
11.0	217.43	137.76	113.66	103.22	98.02	95.24
11.5	219.93	140.64	116.82	106.65	101.65	99.03
12.0	222.45	143.48	120.02	110.11	105.33	102.87

To get a complete picture of your <u>net worth</u>, (total assets minus total liabilities) first add up the rest of your assets, then add up your liabilities.

Table C: Your Net Worth Statement

ASSETS:

Cash	$ _____
Stocks, Bonds, Mutual Funds	$ _____
Keough / IRA Plans	$ _____
Other	$ _____
Total Assets	$ _____

LIABILITIES:

Mortgage	$ _____
Loans	$ _____
Credit Card Balances	$ _____
Other	$ _____
Total Liabilities	$ _____

TOTAL ASSETS $ _____

Minus

TOTAL LIABILITIES $ _____

Equals

NET WORTH $ _____

To be more precise about what you <u>really</u> will be able to afford monthly, use the worksheet below to calculate your monthly expenses. After you have totaled them up, subtract that figure from your gross monthly income. The balance is what you can afford to spend monthly on housing.

ESTIMATED MONTHLY EXPENSES

ITEM A	MONTHLY EXPENSES	ITEM B	MONTHLY EXPENSES
Groceries	_____	Savings	_____
Telephone	_____	Transportation	_____
Gas and Electric	_____	Entertainment	_____
Cable television	_____	Personal grooming	_____
Car payments	_____	Child care costs	_____
Car insurance	_____	Educational expenses	_____
Car maintenace	_____	Clothing costs	_____
Gas expense	_____	Restaurant expenses	_____
Parking expense	_____	Vacation expenses	_____
Medical insurance	_____	Charitable contributions	_____
Dental insurance	_____	Taxes	_____
Life insurance	_____	Other	_____
Disability insurance	_____	Other	_____
Tenant insurance	_____	Other	_____
Other insurance	_____	Subtotal A	_____
Installment loans	_____	Subtotal B	_____
Credit card pmts	_____	ESTIMATED	
		TOTAL EXPENSES	_____

1. Monthly Gross Income: _____

2. Estimated Monthly Expenses: _____

Having done these worksheets, you should be ready to have a mortgage officer prequalify you for a loan. Adding the amount of the down payment you can make to the loan amount, will give you the maximum priced home you can afford.

WHERE TO GET FINANCING

- **BANKS.** Both savings banks and commercial banks offer mortgage loans. Shop around for the best financial deal suitable to your needs.

- **MORTGAGE BROKERS.** Mortgage brokers will be able to find you the lowest interest rate-loan possible; and follow up with the bank for you. Typically they are paid a small fee by the lending institution.

- **HSH ASSOCIATES.** This mortgage update service, located in New Jersey, provides a listing of over 60 major lender's co-op loan rates for the New York City area, including interest rates, points, origination fees, etc. HSH can be reached at 1-800-UPDATES.

NEGOTIATING THE CONTRACT

Once you have found the apartment you wish to buy, the next step is to make an offer. Sales of Condo properties are of public record, and can be looked up in the Experian or Yale Robbins Condo guides. However, co-op prices are not of public record. A broker or appraiser may be able to get comparable sales information for you.

In general, your first offer should be about 15 percent below the asking price, keeping in mind that the owner may be firm in his asking price. Should the seller counter-offer, however, then you may continue to negotiate from there.

When buying a co-op, you will need to meet the standards of the co-op board, who will investigate your financial information and social and business references. A personal interview with some board members is usually required prior to approval.

GETTING PROFESSIONAL HELP

Whether you find and negotiate a co-op or condo purchase by yourself, or with the aid of a broker, there is some professional help that you will need. The legal aspects of your contract should be handled by an attorney who specializes in residential real estate in Manhattan. It should be the attorney's job to check all the documents related to the co-op or condo purchase. Your attorney will protect your legal interests in the contract negotiation with the seller.

Additionally, you may want to consider the help of a good accountant, a mortgage banker, a professional engineer, a real-estate appraiser and an insurance agent. It's best to ask friends for their recommendations.

The BOLD Property Information System is a Manhattan company that prepares property risk reports for specific properties. This company can prepare a customized report for the home you are interested in purchasing, which will tell you about the quality of life in the building and the neighborhood. It will tell you the crime rates, any plans for new construction nearby, any plans for homeless shelters or drug-rehabilitation facilities, etc. The property risk report costs $195; for more information, call (212) 673-7700.

CLOSING

At closing, the buyer, the seller, the buyer and sellers's attorneys, the title closer and the lender's attorney (if the buyer is obtaining a mortgage) are all present. Closing costs are paid by both the buyer and the seller; typical closing costs for Manhattan properties are listed below.

Once closing is completed, title and keys are transferred to the new owner. Now it's time to uncork the champagne.

MANHATTAN CLOSING COSTS & EXPENSES

For Seller

Broker	6%
Seller's Attorney	$1,500 and up
Co-op Attorney or Managing Agent	$450 and up
*Flip Tax	1%-3% of purchase price
Stock Transfer Price	$.05 per share
*Move-out Deposit	$500-$1,000
New York City Transfer Tax	1% of gross purchase price if $500,000 or under (filing fee of $25 also required) 1.425% of gross purchase price if over $500,000
New York State Transfer Tax	$2 per $500 of purchase price
Payoff Bank Attorney	$300 and up
UCC-3 Filing Fee	$20

For Purchaser

Purchaser's Attorney	$1,500 and up
Bank Fees	
*points	0 to 3%
*application, credit & appraisal	$400-$600
*bank attorney	$450-$600
*UCC-1 filing fee	$20
Short-term Interest	up to one month
*Move-in Deposit	$500-$1,000
Managing Agent of Co-op Attorney (Recognition Agreement Fee)	$200 and up
Lien Search	$300
Maintenance Adjustment	up to one month
Mansion Tax	1% of price when price exceeds $1,000,000

NOTES

MOVING
TO
MANHATTAN

Chapter 7

MOVING TO MANHATTAN

Congratulations. You have found an apartment you love in the neighborhood of your choice. So now, keys and lease in hand, it's time to consider your move.

On this and the following pages, all of the steps to take to make your move as easy as possible are listed. You will learn how to make your move, set up utilities and other services, get around, get settled, and find exciting things to do in your new neighbor hood.

ORGANIZING YOUR MOVE

30 Days Before You Move:

❶ Make sure you have a checklist of items that you want to pack, give away, donate or sell. Start packing items that you will not need before your move.

❷ Interview moving companies and purchase insurance coverage on movables.

❸ Make travel arrangements, airline, hotel, and car reservations if necessary.

❹ Be sure to file a change of address with your local post office.

❺ keep a file with all of your moving-related receipts: many expenses are tax-deductible.

2 Weeks Before You Move:

✌ Call all utility companies and have your service stopped at the old address and started at the new address.

> ✍ Phone company
> ✍ Heat/Electric company
> ✍ Cable company
> ✍ Trash removal company
> ✍ Water company

1 Week Before You Move:

☞ Make sure all packing is finished except for the everyday necessities and that all boxes are labeled.

☞ Confirm you moving arrangements and travel plans.

1 Day Before You Move:

☐ Check to make sure that you have the keys and the directions to your new address.

☐ Make sure that everything is accounted for at your old address before you leave.

☐ Pick up rental truck or call moving company to once again confirm your move time.

Here is a checklist to follow when interviewing movers:

☑ Get at least three estimates of moving costs. Also, find out if boxes, wrapping material and tape are included in the moving cost/estimates.

☑ Ask if the movers will put a cap on the estimate, (a figure that the estimate cannot exceed when the job is done).

☑ Check to see if there is a head mover you can speak to if there are any problems.

☑ Get a moving confirmation number, day and time.

☑ Buy insurance on moving belongings and take pictures of all your furnishings before the movers come. Look for damage after the movers have completed work.

BUDGET PLANNING CHART

This chart is designed to help you figure out all your moving related costs. Contact the IRS @ 1-800-829-4477 to find out which expenses are tax-deductible.

Before your move expenses:

Apartment and/or house finding trip   _____

Home inspection fee (if purchasing)   _____

Realtor's fee and/or closing costs   _____

1st and last month's rent/and or security deposits for apartment lease   _____

Utility deposits, if any   _____

House-cleaning supplies or services   _____

Moving expenses:

Packing materials   _____

Professional movers or rental truck   _____

Your personal transportation (airline tickets, auto expenses, etc.)   _____

Other Expenses: _____

Packing Day

☒ You can find boxes in grocery stores, liquor stores or large discount stores , or you can get packing boxes from your mover. Pack everything you intend to take.

☒ Canned foods can be heavy and can be expensive to move, decide if you want to keep them. Also, perishable foods will spoil; make sure you use them or throw them away before your move.

☒ Be careful when moving flammable materials, such as motor oil, cleaning chemicals, pesticides, automotive fluids, and batteries. Call 1-800 Cleanup to find out the nearest locations for the disposal of hazardous wastes and materials.

☒ If you decide not to keep some of your belongings, have a yard sale, or give them to friends or neighbors. You might also donate them to a local church or charity.

☒ Use towels, old newspapers, tissue paper, bubble wrap and paper bags as packing material.

When packing, always remember to:

☒ Reinforce the bottoms of the boxes with heavy- duty tape.

☒ Pack heavy items in small boxes and lighter items in large boxes.

☒ Wrap delicate and breakable items individually, with padding in between the pieces.

☒ Place all lampshades together in one box.

☒ Make sure boxes are not loaded too heavily.

☒ Label all boxes clearly and keep a list of everything that is packed and what room it is going into.

Getting Your  Mail:

- ▤ File a Change of Address Form with your local post office 30 days prior to your moving date.
- ▤ Let everyone know you're moving. Be certain to notify magazine and newspaper subscriptions, banks, businesses, credit card and insurance companies as well as friends and family members.
- ▤ First-class, Priority and Express mail will all be forwarded, at no charge, for 12 months. Periodicals will be forwarded for 60 days.

Getting Reconnected

Contact the following companies to make sure that your new service will be turned on at your new address; turned off at your old address.

Phone Companies: Local and Long-Distance
- ☎ Get your new telephone number from your local carrier. Then call your long-distance company to insure uninterrupted service.

Utilities: Gas and Electric
- 🕯 Have service turned off at your old address the day after you move out and ask to have your deposit returned.
- 🕯 Contact the utility serving your new address to have service turned on. You will need to show proof of new address and have a driver's license or social security number for identification purposes.

Other Services

- √ Make sure that all newspaper deliveries and other services are cancelled and restarted at the new address.
- √ Arrange to have your cable turned off and the box picked up to avoid any penalties. Make sure that the Cable Company knows the new address in order to have the service re-installed.

Getting Around

MTA
Passenger Information
Number:
718-330-1234

For non-english
speakers:
718-330-4847

on BUSes

If you are traveling across town, it is easiest to travel by bus. Copies of bus maps for the five boroughs may be optained by writing to:

New York Transit Authority
Customer Service
370 Jay Street
Seventh Floor
Brooklyn, NY 11201.

MTA Subway and
Bus
Lost and Found:
718-625-6200

Make certain that you know the line or route you were on and the time of travel.

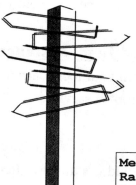

**Metro North
Railroad**
Travel Information:
212-532-4900

**Long Island
Railroad**
Travel Information:
718-217-5477

BY Taxi Cab

If you are traveling in a group of three or four people, taking a taxi may actually be cheaper than traveling by bus or train. Never, however, assume that the driver knows the best route to your destination.

Fares start at $2.00 ($2.50 at night) and increase by 30 cents for every 1/5 mile traveled. A fare card should be posted in the taxi cab. A 15% tip is expected.

If you leave something behind in a cab, the Taxi and Limousine Commission, ((212)302-8294), recommends that you report the lost property to the police precinct nearest to your drop-off point, and call the NYPD's Property Clerk's Office at 374-5084.

on the subway

The subway is the fastest way to travel through New York City. Fares may be purchased in the form of a subway token or a magnetic fare card, the Metrocard. With the card you may transfer from subway to bus or bus to subway for free.

When you purchase a Metrocard of $15 or more, a 10% bonus is added to the value of the card. Seven- and thirty-day unlimited passes are available for $17 and $63, respectively. There is also a single-day unlimited ride card available for $4. Free maps of the subway system are available at all token booths.

What to do

if you're...

LOST

To find an avenue address, drop the last number in the address, divide by two (2), and then add (+) or subtract (-) the key number below from the result. The resulting number is the nearest cross street.

Avenues A, B, C, & D	+3
First Avenue	+3
Second Avenue	+3
Third Avenue	+10
Fourth Avenue	+8
Fifth Avenue	
Up to 200	+13
Up to 400	+16
Up to 600	+18
Up to 775	+20
775 to 1286	...

Cancel the last figure of the house number and subtract 18 (do not divide by 2).

Up to 1500	+45
Up to 2000	+24
Sixth Avenue	-12
Seventh Avenue	+12
Eighth Avenue	+10
Ninth Avenue	+13
Tenth Avenue	+14
Eleventh Avenue	+15
Amsterdam Avenue	+60
Audubon Avenue	+165
Broadway (23 - 192 Sts.)	-30
Columbus Avenue	+60
Convent Avenue	+127
Central Park West	...

Divide house no. by 10 and +60

Edgecombe Avenue	+134
Ft. Washington Avenue	+158
Lenox Avenue	+10
Lexington Avenue	+22
Madison Avenue	+26
Park Avenue	+34
Park Avenue South	+8
Riverside Drive	...

Divide house no. by 10 and +72

West End Avenue	+60
York Avenue	+4

Cross street addresses increase east or west of Fifth Avenue, which runs north to south. The exception is cross streets west of Central Park, which increase from Central Park West.

LOCKED OUt

Generally, locksmiths will charge a flat fee simply for showing up—$15 to $20. Once they have arrived, it may cost anywhere from $35 to $65 to open the door. A fee may also be added for service late at night.

If it is necessary to replace a lock, try changing the cylinder instead of the entire lock. This procedure starts at about $40.

Manhattan
Champion Locksmiths
362-7000
University Locksmiths
627-0777

RObbEd

If you are burglarized, first go to the police—they'll assist in making a list of stolen items and note the points of entry.

For more expensive belongings, Allstate and Nationwide both offer rental insurance policies that cover up to $20,000 of property loss. Premiums are set according to where you live. Manhattan and the Bronx run approximately $160 per year. Brooklyn rates are slightly higher, upstate regions are lower.

Allstate Insurance
32 Union Square East
(b/w 15th & 16th St)
982-6606

60 East 42nd Street
(b/w Madison & Park Ave)
687-8787

Nationwide Insurance
145 West 72nd Street
(b/w Broadway & Columbus Ave)
595-5590

210 East 86th Street
(b/w First & Second Ave)
452-1919

Getting Settled

MUNICIPAL GOVERNMENT

New York voters elect three city-wide officials (the mayor, the public advocate, and the comptroller) as well as a borough president and a City Council member every four years. To register to vote in New York or to find your City Council district, contact the *Board of Elections*, **(212) 487-5300** or the *League of Women Voters*, **(212) 674-8484**. The *Mayor's Action Center* is also available to answer constituents' questions, **(212) 788-7585**. For information on the payment of taxes, call *Citytax Dial*, the *Department of Finances* 24-hour answer line **(718) 935-6736**.

Listings for government offices can be found in the *Blue Pages* section of the NYNEX *White Pages*.

UTILITY INSTALLATION

For gas and electricity, call *Con Edison*, **(212) 338-3000**.
Phone service is offered by *NYNEX*, **(212) 890-2350**.

EDUCATION

New York's public school system is one of the largest in the country. The *Board of Education* can help you find your way through the enrollment process:
Board of Education, 110 Livingston Street, **(212) 935-2000**.

To find out where your child should attend school (Elementary, Junior High or High School), contact:
The Office of Zoning & Intergration, 28-11 Queens Plaza North, Long Island City, NY 11101, **(718) 391-8000**

For information on area parochial schools, contact:
The Archdiocese of New York, **(212) 691-3381**

LICENSE/CAR REGISTRATION

If you are transferring an out-of-state license to a New York State license, both written and road tests may be waived if you hold an out-of-state license that is valid or that expired within the last 12 months. To register a vehicle for the first time, you must bring the following to your local Motor Vehicles office:

- Completed Registration/Title Application
- Proof of insurance in registrant's name
- If the vehicle was purchased from a dealer/leasing company, an Odometer Disclosure Statement
- Proof of registrant's name and date of birth
- Appropriate fee

- Proof of Ownership
- Sales tax clearance
- If the registrant is not the owner of the vehicle, registration authorization from the owner with name and date of birth
- Bill of sale

DEPARTMENT OF MOTOR VEHICLES

141-155 Worth Street (Between Center and Worth Streets, across from City Hall); **Mon-Fri, 9-4:30pm**

300 West 34th Street (Between 8th & 9th Streets); **Mon-Wed 8-5:30pm, Thurs 8-7pm**

2110 Adam Clayton Powell, Jr. Blvd.; **Mon, Tues, Wed and Fri, 9-4:30pm & Thurs 11-7pm**

Important Numbers

EMERGENCIES

Ambulance, Fire, Police	**911**	Customs (24 hrs.)	(800) 697-3662
Arson Hotline	(718) 722-3600	Department of Aging	(212) 442-1000
Battered Women	(800) 621-4673	Disabled Information	(212) 229-3000
Child Abuse	(800) 342-3720	Gay and Lesbian Switchboard	(212) 777-1800
Dental Emergency	(212) 677-2510	Health Department	(212) 442-1999
Domestic Violence	(800) 621-4673	Health Information (24 hrs.)	(212) 434-2000
Drug Abuse	(800) 395-3400	Housing Authority	(212) 306-3000
Emergency Medical (EMT) Information	(718) 416-7000	Immigration/Naturalization	(212) 206-6500
Missing Persons	(212) 719-9000	Legal Aid Society	(212) 577-3300
Rape Hotline	(212) 577-7777	Mayor's Office	(212) 788-7585
Sex Crimes Reports	(212) 267-7273	Medicaid	(718) 291-1900
Suicide Prevention	(212) 532-2400	Medicare	(800) 638-6833
Victim Services Hotline	(212) 577-7777	New York Post Office	(212) 967-8585

SERVICES

AAA	(212) 757-2000	Passport Information	(212) 399-5290
AIDS Hotline	(800) 342-2437	Planned Parenthood	(212) 541-7800
Alcoholics Anonymous	(212) 870-3400	Potholes	(212) 442-7094
All Night Pharmacy	(212) 755-2266	Salvation Army	(212) 337-7200
ASPCA	(212) 876-7700	Sidewalks	(212) 442-7942
Better Business Bureau	(212) 533-6200	Social Security	(800) 772-1213
Borough President	(212) 669-8300	Supreme Court	(212) 374-8500
Bridges and Tunnels	(212) 360-3000	Taxi Complaints	(212) 302-8294
Central Park Events	(212) 360-8126	Telegrams	(800) 325-6000
Chamber of Commerce	(212) 493-7400	Time	(212) 976-8463
City Sanitation	(212) 219-8090	Towaways	(212) 971-0770
Consummer Affairs	(212) 487-4398	Traffic Information	(212) 442-7080
Convention and Visitor's Bureau	(212) 397-8222	Traveler's Aid	(212) 944-0013

24-Hour Locksmith (212) 247-6747

Senior Citizen Services

New York City Department for the Aging
442-1000
—to order this agency's "City Services for Older New Yorkers," a thorough guide of programs and services.

East Side Elder Abuse Prevention Project
289-0601
The project is a collaboration of five agencies serving the Upper East Side of Manhattan to provide a comprehensive response to the problem of elder abuse in the area.

The Burden Center for the Aging
879-7400

Search and Care
860-4145
This organization serves Upper Yorkville and Carnegie Hall as a substitute for family to people who are frail and isolated.

Lenox Hill Neighborhood House
744-5022

Stanley Isaacs Neighborhood Center
Three locations:
360-7620—East 93rd Street
685-5675—East 33rd Street
348-4344—Meals-on-Wheels

Community Law Offices of the Legal Aid Society
426-3000
Provides legal assistance and advice to seniors living uptown of 96th Street.

Legal Services for NYC
431-7200
Referral service for seniors seeking legal help.

Department for the Aging Elderly Crime Victims Resource Center
442-3103
Helps crime victims, provides victim counseling, and assists in senior citizens abuse cases.

BLS Legal Svces. Corp./Senior Citizens Law Office
233-5753
Provides free legal services for Manhattan seniors.

Reduced Fare
(718) 243-4999
Reduced fare on all city subways, buses, and the Staten Island Ferry. This service is available 24 hours a day, seven days a week, for seniors (65 and over). No income restrictions apply.

Senior Citizen Rent Increase Exemption Program (SCRIE)
442-1000
Available to seniors who are 62 and older and living in rent-controlled or stabilized apartments or hotels, and who pay at least one-third of their net monthly income to rent. Income limits may apply.

Elderly Pharmeceutical Insurance Coverage (EPIC)
1 (800) 332-3742
Assists low- and moderate-income seniors, not on Medicaid, with the cost of prescription drugs.

The New York Foundation for Senior Citizen Homesharing Program
962-7559
Refers people (ages 18 and up) to seniors seeking roommates.

New York University Program for Lifelong Learning for University Seniors
998-7130
New York University offers seminars, lectures, and weekly luncheon discussions for seniors. Literature, current events, the arts, and social issues are some of the topics covered.

Stein Senior Center
689-4615
For 23 years, this East Side center has provided a variety of services for senior citizens— such as home-delivered meals, case assistance, nutrition counseling, education, and its Safe Streets program. The center is funded under contract by the city's Department of Aging, city Meals-on-Wheels, and the state Office for the Aging.

Encore Senior Center
581-2910
Provides home meals for West Side seniors, education and health promotion programs, and recreational activities.

Exploring the Cyber City
New York City Online

Government
NYC Link—The Official Guide to
New York City
www.ci.nyc.ny.us

Museums
Metropolitan Museum of Art
www.metmuseum.org

Museum of Natural History
www.amnh.org

Museum Links
www.museum.the-links.com

Museum of Television & Radio
www.mtr.org

Museum of Modern Art
www.moma.org

Sports
New York Yankees
www.yankees.com

New York Mets
*www.majorleaguebaseball.com/
nl/ny*

New York Knicks
www.nba.com/knicks/

New York Rangers
www.nhl.com/teams/nyr/

New York Jets
www.nfl.com/jets/

New York Giants
www.nfl.com/giants/

WNBA
www.nba.com/wnba/

Tourist Attractions
Statue of Liberty
www.nps.gov

Radio City Music Hall
www.radiocity.com

Grand Central Station
www.gcstation.net

Chinatown
www.chinatown.ny.com

Greenwich Village
www.dcny.com/gvo/

Hell's Kitchen
www.hellskitchen.net

Times Square
www.times-square.org

Official Tourism Site of New York
City
www.nycvisit.com

Food
4Dining
*www.4dining.com/new-york-
city-restaurants*

Beer Guide
www.nycbeer.org

New York Flying Pizza Pies
www.flying-pizzas.com

Manhattan Bagel
www.manhattan-bagel.com

Restaurant Report
www.appetitenet.com

Music/Dance/Theatre
New York City Ballet
www.nycballet.com

New York City Opera
www.metopera.org

Theatres and Producers
www.broadway.org

Searches and City Life
Altavista
www.altavista.com

Sidewalk
www.sidewalk.com

Yahoo
www.ny.yahoo.com

New York World
www.newyorkworld.com

Others
New York Firefighters Friend
www.nyfirstore.com

Metropolitan Transit Authority
www.mta.nyc.ny.us

New York Taxi Bill of Rights
www.tricky.com/nytaxi/

New York City Police Dept.
www.ci.nyc.ny.us/html/nypd/

The Empire State Building
www.esbnyc.com

Jazz Central Station: New York City
http://jazzcentralstation.com

RUNNING THE CITY
CITY OFFICIALS

Mayor of the City of New York:

When the office of Mayor was established in 1665, he was little more than a figurehead. At the time, mayors were elected by the Common Council, which would become today's City Council. In 1834, mayors began to be chosen through popular elections.

Rudolph Giuliani
City Hall
New York, NY 10007
Phone: 788-3000
Fax: 406-3587

The office of Mayor acquired more and more power throughout the years. In 1830, they won veto power over the Council. Less than twenty years later (in 1849) the term of office was doubled, from one year to two. It would be doubled again—to four years—in 1905. The Mayors acquired more territory when the five boroughs were consolidated in 1898, although at the time the mayor still shared power with the borough presidents and the Board of Estimate.

Later, in 1961, the mayor was given responsibility for the city's capital budget and oversight of the operating budget. In 1990, the Board of Estimate was abolished, leaving the mayor with the power to award city contracts.

Today, the mayor presides over forty city agencies, recieves $165,000 per year, and has his official residence in Gracie Mansion.

Public Advocate

When the Board of Estimate was abolished in 1990, the President of the City Council's powers were re-defined. The office of Public Advocate was established to replace the Council President.

The Public Advocate is an ombudsman and representative for the users of city services. He presides over City Council meetings and serves on all council committees, however, he may only cast votes to break a tie. He is able to sponsor legislation, and, should the mayor die or resign from office, the Public Advocate succeeds him.

Mark Green
1 Centre Street
15th Floor North
New York, NY 10007
Phone: 669-7200
Fax: 669-4701

Alan Hevesi
1 Centre Street
Room 530
New York, NY 10007
Phone: 669-2508
Fax: 669-8878

Comptroller

Established in 1801, the comptroller is the chief financial officer of the city. In the beginning, the position was filled by appointment; in 1884 it became an elected position. The term in office is four years, which are served concurrently with the mayor.

The comptroller has supervised the Department of Finance since 1931. He audits all city finance matters—such as contracts, budgets, and departmental spending—and publishes the annual financial report for the city. He also sits on the Banking Commision and the state Financial Control Board, and is second in line of succession to the mayor.

Borough President of Manhattan

C. Virginia Fields
1 Centre Street
19th Floor South
New York, NY 10007
Phone: 669-8300
Fax: 669-4900

The Chief Executive Officers of the Boroughs are the Borough Presidents. When the boroughs were consolidated in 1898, some worried over the loss of local rule, and so the office of borough president was created.

However, since that time city services have become more and more centralized, and the borough presidents have been steadily losing power. The presidents used to be members of the Board of Estimate, but when it was abolished in 1990, the borough presidents lost most of their power over the city budget.

Today, the presidents appoint members of the local community board chairs from that borough. Also, each president appoints one member of the Board of Education and the City Planning Board.

Manhattan's borough president's office employs 81 people and has a budget of $5 million. The borough presidents earn $114,000 per year and serve for four years, concurrent with the mayor.

U.S. Representatives
(Districts within Manhattan)

14th District
Carolyn Maloney (D)
1651 Third Avenue
Suite 311
New York, NY 10128
Phone: 860-0606
Fax: 860-0704

New York State Legislators:
State Senate

District 26	District 27
Roy M. Goodman (R)	Catherine M. Abate (D)
270 Broadway	270 Broadway
Room 2400	Room 2301
New York, NY 10007	New York, NY 10007
Phone: 298-5515	Phone: 298-5550
Fax: 298-5518	Fax: 298-5555
	Webpage:
	www.sendem.com

District 28
Olga A. Mendez (D)
87 East 116th Street
New York, NY 10029
Phone: 860-0893
Fax: 831-0530

East Side City Council

City Council District 2	City Council District 4
Margarita Lopez (D)	Andrew S. Eristoff (R-L)
237 First Avenue	370 Lexington Avenue
Suite 405	Suite 2001A
New York, NY 10003	New York, NY 10017
Phone: 614-8751	Phone: 818-0580
Fax: 614-8813	Fax: 818-0706
	Webpage:
	idt.net/ ~ eristoff

City Council District 5
A. Gifford Miller (D)
336 East 73rd Street
Suite C
New York, NY 10021
Phone: 535-5554

Manhattan City Council

The New York City Council is the legislative branch of the city government. There are 51 council seats, ten of which are from Manhattan districts. Nine of the Manhattan Council members are Democrats and one is a Republican. They earn $55,000 per year.

The Community Boards

Community boards act as neighborhood legislatures and advocacy groups. They advise in zoning and land-use issues, community planning, the city budget process, and coordination of municipality services. They do not have any specific jurisdiction, and may look into any aspect of city services. However, they may advise only, they have no binding powers on other agencies.

The boards have up to fifty unsalaried members, which are appointed by the borough president. Each consists of a small staff overseen by a full time district manager.

Board 5
450 Seventh Avenue
Suite 2109
New York, NY 10123
Phone: 465-0907
Fax: 465-1628
Lola Finkelstein, Chair
Kathy Kinsella,
District Manager

Board 6
330 East 26th Street
Room 2H
New York, NY 10010
Phone: 679-0907
Fax: 683-3749
Arnold S. Lehman, Chair
Carol Pieper,
District Manager

Board 8
309 East 94th Street
New York, NY 10128
Phone: 427-4840
Fax: 410-9738
E-mail: cb8@aol.com
Barry Schneider, Chair
Denise Woodin, Distric Manager

State Assembly

District 62	District 63
Sheldon Silver (D)	Steven Sanders (D)
270 Broadway	201 East 16th Street
Suite 1807	New York, NY 10003
New York, NY 10007	Phone: 979-9696
Phone: 312-1420	Fax: 979-0594
Fax: 312-1425	
District 64	**District 65**
Richard N. Gottfried (D)	Alexander Pete Grannis (D)
242 West 27th Street	1672 First Avenue
New York, NY 10001	New York, NY 10128
Phone: 807-7900	Phone: 860-4906
Fax: 243-2035	Fax: 996-3046
District 66	**District 73**
Deborah J. Glick (D)	John A. Ravitz (R)
853 Broadway	251 East 77th Street
Room 2120	Lower Level
New York, NY 10003	New York, NY 10021
Phone: 674-5153	Phone: 861-9061
Fax: 674-5530	Fax: 861-5273
	E-mail: johnravitz@aol.com
	Webpage:
	gramercy.ios.com/ravitz/

City~Wide Community Service Numbers

Civic Groups

Greenwich Village Chamber of Commerce Inc.
27 Barrow Street
(212) 255-5811

Manhattan Bowery Project
8 East 3rd Street
(212) 533-8400

Federation to Preserve the Greenwich Village Waterfront
156 Perry Street
(212) 727-3238

Clean Air Campaign
150 Nassau Street
(212) 349-7255

Community Boards

Community Board 1
49-51 Chambers Street
(212) 442-5050

Community Board 2
3 Washington Square Village
(212) 979-2272

Community Board 3
59 East Fourth Street
(212) 533-5300

Civic Groups

Gay Men's Health Crisis
119 West 24th Street
(212) 367-1000

Gay & Lesbian Anti-Violence Project
647 Hudson Street
(212) 807-0197

Hudson River Park Conservancy
141 Fifth Avenue
(212) 353-0366
at Pier 40 (212) 627-2020

Union Square BID
(212) 460-1200

Public Officials

Councilwoman Kathryn E. Freed
First District
(212) 778-7722

Councilman Antonio Pagan
Second District
(212) 788-7372

Councilman Thomas K. Duane
Third District
(212) 929-5501

State Senator Roy M. Goodman
Twenty-Sixth District
(212) 417-5563

State Senator Catherine Abate
Twenty-Seventh District
(212) 417-5504

State Assemblyman Sheldon Silver
Sixty-Second District
(212) 312-1400

State Assemblyman Deborah Glick
Sixty-Fifth District
(212) 674-5153

State Assemblyman Steven Sanders
Sixty-Third District
(212) 979-9696

Rep. Jerrod Nadler
Eighth District
(212) 334-3207

Rep. Carolyn Maloney
Fourteenth District
(212) 860-0606

Rep. Nydia Velazquez
Twelfth District
(718) 699-2602

PART II

DOWNTOWN

LANDLORD AND

RENTAL MANAGERS

DIRECTORY

PART II

The following list of landlords and agents for Manhattan apartments should interest anyone seeking a rental apartment. These owners and managers represent multiple, diverse properties including luxury high-rise buildings as well as smaller elevator and walk-up buildings. Together they control thousands of rental apartments in Manhattan's Downtown area. Most of these companies can be contacted directly and do not charge a fee.

ACTION GUIDE

Begin your search by calling each real estate company approximately 30 to 60 days in advance of your target move-in date. When you call a real estate firm to find out about available apartments, ask to whom you are speaking and make a note of that person's name. Be polite and courteous as this is the individual who will help you find an apartment. You will be told about apartments in your price range that are immediately available. Ask about the landlord's financial requirements (this may range between 40 - 50 times the monthly rent) and about anything else that may be relevant to your situation.

If a representative tells you that nothing is available when you call, ask if you can be put on a waiting list; then stay in touch by calling regularly. Many apartments become available around the first and the fifteenth of each month, as these are typical lease start dates. You might want to consider being flexible about the location, size and type of apartment in order to have more choices. This will be especially important if you have a limited budget.

You will need to familiarize yourself with current market conditions in order to choose the apartment that you will ultimately rent. To do so, see as many apartments as possible. If an apartment has an application on it, but is still available to be seen, look at it also. The applicant may be turned down or may change his or her mind and you will be next in line if you put a back up application on it.

The following list outlines specific items you will need to take when going to view an apartment.

1. *Fill out the sample application on page 127 entirely, giving the name and telephone number of your present landlord, business references, bank account numbers, etc. (You may be able to use this in lieu of the landlord's application.)*
2. *Have a photo I. D., a check book, $50 cash or an ATM card.*
3. *Have a letter of employment stating salary, position and length of employment plus 3 recent pay stubs.*
4. *If necessary, have a guarantor's letter and application filled out.*
5. *If you are self-employed, have a letter from your accountant and your last two years tax returns.*

When you see an apartment you like, return as soon as possible to the real estate company and fill out their application. Make a note of anything in the apartment that needs repair and ask all pertinent questions. You will need to leave a check for processing costs, which will include checking your credit and references. You should present all of your documentation at this time.

Be prepared to make a good first impression. Remember, the landlord may have other applicants for the apartment. So, having credit card, bank account, and reference telephone numbers is essential. Some landlords, in addition to requiring business and personal references, may ask for specific financial and/or legal references, the name of the applicant's banker and/or attorney. Try to have as much information as possible at your fingertips.

Call your contact person after a week if you have not heard from him or her to check on the status of your application; then stay in touch until you know whether or not your application has been accepted.

MAJOR LANDLORD AND MANAGEMENT COMPANIES
(DOWNTOWN RENTAL BUILDINGS)

Joseph Alpert
27 Madison Ave; NY, NY 10016
(212) 532-4466

Owns and manages buildings throughout Manhattan.

Abington Holding.
950 Third Ave; NY, NY 10022
(212) 759-5000

Owns and manages buildings throughout Manhattan.

A.J. Clarke Mgt Corp.
1881 Broadway; NY, NY 10023
(212) 541-4477

Manages luxury rental & co-op buildings in Manhattan.

Align Mgt Co.
64-35 Yellowstone Blvd; Forest Hills, NY
(718) 896-9600
Also (212) 779-7968 in Manhattan

Owns and manages buildings throughout Manhattan.

B & L Mgt Co.
344 East 63rd Street; NY, NY 10021
(212) 980-0980

Owns and manages buildings throughout Manhattan.

Martin Baumrind.
201 Clinton Street; Brooklyn, NY 11201
(718) 858-8871

Major Landlord in the East Village and the West 40's.

Bernstein Mgt Corp.
855 Sixth Ave; NY, NY 10001
(212) 594-1414

Major Landlord in Chelsea and the West 30's.

Bettina Equities Co.
230 East 85th Street; NY, NY 10028
(212) 744-3330

Owns and manages buildings throughout Manhattan.

Philip Brodsky.
188 Sixth Ave; NY, NY 10013
(212) 219-3990

Owns and manages buildings in the East Village and Chelsea.

Nathan Brodsky.
425 West 59th Street; NY, NY 10019
(212) 315-5555

Owns and manages buildings in Greenwich Village.

Buchbinder & Warren.
1 Union Square; NY, NY 10003
(212) 243-6722

Owns and manages buildings in Greenwich Village.

Building Mgt Corp.
52 Vanderbilt Ave; NY, NY 10017
(212) 557-6700

Owns and manages buildings throughout Manhattan.

Cooper Square Realty.
1860 Fifth Ave; NY, NY 10010
(212) 727-7222

Owns and manages buildings downtown.

Louis Devito.
23 Barrow Street; NY, NY 10014
(212) 924-5924

Owns and manages buildings downtown.

Dezer Properties Co.
89 Fifth Ave; NY, NY 10003
(212) 929-1285

Owns and manages buildings in Chelsea.

Charles E. Duross & Sons.
207 West 14th Street; NY, NY 10011
(212) 242-6800

Owns and manages buildings in Chelsea.

EBB Realty.
323 West 14th Street; NY, NY 10014
(212) 255-3732

Owns and manages buildings in the Greenwich Village and Chelsea.

Feil Organization.
370 Seventh Ave; NY, NY 10001
(212) 563-6557

Owns and manages buildings throughout Manhattan.

Abraham Fierstein.
15 West 30th Street; NY, NY 10001
(212) 736-3229

Owns and manages buildings in Chelsea and the West 30's.

Leslie J. Garfield & Co. Inc.
654 Madison Ave; NY, NY 10021
(212) 371-8200

Owns and manages buildings in Greenwich Village and Chelsea.

Gilman Realty Corp.
350 Merrick Rd.
Rockville Centre; NY 11570
(516) 764-0226

Owns and manages buildings in Lower Manhattan.

Glenwood Mgt.
1200 Union Turnpike
New Hyde Park, NY 11040
(718) 343-6400
in Manhattan: (212) 535-0500

Owns and manages buildings throughout Manhattan.

William Gottlieb.
544 Hudson Street; NY, NY 10014
(212) 989-3100

Owns and manages buildings in Lower Manhattan.

Giurdanella Bros.
4 Bond Street; NY, NY 10012
(212) 674-2097

Owns and manages buildings in Greenwich Village.

Greenthal Mgt.
4 Park Ave; NY, NY 10016
(212) 340-9300

Owns and manages buildings throughout Manhattan.

Helmsley Spear Inc.
60 East 42nd Street; NY, NY 10165
(212) 687-6400 or (212) 880-0406

Owns and manages luxury rental and co-op buildings throughout Manhattan.

Jacobson Properties.
11 Waverly Place; NY, NY 10003
(212) 533-1300

Owns and manages buildings throughout Manhattan.

Justin Enterprises.
1235 Broadway; NY, NY 10001
(212) 684-7573

Owns and manages buildings in Chelsea and the West 30's.

Kinsey Company.
163 West 23rd Street; NY, NY 10011
(212)255-3579

Owns and manages buildings throughout Manhattan.

Kalimian Brothers.
641 Lexington Ave; NY, NY 10022
(212) 371-5050

Owns and manages buildings throughout Manhattan.

Macklowe Organization.
142 West 57th Street; NY, NY 10014
(212) 265-5900

Owns and manages buildings throughout Manhattan.

Matel Realty Co.
303 East 6th Street; NY, NY 10003
(212) 674-0950

Owns and manages buildings in the East Village and the East 20s.

Moskowitz Assoc.
70 Lafayette Street; NY, NY 10013
(212) 732-4040

Owns and manages buildings in Lower Manhattan.

Ogrin Associates.
2280 S. Grand Avenue, Baldwin, NY 11510
(516) 623-4454

Owns and manages buildings in Greenwich Village and the Upper Eastside.

Olnick Organization.
600 Madison Ave; NY, NY 10022
(212) 415-4800

Owns and manages buildings throughout Manhattan.

Orsid Realty Corp.
156 West 56th Street; NY, NY 10107
(212) 247-2603

Owns and manages buildings throughout Manhattan.

Ponte Bros. Inc.
511 Canal Street; NY, NY 10013
(212) 966-5420

Owns and manages buildings Downtown.

R&R Mgt. Co.
P.O. Box 20720; NY, NY 10025
(212) 724-4126

Owns and manages buildings throughout Manhattan.

Jack Resnick & Sons Inc.
110 East 59th Street; NY, NY 10022
(212) 421-1300

Owns and manages buildings throughout Manhattan.

Rockrose Development Corp.
309 East 45th Street; NY, NY 10017
(212) 697-4422

Owns and manages buildings throughout Manhattan.

Michael Romanoff.
7-11 S. Broadway; White Plains NY 10601
(914) 428-4200

Owns and manages buildings in Greenwich Village.

Rose Assoc.
380 Madison Ave; NY, NY 10017
(212) 210-6666

Owns and manages buildings on the East Side.

Sidney Rubell.
348 West 23rd Street; NY, NY 10011
(212) 243-2370

Owns and manages buildings in Lower Manhattan.

Rudin Mgt. Co. Inc.
345 Park Ave; NY, NY 10154
(212) 407-2400

Owns and manages buildings throughout Manhattan.

Sackman Enterprises Inc.
165 West 73rd Street; NY, NY 10023
(212) 595-5565 ext 611

Owns and manages buildings throughout Manhattan.

Shalom Brothers Inc.
102 Madison Ave; NY, NY 10016
(212) 683-0200
*Call Empire Mgt. for information on
available apartments at (212)686-5252

Owns and manages buildings throughout Manhattan.

Solil Mgt. Corp.
640 Fifth Ave; NY, NY 10019
(212) 265-2280 or call leasing department at
(212) 265-1667/8 for further information

Owns and manages buildings throughout Manhattan.

Stahl Mgt. Corp.
277 Park Ave; NY, NY 10172
(212) 826-7060

Owns and manages buildings throughout Manhattan.

Superior Mgt. Inc.
50 Bank Street; NY, NY 10014
(212) 243-7757

Owns and manages buildings in Greenwich Village and Chelsea.

Thurcon Construction.
2700 Grand Ave; Bellmore, NY 11710
(516) 783-6500

Owns and manages buildings Downtown.

Walter & Samuels.
419 Park Ave South; NY, NY 10016
(212) 685-6200
*For further information on available apartments, call (212) 696-7104

Owns and manages buildings throughout Manhattan.

Morton Tabak.
98-41 64th Road; Forest Hills, NY 11374
(718) 275-3919

Owns and manages buildings in the East Village.

NOTES

PART III

DOWNTOWN

BUILDING

DIRECTORY

A STREET BY STREET GUIDE TO FINDING DOWNTOWN'S BEST RENTAL, CO-OP AND CONDO APARTMENTS

HOW TO USE THE BUILDING DIRECTORY

The building directory is organized by street address from East 1st - East 29th Street, Fifth Avenue to the River. Each building listed is a luxury rental, co-op or condo and is attended by a doorman, concierge or elevator operator. Additionally, non-luxury elevator and loft buildings are also listed separately. Complete information is given regarding the building's location, description, amenities and apartment types. Managing agents names, addresses and phone numbers are listed in the index that follows.

The following is an example of a building listing - including explanations:

A.	B.	C.	D.	E.
East Village Area **194 East 2nd Street** @ Avenues A & B *The Villager* **Rental**	Built in 1998 - 7 stories	Doorman, sundeck, closed-circuit TV, advanced T-1 communication lines, laundry on every floor	One-bedrooms, Two-bedrooms, Three-bedrooms, Four-bedrooms	Developer: Shaya B. Development Exclusive Broker: Ardor Realty (212) 794-1330 *Fee

A. ADDRESS: Gives the exact location, name of building, type of building.

B. BUILDING DESCRIPTION: Gives the approximate date built, number of stories and other details.

C. BUILDING AMENITIES: Includes service personnel, parking, exercise facilities, etc.

D. APARTMENT TYPES: Indicates the types of apartments found in the buildings, including the number of rooms or bedrooms.

E. MANAGING AGENT: Gives the name of the management company.

The 1999 Building Directory provides up-to-date information for more than 500 luxury buildings in Manhattan's Downtown area. To look up the address and phone number of management companies, refer to the Management Index that follows this section.

Every effort has been made to verify the accuracy of the information which was compiled from a variety of sources, including:

- inspection of buildings and building personnel

- inspection of apartment floor plans where available

- managing agents and landlords

- newspaper advertisements

Note:

Some information may be incomplete. Managing agents or telephone numbers may have changed from the time the information was originally compiled. The publisher assumes no responsibility for damages caused by inaccuracies or omissions.

LUXURY DOORMAN/CONCIERGE BUILDINGS
EAST NUMBERED STREETS

EAST 1ST STREET - 29TH STREET   FIFTH AVENUE - EAST RIVER

Address	Description	Amenities	Apartment Types	Managing Agent
East Village Area **194 East 2nd Street** @ Avenues A & B *The Villager* **Rental**	Built in 1998 - 7 stories	Doorman, sundeck, closed-circuit TV, advanced T-1 communication lines, laundry on every floor	One-bedrooms, Two-bedrooms, Three-bedrooms, Four-bedrooms	Developer: Shaya B. Development Exclusive Broker: Ardor Realty (212) 794-1330 *Fee
East Village Area **141 East 3rd Street** @ N/W/C Avenue A *Ageloff Towers* **Co-op**	Built around 1930, Converted in the 1980's to co-op - 12 stories	Doorman	Studios, One-bedrooms, Two-bedrooms+	Herman Realty Corp.
East Village Area **14 East 4th Street** @ Broadway/Lafayette *The Silk Building* **Condo**	Built around 1910, Renovated and converted to condo in 1983 - 12 stories	Doorman, concierge, fireplaces, solarium, health club, garden	One and Two- bedroom loft units from 1100 to 2200 square feet	Cooper Sq. Rlty.
East Village Area **172 East 4th Street** @ N/W/C Avenue A **Co-op**	Built around 1930, Converted in the 1980's to a co-op - 12 stories	Doorman	Studios, One-bedrooms, Two-bedrooms+	Buchbinder & Warren
East Village Area **225 East 6th Street** @ Second/Third Ave. *Hudson East* **Rental**	Built in the 1990's	Concierge	Studios, One-bedrooms, Two-bedrooms	N/A
Greenwich Village Area **50 East 8th Street** @ Mercer/Greene St. **Co-op**	Built around 1950, Converted in the 1980's to co-op - 6 stories	Doorman, garage	Studios, One-bedrooms, Two-bedrooms+	Mark Greenberg RE Co.
Greenwich Village Area **60 East 8th Street** @Broadway/University *Georgetown Plaza* **Co-op**	Built in the 1960's - 34 stories	Doorman, pool, garage, roof garden	Studios, One-bedrooms, Two-bedrooms	Rose Assoc.
Greenwich Village Area **20 East 9th Street** @ Fifth/University *The Brevoort East* **Co-op**	Built in the 1960's, converted in the 1970's to co-op - 25 stories	Doorman, concierge, double-entrance, garage	Studios, One-bedrooms, Two-bedrooms, Three-bedrooms+	Insignia Residential Group
Greenwich Village Area **25 East 9th Street** @ Fifth/University Also **26 East 10th St.** *The Beauclaire* **Co-op**	Built in the 1920's - 12 stories	Doorman, fireplaces	Studios, One-bedrooms, Two-bedrooms	Kreisel Co. Inc.
Greenwich Village Area **29-45 East 9th Street** @Broadway/University **Co-op**	Built in the 1920's, Converted in the 1980's to co-op - 11 stories	Doorman	One-bedrooms, Two-bedrooms, Three-bedrooms+	Century Operating Corp.

LUXURY DOORMAN/CONCIERGE BUILDINGS
EAST NUMBERED STREETS

EAST 1ST STREET - 29TH STREET   **FIFTH AVENUE - EAST RIVER**

Address	Description	Amenities	Apartment Types	Managing Agent
Greenwich Village Area **30 East 9th Street** @ S/E/C University Pl. *The Lafayette* Co-op	Built around 1950, Converted in the 1980's to co-op - 6 stories	Doorman, garage	Studios, One- bedrooms, Two- bedrooms+	New Bedford Mgt. Corp.
Greenwich Village Area **40 East 9th Street** @Broadway/University *The Sheraton* Co-op	Built around 1950, Converted in the 1980's to co-op - 13 stories	Doorman, garage, garden	Studios, One- Bedrooms, Two- Bedrooms +	Insignia Residential Group
Greenwich Village Area **55 East 9th Street** @Broadway/University *The Jefferson* Co-op	Built in the 1960's, Converted in the 1980's to co-op - 14 stories	Doorman	Studios, One- bedrooms, Two- bedrooms, Three- bedrooms	Engleman & Co.
Greenwich Village Area **60 East 9th Street** @Broadway/University *The Hamilton* Co-op	Built around 1950, Converted in the 1980's to co-op - 6 stories	Doorman, garage	Studios, One- bedrooms, Two- bedrooms	Century Operating Corp.
Greenwich Village Area **63 East 9th Street** @Broadway/University *Randall House* Co-op	Built around 1960 - 13 stories	Doorman	Studios, One- bedrooms, Two- bedrooms	Dwelling Mgt.
East Village Area **115 East 9th Street** @ Third Avenue *The Saint Mark* Co-op	Built in the 1960's, Converted in the 1980's to co-op - 21 stories	Doorman, garage	Studios, One- bedrooms, Two- bedrooms +	Charles H. Greenthal Mgt. Corp.
East Village Area **601-03 East 9th St.** **Also 143 Avenue B** *Christodora House* Condo	Pre-war renovation, Converted in the 1980's to a condo - 17 stories	Doorman, Art Deco lobby	Studios, One- bedrooms, Two- bedrooms, Quadraplex P.H. of 3000 sq. ft.	Andrews Building Corp.
Greenwich Village Area **23 East 10th Street** @ University Place *The Albert* Co-op/Rental	Built in the 1920's, Converted in the 1980's to co-op - 13 stories	Doorman, landscaped roof garden, exposed brick, sleep lofts and dishwashers	Studios, One- bedrooms, Two- bedrooms, Three- bedrooms	Kreisel Co. Inc.
Greenwich Village Area **28 East 10th Street** @ Fourth/University *Devonshire House* Rental	Pre-war - 15 stories	Doorman	Studios, One- bedrooms, Two- bedrooms	Felder Mgt. Assoc. (212) 685-5250
Greenwich Village Area **40 East 10th Street** @Broadway/University Co-op	Built around 1930, Converted in the 1980's to co-op - 10 stories	Doorman, roof garden	Studios, One- bedrooms, Two- bedrooms	Blue Woods Mgt.

EAST 1ST STREET - 29TH STREET   FIFTH AVENUE - EAST RIVER

Address	Description	Amenities	Apartment Types	Managing Agent
East Village Area **70 East 10th Street** @ Broadway/Fourth *Stewart House* Co-op	Built around 1960, Converted in 1979 to co-op - 21 stories	Doorman, garage, circular drive and landscaped garden, courtyard in the rear	One-bedrooms, Two-bedrooms, Three-bedrooms+	Kreisel Co. Inc.
East Village Area **67 East 11th Street** @ N/W/C Broadway *The Cast Iron Building* Co-op	Built around 1900, Renovated in the 1970's - Converted in the 1980's to co-op - 7 stories	Doorman	Studios, One-bedrooms	Andrews Bldg. Corp.
Greenwich Village Area **18 East 12th Street** @ Fifth Ave/University Condo	Built around 1910, Renovated and converted to condo in 1985 - 10 stories	Doorman, roof garden, laundry room on every floor	Studios, One-bedrooms, Two-bedrooms	WPG Rudd Residential, Inc.
Greenwich Village Area **31 East 12th Street** @ University Place Co-op	Built around 1930, Converted in the 1970's to co-op - 12 stories	Doorman	Studios, One-bedrooms, Two-bedrooms	Buchbinder & Warren
Greenwich Village Area **39 East 12th Street** @Broadway/University *University Mews* Co-op	Built around 1900, Converted in the 1980's to co-op - 9 stories	Doorman, roof garden	Studios, One-bedrooms, Two-bedrooms - Each with additional sleep loft or storage space	Lawrence Properties
Greenwich Village Area **44 East 12th Street** @Broadway/University *Charing Court* Condo	Built in 1985 as condo- 10 stories	Doorman, roof garden	Studios, One-bedrooms, Two-bedrooms+	SDG Mgt. Corp.
East Village Area **60 East 12th Street** @ Broadway/Fourth *Hewlett House* Rental	Post-war - 13 stories	Doorman	Studios, One-bedrooms, Two-bedrooms	N/A
East Village Area **77 East 12th Street** @ N/W/C Fourth Ave Co-op	Built in the 1960's, Converted in the 1980's to co-op - 20 stories	Doorman, garage	Studios, One-bedrooms, Two-bedrooms +	Kreisel Corp.
East Village Area **125 East 12th Street** @ Third/Fourth Aves. *The Zachary* Condo	Built around 1930, renovated in 1989 as condo - 6 stories	Doorman	One-bedrooms, Two-bedrooms, Three-bedrooms	Taranto Assoc. Mgt.
East Village Area **114 East 13th Street** @ Third/Fourth Avenue *American Felt Bldg.* Condo	Built around 1910, renovated in 1985 as condo - 11 stories	Doorman, roof garden	Studio and One-bedrooms Lofts	Elm Mgt.

LUXURY DOORMAN/CONCIERGE BUILDINGS
EAST NUMBERED STREETS

EAST 1ST STREET - 29TH STREET   FIFTH AVENUE - EAST RIVER

Address	Description	Amenities	Apartment Types	Managing Agent
Greenwich Village Area **7 East 14th Street** @ Fifth/University *The Victoria* **Co-op**	Built in the 1960's, Converted in the 1980's to co-op - 21 stories	Doorman, garage	Studios, One-bedrooms	Goodstein Mgt.
Gramercy Park Area **105 East 15th Street** @ Union Square East **Co-op**	Built around 1900, Converted in the 1980's to co-op - 10 stories	Doorman	Studios, One- bedrooms, Two- bedrooms+	Heron Mgt. Ltd.
Gramercy Park Area **145 East 15th Street** @ Irving Place *Gramercy Arms* **Co-op**	Built around 1960, Converted in the 1980's to co-op - 17 stories	Doorman, garage, balconies	Studios, One- bedrooms, Two- bedrooms+	Punia & Marx
Gramercy Park Area **210 East 15th Street** @ Second/Third Aves. *The Peter Stuyvesant* **Co-op**	Built in the 1960's, Converted in the 1980's to co-op - 14 stories	Doorman, garage	Studios, One- bedrooms, Two- bedrooms	Taranto & Assocs.
Gramercy Park Area **230 East 15th Street** @ Second/Third Aves. *The Rutherford* **Co-op**	Built around 1960, Converted in the 1980's to co-op - 13 stories	Doorman, garage	Studios, One-bedrooms	Goodstein Mgt. Inc.
Gramercy Park Area **142 East 16th Street** @ Third Ave/Irving Pl. *The Gramercy Spire* **Co-op**	Built in the 1960's, Converted in 1979 to co-op - 23 stories	Doorman, garage, balconies	Studios, One- bedrooms, Two- bedrooms	Taranto & Assocs.
Gramercy Park Area **145 East 16th Street** @ Third Ave/Irving Pl *The Washington Irving* **Rental**	Post-war - 19 stories	Doorman	Studios, One- bedrooms, Two- bedrooms	Solil Mgt. Corp.: (212) 265-2280 For leasing information: (212) 265-1667 or 8
Gramercy Park Area **200 East 16th Street** @ S/E/C Third Ave *Gramercy Towers* **Co-op**	Built around 1930, Converted in the 1980's to co-op - 20 stories	Doorman	Studios, One- bedrooms, Two- bedrooms	Mark Greenberg RE Co.
Gramercy Park Area **201 East 17th Street** @ N/E/C Third Ave *Park Towers* **Co-op**	Built in the 1970's, Converted in the 1980's to co-op - 31 stories	Doorman, garage, roof garden	Studios, One- bedrooms, Two- bedrooms	Goodstein Mgt. Inc.
Gramercy Park Area **130 East 18th Street** @ Irving Pl./Third Ave *Gramercy Plaza* **Co-op**	Built in the 1960's - 17 stories	Doorman, garage	Studios, One- bedrooms, Two- bedrooms	Century Operating Corp.

LUXURY DOORMAN/CONCIERGE BUILDINGS
EAST NUMBERED STREETS

EAST 1ST STREET - 29TH STREET   **FIFTH AVENUE - EAST RIVER**

Address	Description	Amenities	Apartment Types	Managing Agent
Gramercy Park Area **150 East 18th Street** @ Third Ave **Rental**	Post-war - 14 stories	Doorman, garage	Studios, One-bedrooms, Two-bedrooms	American SIBA Corp. (212) 764-0700
Gramercy Park Area **157 East 18th Street** @ Third Ave *The Gramercy Regent* **Co-op**	Pre-war, converted in the 1980's to co-op - 7 stories	Doorman	Studios, One-bedrooms, Two-bedrooms+	Self-managed
Gramercy Park Area **211 East 18th Street** @ Second/Third Aves. **Co-op**	Built in the 1950's, Converted in the 1980's to co-op - 7 stories	Doorman, garage	Studios, One-bedrooms, Two-bedrooms	Cooper Square Realty
Gramercy Park Area **242 East 19th Street** @ S/W/C Second Ave. **Co-op**	Built in the 1920's, Converted in the 1980's to co-op - 15 stories	Doorman	Studios, One-bedrooms, Two-bedrooms, Three-bedrooms	Vintage Realty
Gramercy Park Area **245 East 19th Street** @ Second Avenue **Rental**	Pre-war -16 stories	Doorman	Studios, One-bedrooms, Two-bedrooms	Harper Mgt. (212) 581-4180
Gramercy Park Area **151 East 20th Street** @ Third Avenue **Gramercy Park Condo** **Condo**	Post-war, built as condo - 4 stories	Doorman	23 units - Mostly studios	Arnold S. Warwick Co.
Gramercy Park Area **201 East 21st Street** @ N/E/C Third Ave *Quaker Ridge* **Co-op**	Built in the 1960's, Converted in the 1980's to co-op - 19 stories	Doorman, garage	Studios, One-bedrooms, Two-bedrooms	Goodstein Mgt. Inc.
Gramercy Park Area **301 East 21st Street** @ Second Avenue *The Petersfield* **Rental**	Pre-war - 16 stories	Doorman	Studios, One-bedrooms, Two-bedrooms	Charles Greenthal Mgt. (212) 340-9300
Gramercy Park Area **5 East 22nd Street** @ N/E/C Broadway *Madison Green* **Condo**	Built in 1983 as condo - 31 stories	Doorman, concierge, balconies, health club, garage, club room, children's play room, laundry room on every floor	Studios, One-bedrooms, Two-bedrooms+	Rose Assoc.
Gramercy Park Area **21 East 22nd Street** @Park Av S/Broadway **Co-op**	Built around 1910, Converted in the 1980's to co-op - 12 stories	Doorman	Studios, One-bedrooms	Wallack Mgt.

LUXURY DOORMAN/CONCIERGE BUILDINGS

EAST NUMBERED STREETS

EAST 1ST STREET - 29TH STREET
FIFTH AVENUE - EAST RIVER

Address	Description	Amenities	Apartment Types	Managing Agent
Gramercy Park Area **205 East 22nd Street** @ Second/Third Ave. *Gramercy Park Habitat* **Condo**	Built in the 1890's, renovated in 1983 as condo - 7 stories	Doorman, some units with fireplaces, garage, laundry room on every floor	Studios, One-bedrooms, Two-bedrooms	RA Cohen Mgt.
Gramercy Park Area **235 East 22nd Street** @ N/W/C Second Ave. *Gramercy House* **Co-op**	Built around 1930, Converted in the 1980's to co-op - 17 stories	Doorman, solarium, fireplaces, private park for tenants	Studios, One-bedrooms, Two-bedrooms, Three-bedrooms+	Equity Mgt. Group
Gramercy Park Area **301 East 22nd Street** @ N/E/C Second Ave. *Gramercy East* **Co-op**	Built in the 1960's, Converted in the 1980's to co-op - 17 stories	Doorman, garage, roof garden	Studios, One-bedrooms, Two-bedrooms+	Goodstein Mgt. Inc.
Gramercy Park Area **321 East 22nd Street** @ First/Second Ave. **Rental**	Post-war - 6 stories	Doorman, duplex and triplex apartments	Studios, One-bedrooms, Two-bedrooms	Thurcon Development: Exlusive Broker: Citi Habitats (212) 685-7300 * Fee
Gramercy Park Area **320 East 23rd Street** @ First/Second Ave. **Rental/Rent stabilized**	Built in the 1960's, renovated in 1984 - 15 stories	Doorman, garage, wall-to-wall windows, kitchens have dishwashers	Studios, One-bedrooms, Two-bedrooms	Goodstein Mgt. (212) 376-8600
Gramercy Park Area **200 East 24th Street** @ S/E/C Third Avenue *Crystal House* **Co-op**	Built in the 1970's, Converted in the 1980's to co-op - 19 stories	Doorman, garage, roof garden	Studios, One-bedrooms, Two-bedrooms+	Elm Mgt.
Gramercy Park Area **215 East 24th Street** @ Second/Third Ave. *Penny Lane* **Co-op**	Built in the 1970's, Converted in the 1980's to co-op - 8 stories	Doorman, garage, double-height windows	Studios, One-bedrooms, Two-bedrooms; Single, Duplex and Triplex Apartments	Walter & Samuels, Inc.
Gramercy Park Area **245 East 24th Street** @ N/W/C Second Ave. *Tracy Towers* **Co-op**	Built around 1960, Converted in the 1980's to co-op - 17 stories	Doorman	Studios, One-bedrooms, Two-bedrooms	Equity Mgt. Group
Gramercy Park Area **305 East 24th Street** @ First/Second Ave. *New York Towers* **Co-op**	Built in the 1960's, Converted in the 1980's to co-op - 20 stories	Doorman, garage, balconies	Studios, One-bedrooms, Two-bedrooms+	Nardoni Rlty. Inc.
Gramercy Park Area **45 East 25th Street** @ Park/Madison Ave. *The Stanford* **Condo/Rental**	Built in 1986 as condo-40 stories	Doorman, concierge, private park and fountain entrance, balconies, private gardens, fitness center, laundry on every other floor	Studios, One-bedrooms, Two-bedrooms, Three-bedrooms	Exclusive Rental Broker: Citi Habitats (212) 685-7300 *Fee

EAST 1ST STREET - 29TH STREET   FIFTH AVENUE - EAST RIVER

Address	Description	Amenities	Apartment Types	Managing Agent
Gramercy Park Area **201 East 25th Street** @ Second/Third Ave. *The Peter James* **Co-op**	Built around 1960, Converted in the 1980's to co-op - 18 stories	Doorman, garage, roof garden	Studios, One-bedrooms, Two-bedrooms	R.A. Cohen Assoc.
Gramercy Park Area **245 East 25th Street** @ N/E/C Second Ave. *Spruce Ridge House* **Co-op**	Built in the 1960's, Converted in the 1980's to co-op - 20 stories	Doorman, garage, sundeck	Studios, One-bedrooms, Two-bedrooms+	Washington Square Mgt.
Gramercy Park Area **145 East 27th Street** @ Third Avenue *The Townsway* **Rental/Rent Stabilized**	Built in the 1960's - 15 stories	Doorman, garage, sundeck	Studios, One-bedrooms, Two-bedrooms	Algin Mgt. (212) 725-0566 or (718) 896-9600
Gramercy Park Area **200 East 27th Street** @ S/E/C Third Ave. *Victoria House* **Co-op**	Built in the 1960's, Converted in the 1980's to co-op - 18 stories	Doorman, roof garden, garage	Studios, One-bedrooms, Two-bedrooms	Akam Associates
Gramercy Park Area **240 East 27th Street** *Parc East Tower* **Rental**	Built in the 1970's - 26 stories	Doorman. garage	One-bedrooms, Two-bedroom	Merit Corp. (212) 628-0560
Gramercy Park Area **140 East 28th Street** @Third/Lexington Ave **Co-op**	Built around 1930, Converted in the 1980's to co-op - 13 stories	Doorman, fireplaces, roof garden	Studios, One-bedrooms, Two-bedrooms	Rose Assoc.
Gramercy Park Area **201 East 28th Street** @ N/E/C Third Ave. *Chesapeake House* **Co-op**	Built in the 1960's, Converted in the 1980's to co-op - 20 stories	Doorman, roof garden, garage	Studios, One-bedrooms, Two-bedrooms, Three-bedrooms	Charles H. Greenthal & Co.
Gramercy Park Area **247 East 28th Street** @ Second/Third Ave. *The Clarendon* **Rental**	Built in the 1970's - 17 stories	Doorman, exercise room	One-bedrooms, Two-bedrooms	Samson Mgt. Exclusive Broker (212) 685-7300 *Fee
Gramercy Park Area **154 East 29th Street** @ Third Avenue *The Habitat* **Rental**	Built in the 1970's - 17 stories	Part-time doorman, apartments have dishwashers	Studios, One-bedrooms	Manhattan Skyline Mgt. (212) 977-4813 Rental Office: (212) 889-1850
Gramercy Park Area **155 East 29th Street** @ Third/Lexington Ave. *The Biltmore Plaza* **Rental/Rent stabilized**	Built around 1980 - 30 stories	Doorman, concierge, garage, health club with rooftop pool, recreation room, sundeck	One-bedrooms, Two-bedrooms, Three-bedrooms	Milford Mgt. Rental Office: (212) 684-5900

NON-LUXURY LOFT AND ELEVATOR BUILDINGS

EAST NUMBERED STREETS

EAST 1ST STREET - 29TH STREET   FIFTH AVENUE - EAST RIVER

Address	Description	Amenities	Apartment Types	Managing Agent
East Village Area **178-184 East 2nd Street** @Avenue A/B **Condo**	Built around 1900, Renovated in 1986 as condo - 6 stories	Elevator building	Studios, One-bedrooms, Two-bedrooms, +	Self-managed
East Village Area **280 East 2nd Street** @ Avenues C/D *CD280* **Rental**	Built in 1998 - 11 stories	Elevator building, on-site superintendent, laundry on ground level, excercise room, outdoor running track & landscaped garden	Studios, One-bedrooms	Manhattan Skyline Mgt. (212) 889-1850
East Village Area **70 East 3rd Street** @ First/Second Ave **Rental/Rent Stabilized**	Prewar - 6 stories	Elevator, exposed brick, fireplaces, high ceilings	Studios, One-bedrooms	Park Square Assoc. (212) 529-9595 *Brokerage fee: 1 month's rent
East Village Area **94 East 4th Street** @ First/Second Ave **Rental**	Renovated in the 1990's - 9 stories	Elevator building with video-security, on-site super, apartments have high ceilings and dishwashers	Studios, One-bedrooms, Two-bedrooms	Bettina Equities Co. (212) 744-3330
East Village Area **99 East 4th Street** @ First/Second Ave **Co-op**	Built around 1930, Converted in 1990 - 6 stories	Elevator building	One-bedrooms, Two-bedrooms, Three-bedrooms	Self-managed
East Village Area **527 East 6th Street** @ Avenue A & B **Rental/Rent Stabilized**	Built around 1910 - 6 stories	Elevator, exposed brick, fireplaces, and dishwashers	Studios, One-bedrooms	Park Square Assoc. (212) 529-9595 *Brokerage fee: 1 month's rent
East Village Area **32-34 East 7th Street** @ Second/Third Ave **Rental/Furnished/ Short-term leases**	Built around 1880 - 6 stories	Elevator, exposed brick, high ceilings	Studios, One-bedrooms, Two-bedrooms, Three-bedrooms, Four-bedrooms	Jakobson Properties (212) 533-1300
East Village Area **299 East 8th Street** @ Avenue B **Rental/Rent Stabilized**	Built around 1910 - 6 stories	Elevator, on-site superintendent, exposed brick, high ceilings, fireplaces, dishwashers	Studios, One-bedrooms, Two-bedrooms	Park Square Assoc. (212) 529-9595 *Brokerage fee: 1 month's rent
East Village Area **315-317 East 9th Street** @ First/Second Ave **Rental/Rent Stabilized**	Built in the 1890's - 6 stories	Elevator, exposed brick, high ceilings, fireplaces	Studios, One-bedrooms	Park Square Assoc. (212) 529-9595 *Brokerage fee: 1 month's rent
East Village Area **320 East 9th Street** @ First/Second Ave **Rental**	Post-war - 6 stories	Elevator building, video security, apartments have fireplaces and dishwashers	Studios, One-bedrooms, Duplexes	Bettina Equities (212) 744-3330

NON-LUXURY LOFT AND ELEVATOR BUILDINGS

EAST NUMBERED STREETS

EAST 1ST STREET - 29TH STREET
FIFTH AVENUE - EAST RIVER

Address	Description	Amenities	Apartment Types	Managing Agent
Greenwich Village Area **15 East 10th Street** @ University Place/ Fifth Ave **Co-op**	Built around 1910 - 6 stories	Elevator building	Studios, One-bedrooms, Two-bedrooms	Eichner Leeds
Greenwich Village Area **21 East 10th Street** @ University/Fifth Ave **Co-op**	Built around 1920, Converted in the 1980's to co-op - 12 stories	Elevator building, TV security	Studios, One-bedrooms, Two-bedrooms	David Eisenstein Realty Co.
Greenwich Village Area **25 East 10th Street** @University Place *The Albert Chambers* **Rental**	Prewar - 10 stories	Loft building, voice intercom security	61 loft units	N/A
Greenwich Village Area **29 East 10th Street** @University Place **Condo**	Prewar - 8 stories	Loft building, video intercom security	Apartments range from 1,800 to 2,000 square ft.	TSL Development (Self-managed)
Greenwich Village Area **34 East 10th Street** @ Broadway/ University Place **Co-op**	Built around 1900, Converted in the 1970's to co-op - 10 stories	Loft building	18 loft units	Self-managed
Greenwich Village Area **35 East 10th Street** @ Broadway/ University Place **Co-op**	Built around 1970, Converted in the 1980's to co-op - 9 stories	Elevator building	Studios, One-bedrooms	Heron Mgt.
Greenwich Village Area **43 East 10th Street** @ Broadway/ University Place **Co-op**	Built around 1900, Converted in the 1980's to co-op - 6 stories	Elevator building	Studios, One-bedrooms, Two-bedrooms	Self-managed
East Village Area **205 East 10th Street** @ Third Ave **Co-op**	Built around 1930 - 6 stories	Elevator building	Studios, One-bedrooms, Two-bedrooms	Bell Realty
East Village Area **254 East 10th Street** @ First Ave **Rental**	Built in 1990 - 6 stories	Elevator building, video security	Studios, One-bedrooms, Two-bedrooms	Bettina Equities (212) 744-3330
Greenwich Village Area **15 East 11th Street** @ University/Fifth Ave **Co-op**	Built around 1900, Converted in the 1980's to co-op - 9 stories	Elevator building	Studios, One-bedrooms	Charles H. Greenthal & Co.

NON-LUXURY LOFT AND ELEVATOR BUILDINGS

EAST NUMBERED STREETS

EAST 1ST STREET - 29TH STREET   FIFTH AVENUE - EAST RIVER

Address	Description	Amenities	Apartment Types	Managing Agent
Greenwich Village Area **17-19 East 11th Street** @University/Fifth Ave *Van Rensselaer* **Co-op**	Built around 1900, Converted in the 1980's to co-op - 9 stories	Elevator building, TV security	Studios, One-bedrooms, Two-bedrooms+	Self-managed
East Village Area **245 East 11th Street** @ Second/Third Ave **Rental**	Built around 1930 - 6 stories	Elevator building, on-site superintendent, apartments have high ceilings, exposed brick and dishwashers	Studios, One-bedrooms, Two-bedrooms, Three-bedrooms	Jakobson Properties (212) 533-1300
Greenwich Village Area **8 East 12th Street** @Fifth Ave **Condo**	Prewar - 12 stories	Loft building, video intercom security	Lofts are 2,330+ square feet	Plymouth Mgt. Group, Inc.
Greenwich Village Area **12 East 12th Street** @Fifth Ave/ University Place **Condo**	Built around 1910, Converted in the 1980's to condo - 12 stories	Multiple-use loft condominium, video intercom security, two passenger elevators	Loft units range from approximately 900 to 3,500 square feet	Andrews Building Corp.
Greenwich Village Area **35 East 12th Street** Also **48 East 13th St** @Broadway/ University Place **Co-op**	Built around 1900, Converted in the 1970's to co-op - 9 stories	Loft building, video intercom security, two passenger elevators	25 loft units	Self-managed
Greenwich Village Area **39 East 12th Street** @ Broadway/ University Place **Co-op**	Built around 1900, Converted in the 1980's to co-op - 8 stories	Elevator building, roof garden	Studios, One-bedrooms, Two-bedrooms+	Lawrence Properties
Greenwich Village Area **49 East 12th Street** @ Fourth Ave/ Broadway **Co-op**	Post-war, Converted around 1980 to co-op - 7 stories	Elevator building	Studios, One-bedrooms, Two-bedrooms	Buchbinder & Warren
East Village Area **70 East 12th Street** @ Fourth Ave **Rental**	Built in the 1980's - 12 stories	Elevator building, on-site superintendent, video security	Studios, One-bedrooms, Two-bedrooms	Bettina Equities Rental Office: (212) 744-3330
East Village Area **121 East 12th Street** @Fourth Ave **Rental**	Prewar - 7 stories	Loft building, voice intercom security	69 loft units	N/A
East Village Area **130 East 12th Street** @Fourth Ave **Condo**	Prewar - 7 stories	A multiple-use condominium	Lofts range from approximately 1,650 to 1,700 square feet	Lawrence Properties

NON-LUXURY LOFT AND ELEVATOR BUILDINGS

EAST NUMBERED STREETS

EAST 1ST STREET - 29TH STREET   FIFTH AVENUE - EAST RIVER

Address	Description	Amenities	Apartment Types	Managing Agent
East Village Area **219 East 12th Street** @Third Ave **Condo**	Prewar - 5 stories	A multiple-use condominium	Lofts range from approximately 1,300 to 1,600 square feet	SMG Const. Inc.
East Village Area **226-30 East 12th St** @Second/Third Ave *Virginia Apartments* **Co-op**	Built in the 1920's, Converted in the 1980's to co-op - 11 stories	Elevator building, Video intercom security	Studios, One-bedrooms, Two-bedrooms+	The Equity Mgt. Group
Gramercy Park Area **234 East 14th Street** @ Second/Third Ave **Co-op**	Converted in the 1980's to co-op - 6 stories	Elevator building	Studios, One-bedrooms, Two-bedrooms	New Bedford Mgt.
Gramercy Park Area **333 East 14th Street** @First/Second Ave **Co-op**	Built in the 1960's, Converted in the 1980's to co-op - 18 stories	Elevator building, TV security, garage	Studios, One-bedrooms+	Jordon Cooper & Assoc., Inc.
Gramercy Park Area **201 East 15th Street** @ Third Ave **Co-op**	Built in the 1960's, Converted in the 1980's to co-op - 7 stories	Elevator building	Studios, One-bedrooms, Two-bedrooms	Andrews Building Corp.
Gramercy Park Area **17 East 16th Street** @ Fifth Ave **Co-op**	Prewar, converted in 1979 to co-op - 12 stories	Loft building, voice intercom security	12 loft units	Buchbinder & Warren
Gramercy Park Area **105 East 16th Street** @Union Square East **Co-op**	Prewar - 10 stories	Loft building, voice intercom security	15 loft units	Buchbinder & Warren
Gramercy Park Area **11 East 17th Street** @Fifth Ave **Rental**	Prewar - 7 stories	Loft building, voice intercom security	N/A	Merlon Mgt., Inc.
Gramercy Park Area **14 East 17th Street** @Fifth Ave **Co-op**	Prewar - 9 stories	Loft building, voice intercom security	N/A	Self-managed
Gramercy Park Area **18 East 17th Street** @Fifth Ave **Co-op**	Prewar - 8 stories	Loft building, voice intercom security	N/A	Self-managed
Gramercy Park Area **40 East 19th Street** @Broadway **Co-op**	Prewar - 9 stories	Loft building	9 loft units	Andrews Building Corp. Mgt.

NON-LUXURY LOFT AND ELEVATOR BUILDINGS

EAST NUMBERED STREETS

EAST 1ST STREET - 29TH STREET

FIFTH AVENUE - EAST RIVER

Address	Description	Amenities	Apartment Types	Managing Agent
Gramercy Park Area **112 East 19th Street** @Park Avenue South *Ruggles House* **Co-op**	Built around 1910 - 12 stories	Loft building	22 loft units	Charles Greenthal Mgt.
Gramercy Park Area **35 East 20th Street** @Broadway **Co-op**	Prewar - 8 stories	Loft building	8 loft units	Gramercy Equities Corp.
Gramercy Park Area **39 East 20th Street** @Broadway **Condo**	Prewar - 11 stories	A multiple-use condominium, voice intercom security	Apartments range from approximately 2,000 to 3,000 square feet	Self managed
Gramercy Park Area **210 East 21st Street** @Second/Third Ave **Co-op**	Built around 1910, Converted in the 1980's to co-op - 6 stories	Elevator building	Studios, One-bedrooms	Self-managed
Gramercy Park Area **12 East 22nd Street** @Broadway/ Park Avenue South *Gramercy 22* **Rental/Rent Stabilized**	Built in the 1970's - 12 stories	Elevator building, on-site superintendent, video intercom security, sundeck, apartments have high ceilings and lofts	Studios, One-bedrooms	Abington Holdings (212) 759-5000
Gramercy Park Area **27 East 22nd Street** @Broadway **Condo**	Prewar - 10 stories	A multiple-use condominium, video intercom security	Apartments range from approximately 1,500 to 2,400 square feet	Self managed
Gramercy Park Area **28 East 22nd Street** @Broadway **Co-op**	Prewar - 9 stories	Loft building, video intercom security, one passenger, one service elevator	7 loft units	Self managed
Gramercy Park Area **29 East 22nd Street** @Broadway/ Park Avenue South **Co-op**	Built around 1910, Converted in 1979 to co-op - 12 stories	Loft building, one passenger elevator, one service elevator, roof deck	21 loft units	ETC Mgt.
Gramercy Park Area **102 East 22nd Street** @ Lexington/Park Ave *Gramercy Arms* **Co-op**	Built around 1930, Converted in the 1980's to co-op - 9 stories	Elevator building	Studios, One-bedrooms, Two-bedrooms+	Diversified Property Group
Gramercy Park Area **312 East 22nd Street** @ Second/First Ave *Gramercy East* **Condo**	Built in the 1990's - 7 stories	Elevator building	Studios, One-bedrooms	Equity Mgt. Group

181

NON-LUXURY LOFT AND ELEVATOR BUILDINGS

EAST NUMBERED STREETS

EAST 1ST STREET - 29TH STREET   FIFTH AVENUE - EAST RIVER

Address	Description	Amenities	Apartment Types	Managing Agent
Gramercy Park Area **131 East 23rd Street** @Park Avenue South/ Lexington Ave **Rental**	12 stories - Renovated in 1996	Elevator building, on-site superintendent, laundry on every floor, sundeck, apartments have high ceilings and lofts	Studios, One-bedrooms, Two-bedrooms	Zucker Org./ Manhattan Skyline Mgt. (212) 889-1850 or (212) 997-4813
Gramercy Park Area **310 East 23rd Street** @ First/Second Ave *The Foundry* **Co-op**	Built around 1900, Renovated and converted to co-op in the 1980's- 12 stories	Elevator building, voice intercom security, on-site superintendent, apartments have exposed brick, lofts, dishwashers and microwave ovens	Studios, One-bedrooms, Two-bedrooms	Rockrose Development
Gramercy Park Area **117 East 24th Street** @Park Avenue South *Madison Square Condo* **Condo**	Prewar - 12 stories	Loft building, voice intercom security	Lofts range from approximately 4,000 to 7,000 square feet	Emanuel & Co.
Gramercy Park Area **214 East 24th Street** @ Second/Third Ave *Gramercy Court* **Rental**	Built around 1980 - 7 stories	Elevator building, video security, on-site superintendent, garage, laundry on lobby level, apartments have fireplaces and skylights	Studios, One-bedrooms, Two-bedrooms	Abington Holdings (212) 759-5000
Gramercy Park Area **220 East 24th Street** @Third Ave **Rental**	Postwar - 8 stories	Loft building	Studio, One-bedroom, Two-bedroom lofts,	Hakimian Organization Exclusive Broker: Bill Robertson (212) 979-1142
Gramercy Park Area **229 East 24th Street** @Third Ave **Condo**	Prewar - 9 stories	A residential condominium, voice intercom security	Studios, One-bedrooms, and Two-bedrooms	Citadel Mgt. Co.
Gramercy Park Area **160 East 26th Street** @ Third/Lexington Ave **Co-op**	Built around 1900, Converted in the 1980's to co-op - 8 stories	Elevator building	Studios, One-bedrooms, Two-bedrooms	Buchbinder & Warren
Gramercy Park Area **150 East 27th Street** @Lexington/Third Ave *Gotham House* **Co-op**	Built around 1960, Converted in the 1980's to co-op - 7 stories	Elevator building, garage	Studios, One-bedrooms+	Carlton Mgt.

NON-LUXURY LOFT AND ELEVATOR BUILDINGS

EAST NUMBERED STREETS

EAST 1ST STREET - 29TH STREET   FIFTH AVENUE - EAST RIVER

Address	Description	Amenities	Apartment Types	Managing Agent
Gramercy Park Area **160 East 27th Street** @Third Ave **Co-op**	Built around 1960, Converted in the 1980's to co-op - 12 stories	Elevator building	Studios, One-bedrooms, Two-bedrooms	Mayerhauser Realty, Inc.
Gramercy Park Area **207 East 27th Street** @ Second/Third Ave **Rental**	Built in the 1980's - 8 stories	Elevator building, TV intercom security, on-site superintendent, apartments have dishwashers	Studios, One-bedrooms, Duplexes	Abington Trust (212) 759-5000
Gramercy Park Area **41 East 28th Street** @ Park Avenue South/ Madison Ave **Co-op**	Built in the 1920's, Converted in the 1980's to co-op - 7 stories	Elevator building	18 apartments	Self-managed
Gramercy Park Area **137-139 East 28th Street** @Third/Lexington Ave **Co-op**	Built in the 1920's, Converted in the 1980's to co-op - 9 stories	Elevator building	Studios, One-bedrooms+	Diversified Property Group, Ltd.
Gramercy Park Area **200 East 28th Street** @Third Ave *Rosehill* **Condo**	Built around 1960, Converted in 1987 to condo - 6 stories	Elevator building	Studios, One-bedrooms	Buchbinder & Warren
Gramercy Park Area **208 East 28th Street** @ Third Ave **Co-op**	Built around 1940, Converted in the 1980's to co-op - 6 stories	Elevator building	Studios, One-bedrooms	RVP Mgt. Corp.
Gramercy Park Area **105 East 29th Street** @Park Avenue South **Co-op**	Prewar - 12 stories	Loft building, video intercom security	12 loft units	Self-managed
Gramercy Park Area **145 East 29th Street** @ Third/Lexington Ave **Co-op**	Built in the 1960's - 6 stories	One passenger elevator	Studios, One-bedrooms	Cornerstone Mgt.
Gramercy Park Area **210 East 29th Street** @ Second/Third Ave **Rental**	Built in the 1980's - 6 stories	Elevator building	Studios, One-bedrooms, Two-bedrooms, Duplexes	Abington Trust (212) 759-5000
Gramercy Park Area **229 East 29th Street** @ Second/Third Ave **Co-op**	Built around 1900, Converted in the 1980's to co-op - 6 stories	Elevator building	Studios, One-bedrooms, Two-bedrooms	RVP Mgt. Corp.

LUXURY DOORMAN/CONCIERGE BUILDNGS
WEST NUMBERED STREETS

WEST 8TH STREET - 29TH STREET   FIFTH AVENUE - HUDSON RIVER

Address	Description	Amenities	Apartment Types	Managing Agent
Greenwich Village Area **35 West 9th Street** @ Fifth/Ave of Americas **Co-op**	Built in the 1920's, converted in the 1980's to a co-op - 10 stories	Doorman	One-bedrooms, Two-bedrooms+	Urban Associates
Greenwich Village Area **50 West 9th Street** Fifth/Ave of Americas **Co-op**	Built around 1890, converted in the 1970's to a co-op - 6 stories	Doorman	Studios, One-bedrooms, Two-bedrooms	Cooper Square Realty
Greenwich Village Area **61 West 9th Street** @ Fifth/Ave of Americas *Windsor Arms* **Co-op**	Built in the 1920's, converted in the 1980's to a co-op - 11 stories	Doorman	Studios, One-bedrooms, Two-bedrooms+	Big City Mgt.
Greenwich Village Area **69 West 9th Street** @ Fifth/Ave of Americas **Co-op**	Built in the 1950's, converted in the 1980's to a co-op - 13 stories	Doorman, garage	Studios, One-bedrooms, Two-bedrooms+	Frederick Lee Real Estate
Greenwich Village Area **45 West 10th Street** @ Fifth/Ave of Americas *The Peter Warren* **Co-op**	Built in the 1950's, converted in the 1970's to a co-op - 10 stories	Doorman, garage, roof deck	Studios, One-bedrooms, Two-bedrooms	Akam Assoc.
Greenwich Village Area **296 West 10th Street** @ Washington Street *River West* **Condo/ Rental**	14 stories	Concierge	Studios, one-bedrooms, two bedrooms	N/A
Greenwich Village Area **15 West 11th Street** @ Fifth/Ave of Americas **Co-op**	Built in the 1920's, converted in the 1970's to a co-op - 10 stories	Attended lobby	One-bedrooms, Two-bedrooms, Three-bedrooms	Penmark Realty Corp.
Greenwich Village Area **55 West 11th Street** @ Fifth/Ave of Americas **Rental**	Postwar - 9 stories	Concierge	Studios, One-bedrooms, Two-bedrooms	N/A
Greenwich Village Area **270 West 11th Street** *Tudor Arms* **Co-op**	Pre-war - Converted in 1990 to a co-op - 6 stories	Doorman	Studios, One-bedrooms, Two-bedrooms	ABC Realty
Greenwich Village Area **366 West 11th Street** @ Washington/West St. **Condo**	Built in 1986 as condo, 13 stories	Concierge, balconies	Studios, One-bedrooms, Two-bedrooms	Salon Realty
Greenwich Village Area **15 West 12th Street** @ Fifth/Ave of Americas **Co-op**	Built around 1960, converted in the 1980's to a co-op - 13 stories	Doorman	Studios, One-bedrooms, Two-bedrooms+	Century Operating Corp.

WEST 8TH STREET - 29TH STREET   FIFTH AVENUE - HUDSON RIVER

Address	Description	Amenities	Apartment Types	Managing Agent
Greenwich Village Area **37 West 12th Street** @ Fifth/Ave of Americas *Butterfield House* **Co-op**	Built in the 1960's - Three buildings of 12 stories each, connected by an interior garden courtyard	Doorman, solarium, garage	Studios, One-bedrooms	Brown Harris Stevens
Greenwich Village Area **49 West 12th Street** @ Fifth/Ave of Americas **Co-op**	Built around 1950, converted in the 1980's to a co-op - 10 stories	Doorman, Concierge	Studios, One-bedrooms, Two-bedrooms+	B & L Mgt. Inc.
Greenwich Village Area **59 West 12th Street** @ Fifth/Ave of Americas **Condo**	Built around 1930, converted to condo in 1986 - 16 stories	Doorman, fireplaces	Studios, One-bedrooms, Two-bedrooms+	Goodstein Mgt. Inc.
Greenwich Village Area **79 West 12th Street** @ N/E/C Ave of the Americas *Lawrence House* **Co-op**	Built around 1960, converted in the 1980's to a co-op - 16 stories	Doorman, roof-top garden	Studios, One-bedrooms, Two-bedrooms+	Elm Mgt.
Greenwich Village Area **100-114 West 12th St.** @ S/W/C Sixth Ave. *Mark Twain Apts.* **Co-op**	Built in the 1950's, converted in the 1980's to a co-op - 6 stories	Doorman, garage	Studios, One-bedrooms, Two-bedrooms+	Maxwell Kates, Inc.
Greenwich Village Area **101 West 12th Street** @ N/W/C Sixth Avenue *The John Adams* **Co-op**	Built in the 1960's, converted in the 1980's to a co-op - 21 stories	Doorman, garage, Concierge	Studios, One-bedrooms, Two-bedrooms, Three-bedrooms	Goodstein Mgt. Inc.
Greenwich Village Area **175 West 12th Street** @ N/E/C Seventh Ave. *Century Towers* **Condo/Rental**	Built around 1960, converted to condo in 1987 - 19 stories	Doorman, garage	Studios, One-bedrooms, Two-bedrooms+	Charles H. Greenthal Mgt. Corp.
Greenwich Village Area **225 West 12th Street** @ Seventh/Greenwich **Rental**	Pre-war- Renovated in the 1990's- 6 stories	Doorman	Studios, One-bedrooms	N/A
Greenwich Village Area **247 West 12th Street** @ Greenwich/Fourth Ave **Co-op**	Built around 1900, converted in the 1980's to a co-op - 6 stories	Doorman, garage	Studios, One-bedrooms	Akam Assoc.
Greenwich Village Area **299 West 12th Street** @ Eighth/Hudson Street **Condo**	Built around 1930, converted to condo in 1986 - 16 stories	Doorman, Concierge	Studios, One-bedrooms, Two-bedrooms+	Goodstein Mgt. Inc.
Greenwich Village Area **302 West 12th Street** @ S/E/C Eighth Avenue **Condo**	Built in the 1930's, converted to condo in 1986 - 16 stories	Doorman, sunken living rooms, fireplaces, sundeck	Studios, One-bedrooms, Two-bedrooms+	Goodstein Mgt. Inc.

WEST 8TH STREET - 29TH STREET   FIFTH AVENUE - HUDSON RIVER

Address	Description	Amenities	Apartment Types	Managing Agent
Greenwich Village Area **344 West 12th Street** @ Hudson Street **Co-op**	Built in the 1920's, converted in 1980's to a co-op - 6 stories	Attended lobby	Studios, One-bedrooms, Two bedrooms	Tudor Realty Svs.
Greenwich Village Area **380 West 12th Street** @ Washington/West St. **Co-op**	Built around 1900, converted around 1980 to a co-op - 7 story loft building	Doorman	52 loft units - 1100+ sq. ft.	Lawrence Properties
Greenwich Village Area **13 West 13th Street** @ Fifth/Sixth Avenue **Co-op**	Built in the 1950's, 7 stories	Doorman	Studios, One-bedrooms, Two-bedrooms	Cooper Square Realty
Greenwich Village Area **25 West 13th Street** @ Fifth/Sixth Avenue **Co-op**	Built around 1960, converted in the 1980's to a co-op - 6 stories	Doorman, garage	Studios, One bedrooms	PRC Mgt.
Greenwich Village Area **60 West 13th Street** *Village House* @ Fifth/Sixth Avenue **Condo**	Built in 1967 as condo, 14 stories	Doorman	Studios, One-bedrooms, Two-bedrooms+	William B. May & Co.
Greenwich Village Area **105 West 13th Street** @ Sixth/Seventh Ave. *Greenwich Towers* **Co-op**	Built around 1960, converted in the 1980's to a co-op - 16 stories	Doorman	One-bedrooms, Two-bedrooms	Gerard J. Picaso, Inc.
Greenwich Village Area **175 West 13th Street** @ N/E/C Seventh Ave. *Cambridge House* **Co-op**	Built around 1960, converted in the 1980's to a co-op - 20 stories	Doorman	Studios, One-bedrooms, Two-bedrooms+	PRC Mgt.
Greenwich Village Area **345 West 13th Street** @ Hudson Street **Condo**	Pre-war - 6 stories	Doorman, high ceilings, exposed columns, brick archways	46 live/work lofts ranging from 1,559 to 4,346 sq. ft., One-bedrooms, Two-bedrooms, Three-bedrooms *Projected occupancy as of summer 1999	Hudson Lofts Assoc. (212) 539-4414
Chelsea Area **7 West 14th Street also 10 West 15th Street** @ Fifth/Sixth Avenue *Parker Gramercy* **Co-op**	Built in the 1960's - Twin 12 story north and south buildings	Doorman, garage	Studios, One-bedrooms, Two-bedrooms	Century Operating
Chelsea Area **55 West 14th Street** @ Fifth/Sixth Avenue *Courtney House* **Rental**	Post-war - 20 stories	Concierge, garage, terraces	Studios, One-bedrooms, Two-bedrooms	N/A

LUXURY DOORMAN/CONCIERGE BUILDNGS
WEST NUMBERED STREETS

WEST 8TH STREET - 29TH STREET   FIFTH AVENUE - HUDSON RIVER

Address	Description	Amenities	Apartment Types	Managing Agent
Chelsea Area **222 West 14th Street** @ Seventh/Eighth Ave. ***The Sequoia*** **Condo**	Built in 1987 as condo - 15 stories	Doorman, concierge garage, balconies, health club	Studios, One-bedrooms, Two-bedrooms+	Sterling Mgt.
Chelsea Area **22 West 15th Street** @ Fifth/Sixth Avenue ***Grosvener House*** **Condo**	Built in 1989 as condo - 22 stories	Doorman	One-bedrooms, Two-bedrooms+	Charles H. Greenthal and Co.
Chelsea Area **155 West 15th Street** @ Sixth/Seventh Ave. **Co-op**	Built around 1950, converted in the 1980's to a co-op - 6 stories	Doorman	Studios, One-bedrooms, Two-bedrooms	Lawrence Prop.
Chelsea Area **205 West 15th Street** @ Seventh Avenue ***Chelsmore Apartments*** **Rental**	Pre-war - 6 stories	Concierge	Studios, One-bedrooms, Two-bedrooms	Agent on Premises Joan Rahav 212-989-4677
Chelsea Area **16 West 16th Street** @ Fifth/Ave of Americas ***Chelsea Lane*** **Co-op**	Built in the 1960's, converted in the 1980's to a co-op - 14 stories	Doorman, garage, balconies	Studios, One-bedrooms, Two-bedrooms+	Akam Assoc.
Chelsea Area **161 West 16th Street** @ N/E/C Seventh Ave. **Co-op**	Built around 1930, converted in the 1980's to a co-op - 18 stories	Doorman, garage	Studios, One-bedrooms, Two-bedrooms	Wiener Rlty.
Chelsea Area **200 West 16th Street** @ Seventh Avenue **Rental**	19 stories	Concierge	Studios, One-bedrooms, Two-bedrooms	N/A
Chelsea Area **201 West 16th Street** @ N/W/C Seventh Ave. **Co-op**	Built around 1930, converted in the 1980's to a co-op - 19 stories	Doorman	Studios, One-bedrooms, Two-bedrooms+	Tudor Rlty Svcs.
Chelsea Area **121 West 17th Street** @ Sixth/Seventh Ave. **Co-op**	Built around 1910, converted in the 1980's to a co-op - 9 stories	Concierge	Studios, One-bedrooms, Two-bedrooms	Self-managed
Chelsea Area **257 West 17th Street** @ Seventh/Eighth Ave. ***Steiner Building*** **Condo**	Built around 1900, renovated in 1995 to condo - 9 stories	Concierge	Two-bedrooms, Three-bedrooms	Taranto & Assoc.
Chelsea Area **270 West 17th Street** @ Seventh/Eighth Ave. ***Grand Chelsea*** **Condo**	Built in 1988 as condo - 21 stories	Doorman, Concierge, balconies, sundeck	One-bedrooms, Two-bedrooms, Three-bedrooms	Mark Greenburgh R. E. :

WEST 8TH STREET - 29TH STREET   FIFTH AVENUE - HUDSON RIVER

Address	Description	Amenities	Apartment Types	Managing Agent
Chelsea Area **250 West 19th Street** @ Seventh/Eighth Ave. *Chelsea Court* **Rental**	Built in the 1980's - 16 stories	Doorman, garage, health club, pool	Studios, One-bedrooms, Two-bedrooms, Duplexes, High ceilings and exposed brick in apartments	B&L Mgt. Co. (212) 980-0980
Chelsea Area **251 West 19th Street** @ Seventh/Eighth Ave. **Rental**	Post-war - 11 stories	Doorman	Studios, One-bedrooms, Two-bedrooms	Z&R Mgt. Corp. (212) 691-9542
Chelsea Area **121 West 20th Street** @Sixth & Seventh Ave. *Chelsea 121* **Condo**	Built around 1870 - 5 stories	Doorman	Studios, One-bedrooms, Two bedrooms	Hoffman Mgt.
Chelsea Area **200 West 20th Street** @ S/E/C Seventh Ave. *Kensington House* **Co-op**	Built in the 1930's, converted in the 1980's to a co-op - 15 stories	Concierge	Studios, One-bedrooms+	Hansen Mgt. Inc.
Chelsea Area **365 West 20th Street** @ Eighth/Ninth Ave. *Chelsea Court Tower* **Co-op**	Built around 1930, converted in the 1980's to a co-op - 16 stories	Part-time doorman	Studios, One-bedrooms, Two-bedrooms	Weinreb Mgt. Co.
Chelsea Area **201 West 21st Street** @ N/W/C Seventh Ave. The Piermont **Co-op**	Built around 1960, converted in the 1980's to a co-op - 13 stories	Doorman, solarium	Studios, One-bedrooms+	New Bedford Mgt. Corp.
Chelsea Area **305-313 West 22nd St.** @ Eighth/Ninth Ave. *Chelsea Commons* **Condo**	Built in the 1870's, converted in 1985 to condo - 6 stories	Concierge, fireplaces, Washer/Dryers in apartments	One-bedrooms, Two-bedrooms+	American Landmark Mgt.
Chelsea Area **360 West 22nd Street** @ Eighth/Ninth Ave. *London Towne House* **Co-op**	Built around 1960, converted in 1990 to a co-op - 15 stories	Doorman	Studios, One-bedrooms, Two-bedrooms, Three-bedrooms+	Penmark Realty Corp.
Chelsea Area **525 West 22nd Street** @ Tenth /Eleventh Ave. *Spears Building* **Condo**	Built around 1890, renovated in 1996 as condo - 6 stories	Doorman	Studios, One-bedrooms, Two-bedrooms	Equity Mgt. Group
Chelsea Area **101 West 23rd Street** @ Cor. Sixth Avenue **Co-op**	Built around 1920, converted in 1980 to a co-op - 6 stories	Concierge	Studios, One-bedrooms, Two-bedrooms	Lawrence Properties

LUXURY DOORMAN/CONCIERGE BUILDNGS
WEST NUMBERED STREETS

WEST 8TH STREET - 29TH STREET			**FIFTH AVENUE - HUDSON RIVER**	
Address	Description	Amenities	Apartment Types	Managing Agent
Chelsea Area **120 West 23rd Street** @ Sixth/Seventh Ave. ***The Milan*** **Rental**	Post-war - 10 stories	Concierge	Studios, One-bedrooms+	N/A
Chelsea Area **148 West 23rd Street** @ Sixth/Seventh Ave. ***Chelsea Mews*** **Co-op**	Built around 1920, converted in the 1980's to a co-op - 12 stories	Concierge, garage	One-bedrooms, Two-bedrooms, Three-bedrooms+	Tudor Realty Svc. Corp.
Chelsea Area **170 West 23rd Street** @ Sixth/Seventh Ave. ***Chelsea Seventh*** **Condo**	Built in the 1970's, converted in 1985 to condo - 6 stories	Doorman, balconies, garage	Studios, One-bedrooms	Newmark & Co.
Chelsea Area **208 West 23rd Street** @ Seventh/Eighth Ave. ***The Carteret*** **Rental/ Furnished** **short -term leases**	Built in the 1920's - 17 stories	Doorman, apartments have high ceilings, dishwashers, microwave ovens	Studios, One-bedrooms, Two-bedrooms	Owner/Manager: Jakobson Properties On-site Rental office: (212) 929-7060 or (212) 533-1300
Chelsea Area **225 West 23rd Street** @ Seventh/Eighth Ave. **Rental**	Pre-war - 6 stories	Doorman	Studios, One-bedrooms, Two-bedrooms	Helmsley Spear
Chelsea Area **255 West 23rd Street** also **250 West 24th St.** @ Seventh/Eighth Ave. **Co-op**	Built around 1950, converted in the 1980's to a co-op - 6 stories	Doorman	Studios, One-bedrooms, Two-bedrooms, Three-bedrooms	WPG/Rudd Residential Mgt.
Chelsea Area **300 West 23rd Street** @ Cor. Eighth Avenue **Condo**	Built in the 1920's, converted in the 1980's to a condo - 19 stories	Concierge	Studios, One-bedrooms, Two-bedrooms	R. A. Cohen & Assoc., Inc.
Chelsea Area **315 West 23rd Street** @ Eighth/Ninth Avenue ***The Broadmoor*** **Co-op**	Built around 1930, converted in the 1980's to a co-op - 13 stories	Doorman	Studios, One-bedrooms, Two-bedrooms, Three-bedrooms	Gerard J. Picaso, Inc.
Chelsea Area **324 West 23rd Street** @ Eighth/Ninth Avenue **Condo/Rental**	Post-war - 7 stories	Part-time doorman	Studios, One-bedrooms, Two-bedrooms	Stillman Org.
Chelsea Area **344 West 23rd Street** @ Eighth/Ninth Avenue ***Cheyney*** **Condo**	Built in 1983 as a condo - 10 stories	Doorman, some fireplaces, roof deck	One-bedrooms, Two-bedrooms, +	Taranto & Assoc.

WEST 8TH STREET - 29TH STREET   FIFTH AVENUE - HUDSON RIVER

Address	Description	Amenities	Apartment Types	Managing Agent
Chelsea Area **405/465 West 23rd Street** @ Ninth/Tenth Avenue *London Terrace Towers* **Co-op**	Built around 1930, converted in the 1980's to a co-op - Four 19 story buildings occupying an entire square block	Doorman, elevator operators, 75 ft. pool, garage, garden courtyard, some fireplaces	Studios, One-bedrooms, Two-bedrooms, Three-bedrooms+	Insignia Residential Group On-site Agent
Chelsea Area **415-455 West 23rd St.** @ Ninth/Tenth Avenue *London Terrace Gardens* **Rental**	17 stories	Doorman, elevatorman, garage	Studios, One-bedrooms, Two-bedrooms, Three-bedrooms	Self-managed On-site Agent
Chelsea Area **420 West 23rd Street** @ Ninth/Tenth Avenue **Condo**	Built in 1985 as condo - 12 stories	Doorman, sun deck, balconies	Studios, One-bedrooms, Two-bedrooms	Taranto & Associates, Inc
Chelsea Area **160 West 24th Street** @ Cor. Seventh Ave. *The Chelsea* **Rental**	Post-war - 17 stories	Concierge	Studios, One-bedrooms, Two-bedrooms, Three-bedrooms	Cambridge Mgt. (212) 889-3500

NON-LUXURY LOFT AND ELEVATOR BUILDINGS

WEST NUMBERED STREETS

WEST 8TH STREET - 29TH STREET   FIFTH AVENUE - HUDSON RIVER

Address	Description	Amenities	Apartment Types	Managing Agent
Greenwich Village Area **126 West 11th Street** @Sixth Ave **Co-op**	Built around 1900, converted in the 1980's to a co-op - 7 stories	Elevator building	Studios, one bedrooms, two bedrooms	Carole Ferrara Assoc.
Greenwich Village Area **125 West 12th Street** @Sixth/Seventh Ave **Co-op**	Built around 1920, converted in 1979 to a co-op - 6 stories	Elevator building	Studios, one bedrooms, two bedrooms	Advanced Mgt.
Greenwich Village Area **137-49 West 12th Street** @Sixth/Seventh Ave **Co-op**	Built around 1930, converted in the 1980's to a co-op - 6 stories	Elevator building	Studios, one bedrooms, two bedrooms	Buchbinder & Warren
Greenwich Village Area **350-4 West 12th Street** @Hudson St **Co-op**	Prewar, converted in the 1980's to a co-op - 5 stories	Elevator building	10 apartments	Tudor Realty
Greenwich Village Area **8 West 13th Street** @Fifth/Sixth Ave **Co-op**	Built around 1910, converted in the 1970's to a co-op - 11 stories	Elevator building	Studios, one bedrooms, two bedrooms	N/A
Greenwich Village Area **13 West 13th Street** @Fifth/Sixth Ave **Co-op**	Prewar, converted in the 1980's to a co-op - 7 stories	Elevator building	Studios, one bedrooms, two bedrooms	Cooper Square Realty
Greenwich Village Area **30-34 West 13th Street** @Fifth/Sixth Ave **Co-op**	Built around 1910, converted in the 1970's to a co-op - 6 stories	Elevator building	Studios, one bedrooms, two bedrooms	N/A
Greenwich Village Area **36-40 West 13th Street** @Fifth Ave *The Rambusch Building* **Condo**	Prewar - 9 stories	Direct elevator access, gothic details, unique layouts, huge windows, high ceilings, terraces	All new full floor lofts - 2700+ square feet, one to four bedrooms	Contact: Jami Lieberman, Alchemy Properties (212) 972-0055
Greenwich Village Area **42 West 13th Street** @Fifth/Sixth Ave **Co-op**	Built around 1960, converted in the 1980's to a co-op - 6 stories	Elevator building	Studios, one bedrooms, two bedrooms	Wallack Mgt. Co.
Greenwich Village Area **321-23 West 13th Street** @Eighth Ave/Hudson St *Gansevoort* **Condo**	Built around 1900, renovated in 1987 as a condo - 7 stories	Elevator building	21 studios	RMA Mgt.

191

NON-LUXURY LOFT AND ELEVATOR BUILDINGS

WEST NUMBERED STREETS
WEST 8TH STREET - 29TH STREET   FIFTH AVENUE - HUDSON RIVER

Address	Description	Amenities	Apartment Types	Managing Agent
345 West 13th Street Condo	6 stories		One bedroom, two bedroom, and three bedroom lofts, which range from 1,550 to 4,300 square feet.	Hudson Lofts Assoc. (212) 539-4414
Chelsea Area **116 West 14th Street** *Union Lane* Condo	Built around 1910, converted in the 1990's to a condo - 12 stories	Elevator building	16 two bedroom apartments	Andrews Bldg. Corp.
Chelsea Area **350 West 14th Street** @Eighth/Ninth Ave *Village Pointe* Condo	Built in 1988 as a condo - 8 stories	Elevator building	Studios, One-bedrooms, Two-bedrooms	Buchbinder & Warren
Chelsea Area **30 West 15th Street** @Fifth Ave/Sixth Ave Co-op	Built around 1910 - 12 stories	One passenger and one service elevator	19 loft units	Plymouth Mgt. Group, Inc.
Chelsea Area **77 West 15th Street** @Sixth Ave **Rental**	Built in the 1970's - 6 stories	Elevator building, on-site superintendent, laundry on the ground floor	Studios, one bedrooms	Manhattan Skyline Mgt. (212) 889-1850 or (212) 977-4813
Chelsea Area **161 West 15th Street** also **89 Seventh Avenue** @N/E/C Seventh Ave Co-op	Built around 1920, converted in the 1980's to a co-op - 7 stories	Loft building, TV security, two passenger elevators	62 loft units	WPG Residential Inc.
Chelsea Area **250 West 15th Street** @Seventh/Eighth Ave Co-op	Built around 1930, converted in the 1980's to a co-op - 6 stories	Elevator building	Studios, one bedrooms	Lawrence Properties
Chelsea Area **4 West 16th Street** @Fifth Ave/Sixth Ave Co-op	Built around 1900, converted in the 1980's to a co-op - 10 stories	Loft building, one passenger elevator	15 loft units	Excelsior Mgt. Co.
Chelsea Area **54 West 16th Street** also **570 Sixth Ave** @S/E/C Sixth Avenue Co-op	Built in the 1950's, converted in the 1980's to a co-op - 15 stories	Elevator building, garage	Studios, one bedrooms, two bedrooms, +	Charles H. Greenthal Mgt.
Chelsea Area **111 West 16th Street** @Sixth/Seventh Ave Co-op	Built in the 1920's, converted in the 1980's to a co-op - 6 stories	Elevator building	Studios, one bedrooms	Bernard Gans Mgt.

NON-LUXURY LOFT AND ELEVATOR BUILDINGS

WEST NUMBERED STREETS

WEST 8TH STREET - 29TH STREET   FIFTH AVENUE - HUDSON RIVER

Address	Description	Amenities	Apartment Types	Managing Agent
Chelsea Area **130 West 16th Street** @Sixth/Seventh Ave **Co-op**	Prewar, converted in the 1980's to a co-op - 6 stories	Elevator building	One bedrooms, Two bedrooms	Joseph Alpert
Chelsea Area **135 West 16th Street** @Sixth/Seventh Ave **Condo**	Built around 1920, converted in 1984 to a condo - 6 stories	Elevator building	Studios, one bedrooms, two bedrooms	Lawrence Properties
Chelsea Area **250 West 16th Street** @Seventh/Eighth Ave **Co-op**	Prewar, converted in the 1980's to a co-op - 6 stories	Elevator building	Studios, one bedrooms, two bedrooms	Plymouth Mgt. Group
Chelsea Area **253 West 16th Street** @Seventh/Eighth Ave **Co-op**	Built around 1940, converted in the 1980's to a co-op - 6 stories	Elevator building	Studios, one bedrooms, two bedrooms	Carlton Mgt.
Chelsea Area **113 West 17th Street** @Sixth/Seventh Ave ***Brooks-VanHorn Bldg.*** **Condo**	Built around 1910, renovated in 1982 to a condo - 6 stories	Elevator building, washer/dryers in apartments	35 Studios	Becker & Rubin
Chelsea Area **12-14 West 18th Street** @Fifth/Sixth Avenue ***Chelsea East*** **Condo**	Built around 1890, converted in the 1980's to a condo - 9 stories	One passenger and one service elevator, TV security, solarium	14 loft units	Excelsior Mgt. Co.
Chelsea Area **154 West 18th Street** @Sixth/Seventh Ave **Co-op**	Built around 1910, converted in the 1980's to a co-op - 8 stories	One passenger and one service elevator	30 loft units	Plymouth Mgt. Group
Chelsea Area **305-313 West 18th St** @Eighth/Ninth Ave **Condo**	Built around 1950, converted in 1984 to a condo - 6 stories	Elevator building	Studios, one bedrooms, two bedrooms	Buchbinder & Warren
Chelsea Area **139 West 19th Street** @Sixth/Seventh Ave **Co-op**	Built around 1920, converted in the 1970's to a co-op - 8 stories	Loft building	N/A	Self managed
Chelsea Area **205 West 19th Street** @Seventh/Eighth Ave **Co-op**	Built around 1915, converted in the 1970's to a co-op - 12 stories	Two passenger and one service elevator, solarium	21 loft units	Plymouth Mgt. Group, Inc.
Chelsea Area **210 West 19th Street** @Seventh/Eighth Ave **Condo**	Built in the 1930's, converted in 1985 to a condo - 6 stories	Elevator building	Studios, one bedrooms	Charles H. Greenthal

NON-LUXURY LOFT AND ELEVATOR BUILDINGS

WEST NUMBERED STREETS
WEST 8TH STREET - 29TH STREET   FIFTH AVENUE - HUDSON RIVER

Address	Description	Amenities	Apartment Types	Managing Agent
223 West 19th Street Condo	7 stories		Loft units, which range from 2,325 to 3,280 square feet	B&D Leistner Properties (212) 965-6008
Chelsea Area **434 West 19th Street** @Ninth/Tenth Ave **Rental**	Built in the 1980's - 8 stories	Elevator building, on-site superintendent, apartments have exposed brick walls	Studios, one bedrooms, duplexes	B&L Mgt. (212) 980-0980
Chelsea Area **445 West 19th Street** @Ninth/Tenth Ave *Chatham in Chelsea* **Condo**	Built in 1987 as a condo - 10 stories	Elevator building	Studios, One-bedrooms, Two-bedrooms, three bedrooms	American Landmark Mgt. Corp.
Chelsea Area **32 West 20th Street** @Fifth/Sixth Ave **Co-op**	Built around 1910, converted in 1979 to a co-op - 11 stories	Elevator building	20 loft units	American Landmark Mgt.
Chelsea Area **121 West 20th Street** @Sixth/Seventh Ave *Chelsea 121* **Condo**	Built around 1870, renovated in 1989 to a condo - 5 stories	Elevator building, video security, sundeck, apartments have washer/dryers	One bedrooms, two bedrooms, and three bedrooms	Hoffman Mgt.
Chelsea Area **129 West 20th Street** *The Chelsea Quarter* **Co-op**	Loft Building - 7 stories	Huge windows, health club, balconies, apartments have 9 ft. windows, very high ceilings, and hardwood floors	15 Lofts from 1,548+ sq. ft, 2 full baths, washer/dryers, and Chef's kitchens	Alchemy Properties (212) 965-6008
Chelsea Area **155-165 West 20th St** @Sixth/Seventh Ave **Co-op**	Built around 1940, converted in the 1980's to a co-op - 6 stories	Elevator building	Studios, one bedrooms, two bedrooms	Big City Mgt.
Chelsea Area **223-31 West 21st Street** @Seventh/Eighth Ave **Co-op**	Prewar, converted in the 1980's to a co-op - 6 stories	Elevator building	Studios, one bedrooms, two bedrooms	Wolff Mgt.
Chelsea Area **233 West 21st Street** @Seventh/Eighth Ave **Co-op**	Built in the 1920's, converted in the 1980's to a co-op - 6 stories	Elevator building	Studios, one bedrooms, two bedrooms	Wolff Mgt.
Chelsea Area **234 West 21st Street** @Seventh/Eighth Ave **Co-op**	Prewar, converted in the 1980's to a co-op - 7 stories	Elevator building	Studios, one bedrooms, two bedrooms	Carole Ferrara Assoc.

NON-LUXURY LOFT AND ELEVATOR BUILDINGS

WEST NUMBERED STREETS

WEST 8TH STREET - 29TH STREET   **FIFTH AVENUE - HUDSON RIVER**

Address	Description	Amenities	Apartment Types	Managing Agent
Chelsea Area **129 West 22nd Street** @Sixth/Seventh Ave **Co-op**	Built around 1910, converted in 1979 to a co-op - 12 stories	One passenger elevator and one service elevator	11 loft units	Self managed
Chelsea Area **240 West 23rd Street** @Seventh/Eighth Ave **Co-op**	Built around 1930, converted in the 1980's to a co-op - 7 stories	Elevator building	Studios, one bedrooms, two bedrooms	N/A
Chelsea Area **400-10 West 23rd Street** @Ninth/Tenth Ave **Co-op**	Built in the 1970's, conveted in the 1980's to a co-op - 6 stories	Elevator building	Studios, one bedrooms, two bedrooms	Vintage RE. Svcs.
Chelsea Area **40 West 24th Street** @Fifth/Sixth Ave **Co-op**	Built around 1905, converted in the 1970's to a co-op - 10 stories	Elevator building	24 units	Self managed
Chelsea Area **425-33 West 24th Street** @Ninth/Tenth Ave **Co-op**	Prewar, converted in the 1980's to a co-op - 5 stories	Elevator building	Studios, one bedrooms, two bedrooms	Taranto & Assoc.
Chelsea Area **107 West 25th Street** @Sixth/Seventh Ave **Co-op**	Built around 1910, converted in the 1980's to a co-op - 6 stories	Elevator building	Studios, one bedrooms, two bedrooms	Carole Ferrara Assoc.
Chelsea Area **412 West 25th Street** @Ninth/Tenth Ave **Rental/Rent Stabilized**	6 stories	Elevator building, on-site superintendent	Studios, one bedrooms, two bedrooms, duplexes	Abington Trust (212) 759-5000
Chelsea Area **22 West 26th Street** @Broadway/Sixth Ave **Co-op**	Built around 1910 - 12 stories	One passenger elevator and one service elevator	20 loft units	Argo Corp.
Chelsea Area **233 West 26th Street** @Seventh/Eighth Ave **Co-op**	Built around 1900, converted in the 1980's to a co-op - 9 stories	Elevator building	18 loft units	Arthur Leeds Realty
Chelsea Area **250 West 27th Street** @Seventh/Eighth Ave **Co-op**	Built around 1910, converted in the 1980's to a co-op - 6 stories	Elevator building	N/A	Gerard J. Picasso, Inc.
Chelsea Area **46-50 West 29th Street** @Sixth Ave/Broadway **Co-op**	Built in the 1920's, converted in the 1970's to a co-op - 14 stories	Two passenger and one service elevator	23 loft units	Self managed

NON-LUXURY LOFT AND ELEVATOR BUILDINGS

WEST NUMBERED STREETS
WEST 8TH STREET - 29TH STREET   FIFTH AVENUE - HUDSON RIVER

Address	Description	Amenities	Apartment Types	Managing Agent
Chelsea Area **146 West 29th Street** @Sixth/Seventh Ave **Co-op**	Built around 1910, converted in the 1980's to a co-op - 12 stories	Two passenger and one service elevator	38 loft units	Berik Mgt.
Chelsea Area **249 West 29th Street** @Seventh/Eighth Ave **Co-op**	Built in the 1920's, converted in 1979 to a co-op - 15 stories	One passenger and one service elevator, TV security	27 loft units	Maxwell-Kates Inc.

LUXURY DOORMAN/CONCIERGE BUILDINGS
DOWNTOWN STREETS AND AVENUES IN ALPHABETICAL ORDER

Address	Description	Amenities	Apartment Types	Managing Agent
Battery Park City **300 Albany Street** @ /South End Ave. *Hudson View West* **Condo**	Built in 1988 as condo - 9 stories	Doorman, concierge, garage	Studios, One-bedrooms, Two-bedrooms +	Akam Associates
Battery Park City **350 Albany Street** @ Hudson River *Hudson Tower* **Condo**	Built in 1986 as condo - 15 stories	Concierge, garage, sundeck, laundry rooms on every floor, private garden	One-bedrooms, Two-bedrooms, Three-bedrooms +	R & Y Mgt. Co., Inc.
East Village Area **One Astor Place** @ Broadway/East 8th St. **Rental**	Pre-war - 12 stories	Doorman	Studios, One-bedrooms, Two-bedrooms	N/A
Greenwich Village Area **75 Bank Street** @ N/E/C Bleeker Street *Abingdon Court* **Co-op**	Built in the 1930's, converted in the 1980's to co-op - 6 stories	Doorman	Studios, One-bedrooms, Two-bedrooms+	Ditmas Mgt. Corp.
Greenwich Village Area **99 Bank Street** @ Hudson/Greenwich *The Left Bank* **Co-op**	Built in the 1960's, converted in 1980 to co-op - 7 stories	Doorman	Studios, One-bedrooms, Two-bedrooms+	Andrews Bldg. Corp.
Greenwich Village Area **9 Barrow Street** @ S/W/C West 4th St **Co-op**	Built around 1930, converted in the 1980's to co-op - 9 stories	Part-time Doorman	Studios, One-bedrooms, Two-bedrooms +	Justis Properties Mgt.
Greenwich Village Area **111 Barrow Street** @N/W/C Greenwich St *The Greenwich Villager* **Co-op**	Built around 1920, converted in the 1980's to co-op - 8 stories	Doorman	One-bedrooms, Two-bedrooms, Three-bedrooms	Manhattan Skyline Mgt.
Battery Park City **99 Battery Place** @ West/Thames Street *Liberty View* **Condo/Furnished Short-Term Rentals**	Built in 1988 as condo - 28 stories	Doorman, concierge, health club, laundry on every floor, recreation room, sundeck, garage, apartments have high ceilings, dishwashers and microwave ovens	Studios, One-bedrooms, Two-bedrooms, Three-bedrooms +	Milford Mgt. On-site Rental Office: (212) 898-4800
Chinatown/ Little Italy Area **50 Bayard Street** @ Bowery/Elizabeth St *Bridgeview House* **Condo**	Built in the 1960's, converted in the 1980's to condo - 8 stories	Doorman	Studios, One-bedrooms, Two-bedrooms	Irving R. Raber Co. Inc.
Wall Street/South Street Seaport Area **117 Beekman Street** @ Pearl/Water St *Seaport Park* **Condo**	Built around 1920, converted in the 1980's to condo - 8 stories	Doorman	Studios, One-bedrooms, Two-bedrooms	Charles H. Greenthal & Co.

Address	Description	Amenities	Apartment Types	Managing Agent
Greenwich Village Area **77 Bleecker Street** @ Broadway/Mercer St. *Bleeker Court* **Co-op/Rental**	Built around 1980, converted to co-op in the 1980's - 14 stories	Doorman, garden & sunken court, some apartments with fireplaces/some with skylights, exposed brick, kitchens have dishwashers and microwave ovens	Studios, One-bedrooms, Two-bedrooms, Duplexes	Century Operating Corp.
Greenwich Village Area **160 Bleeker Street** @ Sullivan/Thompson St. *The Atrium* **Co-op**	Built in the 1970's, converted in the 1980's to co-op - 10 stories	Doorman	Studios, One-bedrooms, some Loft spaces on the first and tenth floors	Self-managed
Greenwich Village Area **350 Bleecker Street** @ West 10th/Charles St. **Co-op**	Built around 1950, converted in 1980's to co-op - 7 stories	Doorman, garage	Studios, One-bedrooms, Two-bedrooms	Self-managed
Wall Street Area **25 Broad Street** @ Exchange Place/ Beaver Street *The Exchange* **Rental/Rent Stabilized**	Built around 1900 - Historic Landmark - Renovated in 1997 - 21 stories	Doorman, concierge, free health club, sundeck, business center, laundry - every floor, washer/dryers in Three-bedroom apts.	Studios, One-bedrooms, Two-bedrooms, Three-bedrooms	Insignia Mgt. On-site Rental Office: (212) 217-2901
Wall Street Area **71 Broadway** @ Exchange Place/ Rector Street **Rental**	Landmark building, built around 1900, Renovated in 1997 - 23 stories	Concierge, free health club, recreation room, sundeck, laundry on the 21st floor, wiring for fiber optic, ISDN, and T1 capabilities	Studios, One-bedrooms, Two-bedrooms; apartments are also available with lofts	NRK Mgt. On-site Rental Office: (212) 344-7171
Wall Street Area **176 Broadway** @ John St. & Mdn. Lane **Co-op**	Built around 1900 - 14 stories	Doorman, solarium	72 loft units	John J. Grogan & Assoc. Inc.
Lower Manhattan Area **258 Broadway** @ S/W/C Warren Street **Co-op**	Built around 1910, converted in the 1980's to co-op - 9 stories	Doorman	48 loft units	Taranto and Assoc.
Tribeca **354 Broadway** *D'Arte House* **Condo**	Prewar office building, recently renovated to residential lofts - 12 stories	Doorman, 12 to 15 foot ceilings, terraces, oak flooring, fireplaces	12 full floor loft units ranging from 2,800 to 4,200 square feet.	N/A
Chinatown/ Little Italy Area **376 Broadway** @ White/Franklin Street *Mandarin Plaza* **Condo**	Built in 1988 as condo - 25 stories	Doorman, sundeck	Studios, One-bedrooms, Two-bedrooms+	Bethel Mgt. Inc.
Soho Area **578 Broadway** @ Prince Street **Rental**	Pre-war - 12 stories	Attended lobby	Studios, One-bedrooms, Two-bedrooms	Winoker Realty Co. Mgt. Number: (212) 764-7666

LUXURY DOORMAN/CONCIERGE BUILDINGS
DOWNTOWN STREETS AND AVENUES IN ALPHABETICAL ORDER

Address	Description	Amenities	Apartment Types	Managing Agent
Greenwich Village Area **808 Broadway** @ West 11th Street *The Renwick* **Co-op**	Built around 1900, converted in the 1980's - 8 stories	Doorman, roof garden	Studios, One-bedrooms, Two-bedrooms, Simplexes and Duplexes	Tudor Realty Svs.
East Village Area **51-53 Canal Street** @ Ludlow/Orchard St *Canal Condominium*	Built around 1910, renovated in 1987 as a condo - 6 stories	Doorman	Mostly one-bedrooms	Self managed
Lower Manhattan Area **240 Centre Street** @ Broome/Grand Street *The Police Building* **Co-op**	Built around 1900, converted in the 1980's to co-op - 6 stories	Doorman, garden, healthclub	Studios, One-bedrooms, Two-bedrooms	Equity Mgt. Group
Greenwich Village Area **165 Chambers Street** @ Hudson/Greenwich **Condo**	Built in the 1980's - 11 stories	Doorman	Studios, One-bedrooms, Two-bedroom, Three-bedrooms	L M Dalton Corp.
Greenwich Village Area **15 Charles Street** @ Greenwich/Waverly Pl *Waverly Place Condo* **Condo**	Built in the 1960's, converted in 1992 to co-op - 17 stories	Doorman, concierge, garage	Studios, One-bedrooms, Two-bedrooms+	Knott Harbor Corp.
Greenwich Village Area **140 Charles Street** @ S/E/C Washington St. *Memphis Downtown* **Condo**	Built in 1985 as condo - 22 stories	Doorman, roof-top sundeck, balconies, some apartments with fireplaces	Studios, One-bedrooms	Lawrence Properties
Soho Area **2 Charlton Street** @ S/W/C Sixth Avenue *Charlton House* **Co-op**	Built in the 1960's, converted in the 1980's to co-op - 17 stories	Doorman, garage	Studios, One-bedrooms, Two-bedrooms+	Orsid Realty Corp.
Greenwich Village Area **1 Christopher Street** @ Corner of Greenwich **Rental**	Built in the 1920's - 16 stories	Doorman	Studios, One-bedrooms, Two-bedrooms	N/A
Greenwich Village Area **45 Christopher Street** @ Waverly Place/ Seventh Avenue South **Condo**	Built around 1930, converted in 1987 to condo - 18 stories	Doorman, sundeck	Studios, One-bedrooms, Two-bedrooms+	Goodstein Mgt. Inc.
Greenwich Village Area **95 Christopher Street** @ Bleecker/Hudson *The Gansvoort* **Rental**	Pre-war - 16 stories	Doorman	Studios, One-bedrooms, Two-bedrooms	N/A
Greenwich Village Area **165 Christopher Street** @ Greenwich/Washington **Co-op**	Built in the 1960's, converted in the 1980's to co-op - 7 stories	Doorman, garage	One-bedrooms, Two-bedrooms	Jal Mgt.

LUXURY DOORMAN/CONCIERGE BUILDINGS
DOWNTOWN STREETS AND AVENUES IN ALPHABETICAL ORDER

Address	Description	Amenities	Apartment Types	Managing Agent
Greenwich Village Area **2 Cornelia Street** @ S/W/C Sixth Avenue *Cornelia Street Condo* Condo	Built around 1900, renovated in 1982 as condo - 12 stories	Doorman, laundry on lobby level	One-bedrooms, Two-bedrooms+	Maxwell Kates Inc.
Greenwich Village Area **63 Downing Street** @ Bedford/Varick St *Downing Court* Condo	Built in 1987 as condo - 10 stories	Doorman, balconies	Studios, One-bedrooms, Two-bedrooms, Three-bedrooms	Plymouth Mgt. Group, Inc.
Tribeca Area **105 Duane Street** @ Church Street/ Broadway *Tribeca Tower* **Rental/Rent Stabilized**	Built in 1990 - 52 stories	Doorman, concierge, health club and pool, garage, party room, roof deck, landscaped plaza & garden, laundry on 2nd floor	Studios, One-bedrooms, Two-bedrooms	Related Companies On-site Rental Office: (212) 346-7900
Chelsea Area **85 Eighth Avenue** @ West 14th/15th St. *The Thomas Eddy* Co-op	Built in the 1970's, converted in the 1980's to co-op - 6 stories	Doorman, garage	Studios, One-bedrooms	Mark Greenberg R.E. Co.
Chinatown/ Little Italy Area **80 Elizabeth Street** @ Hester/Grand Street *Royal Elizabeth* Condo	Built around 1930, renovated in 1989 as condo - 7 stories	Doorman	Studios, One-bedrooms, Two-bedrooms	Bethel Mgt.
Chinatown/ Little Italy Area **259 Elizabeth Street** @ Houston/Prince Street *Empire* Condo	Built in 1988 as condo - 8 stories	Part-time Doorman	Studios, One-bedrooms, Two-bedrooms, Three-bedrooms	Chou Mgt.
Greenwich Village Area **1 Fifth Avenue** @ East 8th Street & Washington Mews *Hotel One Fifth Avenue* Co-op	Built in the 1920's, 27 stories - Converted hotel	Doorman	Studios, One-bedrooms, Two-bedrooms+	Insignia Residential Group Inc.
Greenwich Village Area **2 Fifth Avenue** @ Washington Square/ West 8th Street Co-op	Built around 1950, converted in the 1980's to co-op, 20 stories	Doorman, garage, landscaped circular drive	Studios, One-bedrooms, Two-bedrooms+	Rudin Mgt. Co. Inc.
Greenwich Village Area **11 Fifth Avenue** @ East 8th/9th Streets *The Breevort* Co-op	Built in the 1950's, converted in the 1980's to co-op - 19 story residential complex divided into a north and south building	Doorman, concierge, garage, balconies	Studios, One-bedrooms, Two-bedrooms, Three-bedrooms	Kreisel Co. Inc.

LUXURY DOORMAN/CONCIERGE BUILDINGS
DOWNTOWN STREETS AND AVENUES IN ALPHABETICAL ORDER

Address	Description	Amenities	Apartment Types	Managing Agent
Greenwich Village Area **20 Fifth Avenue** @ West 8th Street **Rental**	Pre-war - 17 stories	Doorman	Studios, One-bedrooms, Two-bedrooms	Solil Mgt. (212) 265-2280 Or, for leasing information, call: (212) 267-1667 or 8
Greenwich Village Area **24 Fifth Avenue** @ West 9th/10th Streets *Fifth Avenue Hotel* **Co-op**	Built in the 1920's, converted in the 1980's to co-op - 18 stories	Doorman	Studios, One-bedrooms, Two-bedrooms, Three-bedrooms	Urban Assoc.
Greenwich Village Area **25 Fifth Avenue** @ East 9th/10th Streets **Rental**	Pre-war - 13 stories	Doorman	Studios, One-bedrooms, Two-bedrooms	N/A
Greenwich Village Area **30 Fifth Avenue** @ West 9th/10th Streets **Co-op**	Built in the 1920's, converted in 1970 to co-op - 17 stories	Doorman, roof garden	Studios, One-bedrooms, Two-bedrooms+	Equity Mgt. Group
Greenwich Village Area **33 Fifth Avenue** @ S/E/C East 10th Street **Co-op**	Built in the 1920's, converted in the 1980's to co-op - 16 stories	Doorman	Studios, One-bedrooms, Two-bedrooms+	Century Operating Corp.
Greenwich Village Area **40 Fifth Avenue** @ S/E/C West 11th Street **Co-op**	Built around 1930 - 15 stories	Doorman, garage, health club, fireplaces	Two-bedrooms, Three-bedrooms+	Insignia Residential Group Inc.
Greenwich Village Area **41 Fifth Avenue** @ S/E/C East 11th Street **Co-op**	Built in the 1920's, converted in the 1980's to co-op - 16 stories	Doorman, roof deck	Studios, One-bedrooms, Two-bedrooms+	Maxwell Kates, Inc.
Greenwich Village Area **43 Fifth Avenue** @ N/E/C East 11th Street **Co-op**	Built around 1900, converted in the 1980's to co-op - 11 stories	Doorman	Studios, One-bedrooms, Two-bedrooms, Three-bedrooms+	Cooper Square Realty
Greenwich Village Area **51 Fifth Avenue** @ East 11th/12th Streets **Co-op**	Built in the 1920's, converted in the 1980's to co-op - 16 stories	Doorman	Studios, One-bedrooms, Two-bedrooms	John J. Grogan and Assoc.
Chelsea Area **69 Fifth Avenue** @ N/E/C East 14th Street *Wedgwood House* Coop	Built around 1960, converted in 1980's to co-op - 20 stories	Doorman, sundeck, garage	Studios, One-bedrooms, Two-bedrooms, Three-bedrooms	Argo Corp.
Chelsea Area **96 Fifth Avenue** @ East 14th Street *The Mayfair Fifth* **Rental**	Post-war - 18 stories	Doorman	Studios, One-bedrooms, Two-bedrooms	Solil Mgt. (212) 265-2280 Or, for leasing information, call: (212) 267-1667 or 8

LUXURY DOORMAN/CONCIERGE BUILDINGS
DOWNTOWN STREETS AND AVENUES IN ALPHABETICAL ORDER

Address	Description	Amenities	Apartment Types	Managing Agent
Chelsea Area **108 Fifth Avenue** @ S/W/C West 16th St. **Condo**	Built in 1986 as condo - 20 stories	Doorman, balconies, some fireplaces and washer/dryers in apartments	Studios, One-bedrooms, Two-bedrooms+	R.A. Cohen & Assoc.
Chelsea Area **260 Fifth Avenue** @ East 28th Street **Co-op**	Built around 1900, converted in 1979 to co-op - 16 stores	Doorman	One-bedrooms, Two-bedrooms	Hoffman Mgt.
East Village Area **70 Fourth Avenue** @ Bet 9th & 10th Streets *Stewart House* **Co-op**	Built around 1960 as a co-op - 22 stories	Doorman, garage	Studios, One-bedrooms, Two-bedrooms	Insignia Residential Group
East Village Area **85 Fourth Avenue** @ Bet 10th & 11th Streets **Rental**	Built in the 1950's - 7 stories	Doorman	Studios, One-bedrooms	N/A
East Village Area **111 Fourth Avenue** @ S/E/C East 12th Street **Co-op**	Built around 1920, converted in 1980 to co-op - 13 stories	Doorman, roof garden	Studios, One-bedrooms, Two-bedrooms with sleep lofts	Insignia Residential Group, Inc.
East Village Area **115 Fourth Avenue** @ N/E/C East 12th Street *Petersfield* **Condo**	Built in 1987 as condo - 8 stories	Doorman, concierge, roof garden, washer/dryers in apartments	Studios, One-bedrooms, Two-bedrooms	Kreisel Co. Inc.
Gramercy Park Area **7 Gramercy Park West** @ East 20th Street *A Condo on the Park* **Condo**	Built around 1930, renovated in 1985 as condo - 8 stories	Doorman, concierge, sundeck	Studios, One-bedrooms, Two-bedrooms+	Bellmarc Realty
Gramercy Park Area **24 Gramercy Park So.** @ East 20th Street **Co-op**	Built around 1900 - 12 stories	Doorman	Studios, One-bedrooms, Two-bedrooms	ETC Mgt.
Gramercy Park Area **26 Gramercy Park So.** @ East 20th Street *Irving House* **Co-op**	Built around 1920, converted in the 1980's to co-op - 9 stories	Doorman	Studios, One-bedrooms, Two-bedrooms	Lawrence Properties
Gramercy Park Area **32 Gramercy Park So.** @ S/E/C East 20th Street *Gramercy Towers* **Co-op**	Built in the 1950's, converted in the 1980's to co-op - 18 stories	Doorman, garage	Studios, One-bedrooms, Two-bedrooms+	W.P.G./Rudd Residential Mgt.
Gramercy Park Area **34 Gramercy Park So.** @ S/S East 21st St. **Co-op**	Built around 1900, converted in 1978 to co-op - 9 stories	Doorman	Studios, One-bedrooms, Two-bedrooms	Buchbinder & Warren

LUXURY DOORMAN/CONCIERGE BUILDINGS
DOWNTOWN STREETS AND AVENUES IN ALPHABETICAL ORDER

Address	Description	Amenities	Apartment Types	Managing Agent
Gramercy Park Area **36 Gramercy Park East** @S/S East 21st St. **Rental**	Built around 1910 - 13 stories	Doorman	Studios, One-bedrooms, Two-bedrooms	A.J. Clarke Mgt. Number: (212) 541-4477
Gramercy Park Area **39 Gramercy Park No.** @ N/W/C Third Avenue **Co-op**	Built in the 1950's, converted in the 1980's to co-op - 17 stories	Doorman, balconies	Studios, One-bedrooms, Two-bedrooms+	Insignia Residential Group, Inc.
Gramercy Park Area **44 Gramercy Park North** @ Third/Lexington Ave. **Co-op**	Built around 1930, converted in the 1970's to co-op - 16 stories	Doorman, fireplaces	Studios, One-bedrooms, Two-bedrooms+	Church Mgt.
Gramercy Park Area **45 Gramercy Park North** @ Third/Lexington Ave. **Co-op**	Built around 1930, converted in the 1960's to co-op - 16 stories	Doorman	Studios, One-bedrooms, Two-bedrooms	W.P.G./Rudd Residential Mgt.
Gramercy Park Area **60 Gramercy Park North** also **120 East 22nd St.** @ Lex. & Park Ave. So. **Co-op**	Built around 1930, converted in the 1980's to co-op - Two-buildings connected by a stone-pathed courtyard with benches and fountains	Doorman, elevatorman, fireplaces	Studios, One-bedrooms, Two-bedrooms, Three-bedrooms+	William B. May Co. Inc.
Greenwich Village Area **33 Greenwich Avenue** @ N/W/C 10th Street *Saint Germaine* **Co-op**	Built around 1960, converted in the 1980's to co-op - 15 stories	Doorman, garage	Studios, One-bedrooms, Two-bedrooms+	Wiener Rlty
Tribecca Area **269-83 Greenwich St.** @Chambers/Warren St. **Condo**	Built in the 1980's as condo - 11 stories	Doorman	Studios, One-bedrooms, Two bedrooms	Insignia Residential Group, Inc.
Tribeca Area **275-295 Greenwich St.** @ Warren/Chambers St. *Greenwich Court* **Condo**	Built in 1986 as condo - 11 stories	Concierge, sundeck, private garden	Studios, One-bedrooms, Two-bedrooms, Three-bedrooms+	Insignia Residential Group, Inc.
Tribeca Area **303 Greenwich Street** @ Chambers/Reade St *Dalton on Greenwich* **Condo**	Built in 1987 as condo - 10 stories	Concierge, sundeck, private garden	Studios, One-bedrooms, Two-bedrooms	Cooper Square Rlty, Inc.
Tribeca Area **311 Greenwich Street** @ S/E/C Reade Street *Reade House* **Condo**	Built in 1988 as condo - 11 stories	Doorman, concierge, sundeck, laundry room on 2nd floor	Studios, One-bedrooms, Two-bedrooms, Three-bedrooms	Cooper Square Realty

LUXURY DOORMAN/CONCIERGE BUILDINGS
DOWNTOWN STREETS AND AVENUES IN ALPHABETICAL ORDER

Address	Description	Amenities	Apartment Types	Managing Agent
Tribeca Area **429 Greenwich Street** @ Laight Street *Dietz Lantern Building* **Condo**	Built around 1890, converted in 1996 as condo - 11 stories	Doorman, garage	28 Three-bedroom units	Arnold S. Warwick Co.
Greenwich Village Area **666 Greenwich Street** @ Barrow/Christopher St. *The Archive* **Rental/Rent Stabilized**	Built around 1890 - Landmark Building - Renovated in 1988 - 10 stories	Doorman, concierge, fitness center, garage, sundeck, laundry on every floor. Apartments have high ceilings and oversized, arched windows.	Over 200 layouts - One and Two-bedroom units with sleep lofts	Rockrose Dev. Co. On-site Rental Office: (212) 691-9800
Greenwich Village Area **720 Greenwich Street** @ Perry/Charles Street *The Towers* **Co-op**	Built around 1900, converted in the 1980's to co-op - 10 stories	Doorman, garage	Studios, One-bedrooms, Two-bedrooms+	American Landmark Mgt. Corp
Wall Street Area **3 Hanover Square** @ Stone/Beaver Street **Co-op**	Built in the 1920's, converted in the 1980's to a co-op - 24 stories	Doorman, 20 foot ceilings	Studio, One-bedroom, Two-bedroom, and Three-bedroom Mini Lofts	Rose Assoc.
East Village Area **60 Henry Street** @ Market Street *Honto 88* **Condo**	Built around 1990 as condo - 15 stories	Doorman, health club	Studios, One-bedrooms	Century 21 New Golden Age Realty
Greenwich Village Area **2 Horatio Street** @ Eighth/Greenwich St. **Co-op**	Built around 1930, converted in the 1980's to co-op - 18 stories	Doorman	Studios, One-bedrooms, Two-bedrooms+	Goodstein Mgt., Inc.
Greenwich Village Area **14 Horatio Street** @ S/E/C Eighth Avenue *The Van Gogh* **Co-op**	Built around 1960, converted in the 1980's to co-op - 17 stories	Doorman	Studios, One-bedrooms, Two-bedrooms+	W.P.G./Rudd Residential Mgt.
Greenwich Village Area **95-97 and 110-114 Horatio Street** @ Washington/West St *The West Coast Apts* **Rental**	Built around 1990 - 10 stories	Concierge, garage, healthclub, rooftop deck, laundry on first floor, apartments have high ceilings, skylights, exposed brick and fireplaces	Studios, One-bedrooms, Two-bedrooms, Three-bedrooms, Four-bedrooms, Duplexes and Triplexes	Rockrose Development On-site Rental Office: (212) 727-3500
East Village Area **250 E. Houston Street** @ Avenue A & B *Red Square* **Rental**	Built around 1990 - 13 stories	Doorman, concierge, recreation room, private garden, sundeck, balconies	Studios, One-bedrooms, Two-bedrooms	Park Square Assoc. On-site Rental Office: (212) 529-9595

LUXURY DOORMAN/CONCIERGE BUILDINGS
DOWNTOWN STREETS AND AVENUES IN ALPHABETICAL ORDER

Address	Description	Amenities	Apartment Types	Managing Agent
Tribeca Area **195 Hudson Street** @ Vestry Street **Condo**	New loft conversion - 7 stories	Doorman, roof garden, private storage rooms on each floor, heated parking garage, wood burning fireplaces	Raw lofts - Live/Work - "Build to suit" spaces with 1800-4600 Sq. Ft.; 12' - 20' ceilings	Self-Managed
Greenwich Village Area **421 Hudson Street** @ N/W/C Clarkson Street *Printing House* **Condo/Rental**	Built around 1910, converted in 1987 to condo - 8 stories	Doorman, concierge health club and pool, sundeck, apartments have high ceilings with sleep lofts	One-bedrooms, Two-bedrooms, Three-bedrooms	Orb Mgt. Ltd. On-site Rental Office: (212) 243-1320 ext 222
Gramercy Park Area **1 Irving Place** @ East 14th/15th Street *Zeckendorf Towers* **Condo/Furnished Short-Term Rentals**	Built in 1987 as condo - 26 stories	Doorman, concierge, garage, free health club and pool, sundeck, children's playroom, laundry on 7th floor	Studios, One-bedrooms, Two-bedrooms+	Maxwell-Kates Realty, Broker: Irving Pl. Realty On-site Rental Office: (212) 674-9150 *Broker Fee
Gramercy Park Area **58 Irving Place** Also 127 E. 17th St & **130 East 18th St.** @S/E/C East 18th St. **Co-op**	Built in 1960's, converted in the 1980's to co-op - 16 stories	Doorman, garage	Studios, One-Bedrooms, Two-bedrooms	Century Operating Co.
Gramercy Park Area **61 Irving Place** @ S/E/C East 18th Street *The Gramercy* **Co-op**	Built around 1950, converted in the 1980's to co-op - 7 stories	Doorman	Studios, One-bedrooms, Two-bedrooms+	Big City Mgt.
Gramercy Park Area **81 Irving Place** @ N/E/C East 19th Street **Co-op**	Built around 1930, converted in the 1980's to co-op - 16 stories	Doorman	Studios, One-bedrooms, Two-bedrooms+	Eichner-Leeds Mgt.
Greenwich Village Area **31 Jane Street** @ Eighth Avenue *The Rembrandt* **Co-op**	Built in the 1960's, converted in 1990 to co-op - 18 stories	Doorman	Studios, One-bedrooms, Two-bedrooms	W.P.G./Rudd Residential
Greenwich Village Area **61 Jane Street** @ Greenwich/Hudson St. *The Cezanne* **Co-op**	Built in the 1960's, converted in the 1980's to co-op - 20 stories	Doorman, garage	Studios, One-bedrooms, Two-bedrooms+	W.P.G./Rudd Residential
Greenwich Village Area **99 Jane Street** @ Washington Street **Condo**	Built in 1999 - 11 stories	Roof-top terraces, 11 ft ceilings, 30 ft living rooms and loft-like proportions	84 Two-bedroom, Three-bedroom and Four-bedroom Loft units. Each unit has a river view.	Rockrose Development (212) 727-8999
Greenwich Village Area **130 Jane Street** @ West/Washington St. *Harbor House* **Co-op**	Built around 1930, converted in the 1980's to co-op - 6 stories	Doorman	Studios, One-bedrooms+	Cantor Mgt. Co.

LUXURY DOORMAN/CONCIERGE BUILDINGS
DOWNTOWN STREETS AND AVENUES IN ALPHABETICAL ORDER

Address	Description	Amenities	Apartment Types	Managing Agent
17 John Street *The Tyler Building* **Condo**	Recent renovation - Scheduled for occupancy in the summer of 1999 - 16 stories	Doorman	57 units will range from studios of 580 square feet through three bedrooms of 2,900 square feet.	N/A
Wall Street Area **80 John Street** @ Williams/Gold Street **Rental**	Built in the 1920's - Art Deco Bldg. Renovated in 1997 - 23 stories	Concierge, garage, sundeck, laundry on every floor, good layouts for home/offices	Studios, One-bedrooms, Two-bedrooms, Three-bedrooms	N/A
Wall Street Area **100 John Street** *Renaissance* @ Gold/Pearl Street **Rental**	Renovated in 1998 - 30 stories	Concierge, club room & lounge, garage, sundeck, Internet access, business center services, unique apartment layouts	Studios, One-bedrooms, Two-bedrooms	Insignia Residential Group On-site Rental Office: (212) 489-6666
Soho Area **50 King Street** @ Varick/Sixth Avenue **Co-op**	Built in the 1950's, converted in the 1980's to co-op - 10 stories	Doorman, garage	Studios, One-bedrooms+	A. J. Clarke Mgt. Corp.
Soho Area **285 Lafayette Street** @ Prince Street **Condo**	Renovated pre-war loft building - 8 stories Occupancy as of April 1999	Full-time Concierge, 2,500 sq. ft. landscaped roof garden, set-back terraces, fireplaces, high ceilings, gourmet open plan kitchens, hardwood floors	21 fully finished lofts ranging from 1,800 - 4,460 Sq. Ft., Two to Five bedroom units with double height ceilings	Allied Partners (212) 965-6008
Gramercy Park Area **1 Lexington Avenue** @ N/E/C Gramercy Park North **Co-op**	Built around 1910, converted to co-op in the 1980's - 12 stories	Doorman	27 Duplex Apartments	Insignia Residential Group
Gramercy Park Area **4 Lexington Avenue** @ S/W/C East 22nd St. *Sage House* **Co-op**	Built around 1920, converted in the 1980's to a co-op - 10 stories	Doorman	Studios, One-bedrooms, Two-bedrooms +	Cooper Square Realty, Inc.
Gramercy Park Area **7 Lexington Avenue** @ S/E/C East 22nd St. *Park Gramercy* **Co-op**	Built around 1950, converted in the 1990's to co-op - 12 stories	Doorman	Studios, One-bedrooms+	Rose Associates
Gramercy Park Area **50 Lexington Avenue** @ N/W/C East 24th St. *The Lex* **Co-op**	Built in the 1980's as co-op, 26 stories	Doorman, healthclub, & pool	Studios, One-bedrooms, Two-bedrooms	Charles H. Greenthal & Co.
Gramercy Park Area **88-90 Lexington Avenue** @ East 26th/27th Streets **Rental**	Originally built as an office building and renovated in 1979 to residential units	Doorman, terraces	Studios, One-bedrooms, Two-bedrooms, and full-floor Lofts of 2,500 square feet	Caran Properties, Inc. (212) 207-8118

LUXURY DOORMAN/CONCIERGE BUILDINGS
DOWNTOWN STREETS AND AVENUES IN ALPHABETICAL ORDER

Address	Description	Amenities	Apartment Types	Managing Agent
Wall Street Area **55 Liberty Street** @ S/W/C Nassau Street *Liberty Tower* **Co-op**	Landmark building, built around 1910, converted in 1980 to co-op - 32 stories	Doorman	Studios, One-bedrooms, Two-bedrooms, Three-bedrooms	Blue Woods Mgt. Group, Inc.
Gramercy Park Area **66 Madison Avenue** @ East 27th/28th Streets **Co-op/Rental**	Built around 1920, converted in the 1980's to co-op - 12 stories	Doorman	Studios, One-bedrooms, Two-bedrooms+	ABC Realty
Greenwich Village Area **250 Mercer Street** @ West 3rd/4th Streets **Co-op**	Built around 1890, converted in the 1980's to co-op - 6 stories	Doorman	Studios, One-bedrooms, Two-bedrooms, Three-bedrooms	Casdal Realty Corp.:
Greenwich Village Area **300 Mercer Street** @ Waverly Place **Rental**	Post-war - 35 stories	Doorman	Studios, One-bedrooms, Two-bedrooms	Algin Mgt. Rents through area brokers--Not direct to the public.
Greenwich Village Area **297-303 Mercer Street** Also **258-262 Green St** @ Waverly Place **Co-op**	Built around 1910, converted in 1979 to co-op - 6 stories	Doorman	Studios, One-bedrooms, Two-bedrooms	John J. Grogan & Assoc.
Greenwich Village Area **71 Murray Street** *The Hastings Building* **Condo**	Pre-war, converted to condo in 1997 - 12 stories	Attended lobby, keyed elevators, hardwood floors, oversized windows, wood-burning fireplaces, gourmet kitchens, 11.5 ft beamed ceilings	Live/Work 4,000 Sq. Ft. lofts with Two to Three bedrooms--only one unit per floor	Tishray Realty (212) 233-7171
Battery Park City **450 North End Ave** @ Warren/Chambers St *Tribeca Bridge Tower* **Rental**	Built in the 1998 - 26 stories	Concierge, fitness center, high speed Internet access, high ceilings, washer/dryers, laundry on 2nd floor	One-bedrooms, Two-bedrooms, Three-bedrooms	On-site Agent: Feathered Nest (212) 217-6001
Gramercy Park Area **280 Park Ave South** @ S/W/C East 22nd St. *Gramercy Place* **Condo/Furnished Short-Term Rentals**	Built in 1986 as condo, 25 stories	Doorman, concierge, health club and roof-top pool, private garden, recreation lounge, sundeck	One-bedrooms, Two-bedrooms	Insignia Residential Group Mgt. Broker: Citi Habitats On-site Office: (212) 529-8888 *Rental Fee
Gramercy Park Area **295 Park Avenue South** @ East 22nd/23rd St *Park 23* **Rental**	Pre-war, Renovated in the 1980's - 17 stories	Doorman, Concierge, apartments have high ceilings and sleep lofts, Eat-in-kitchens with dishwashers	Studios, One-bedrooms, Two-bedrooms, Duplexes	Owner/Manager: Abington Trust (212) 759-5000
Gramercy Park Area **407 Park Ave South** @ N/E/C East 28th St. *The Ascot* **Co-op**	Built in the 1980's as co-op - 27 stories	Doorman, garage, balconies, garden entrance, plaza leads to a two-story lobby	Studios, One-bedrooms, Two-bedrooms+	Hoffman Mgt. Co.

LUXURY DOORMAN/CONCIERGE BUILDINGS
DOWNTOWN STREETS AND AVENUES IN ALPHABETICAL ORDER

Address	Description	Amenities	Apartment Types	Managing Agent
Gramercy Park Area **425 Park Ave South** @ N/E/C East 29th St. *Park South Tower* Co-op	Built in the 1920's, converted in the 1980's to co-op - 21 stories	Doorman, Roof Deck	74 Loft Units	Goodman Mgt. Co.
Wall Street Area **35 Park Row** @ N/E/C Beekman Street *Beekman Spruce* Co-op	Built around 1900, converted in the 1980's to co-op - 11 stories	Elevatorman	45 Loft Units	Wallack Mgt. Inc.
East Village Area **165, 185, 215, 217-231** **Park Row** also **1 Madison Street** *Chatham Green* Co-op	Built around 1960, converted in the 1990's to co-op - 21 stories	Doorman, garage	Studios, One- bedrooms, Two- bedrooms, Three- bedrooms+	Century Operating Corp.
Greenwich Village Area **155 Perry Street** @ Washington/West St. Condo	Built around 1920, converted in 1985 to condo - 8 stories	Elevatorman, solarium, health club, roof garden, fireplaces	Studios, One- bedrooms, Two- bedrooms	ABC Realty
Greenwich Village Area **167 Perry Street** @ Washington/West St. Co-op	Built in the 1980's as co-op - 6 stories	Doorman, roof deck	Studios, One- bedrooms+	Akam Assoc.
Soho Area **14 Prince Street** @ Elizabeth Street *Prince 14 Condo* Condo	Built around 1915, renovated in 1984 as condo - 6 stories	Doorman	One-bedrooms, Two- bedrooms, Three- bedrooms	Andrews Bldg. Corp.
Battery Park City **200 Rector Place** @ West Street *Liberty Court* Condo/Furnished Short-Term Rentals	Built in 1987 as condo - 44 stories	Doorman, concierge, garage, health club & pool, roof deck, recreation room, laundry every floor	Studios, One- bedrooms, Two- bedrooms, Three- bedrooms	Milford Mgt. On-site Rental Office: (212) 898-4800
Battery Park City **225 Rector Place** @ Albany/South End Ave *Parc Place* Rental/Rent Stabilized	Built in the 1980's - 24 stories	Doorman, concierge, garage, health club, sundeck, recreation room, laundry on 2nd floor	Studios, One- bedrooms, Two- bedrooms	Related Companies On-site Rental Office: (212) 945-0500
Battery Park City **280 Rector Place** @ /South End Ave *The Soundings* Condo	Built in 1987 as condo - 9 stories	Doorman, Concierge, health club and pool, sundeck, laundry on every floor	Studios, One- bedrooms, Two- bedrooms+	American Landmark Mgt. Corp.
Battery Park City **300 Rector Place** @ S/W/C South End Ave *Battery Pointe* Condo	Built in 1987 as condo - 9 stories	Doorman, health club, children's playroom, sundeck, private garden, laundry room on every floor	Studios, One- bedrooms, Two- bedrooms+	American Landmark Mgt. Corp.

LUXURY DOORMAN/CONCIERGE BUILDINGS
DOWNTOWN STREETS AND AVENUES IN ALPHABETICAL ORDER

Address	Description	Amenities	Apartment Types	Managing Agent
Battery Park City **333 Rector Place** @ South End Avenue/ Esplanade *River Rose* **Rental** - Rent Stabilized	Built in the 1980's - 16 stories	Doorman, garage, sundeck, some terraces	Studios, One-bedrooms, Two-bedrooms, Three-bedrooms	Rockrose Development On-site Rental Office: (212) 786-0537
Battery Park City **377 Rector Place** @ Esplanade *Liberty House* **Condo/Furnished Short-Term Rentals**	Built in 1986 as condo - 25 stories	Doorman, concierge, laundry on lobby level, sundeck, dishwashers and microwave ovens in apartments	Studios, One-bedrooms, Two-bedrooms, Three-bedrooms	Milford Mgt. On-site Rental Office: (212) 898-4800
Battery Park City **380 Rector Place** @ South End Ave. *Liberty Terrace* **Condo/Rental**	Built in 1986 as condo - 26 stories	Doorman, concierge, health club and pool, recreation room, laundry on every floor, sundeck, apartments have high ceilings, dishwashers and microwave ovens	Studios, One-bedrooms, Two-bedrooms, Three-bedrooms	Milford Mgt. On-site Rental Office: (212) 898-4800
Battery Park City **34 River Terrace** *Tribeca Park* **Rental**	Built in 1999 - 28 stories - Scheduled to open May 1999	Concierge	Studios, One-bedrooms, Two-bedrooms	Owner: Related Companies
Battery Park City **41 River Terrace** also **401 Chambers St** *Tribeca Pointe* **Rental/Rent Stabilized**	Built in 1998 - 43 stories	Concierge & valet services, free fitness club, roof deck, children's playroom, high tech wiring	Studios, One-bedrooms, Two-bedrooms, Three-bedrooms	Owner: Rockrose Development Agent on Premises: (212) 370-4141
East Village Area **166 Second Avenue** @ E/S 10th Street **Rental**	Post-war - 16 stories	Doorman	Studios, One-bedrooms	N/A
East Village Area **170 Second Avenue** @East 24th Street **Co-op**	Built in the 1920's, the first luxury high-rise on the Lower East Side, converted in the 1980's to co-op - 16 stories	Elevatorman	Studios, One-bedrooms, Two-bedrooms, Three-bedrooms	ABC Realty
Gramercy Park Area **305 Second Avenue** @ East 17th/18th Street *Rutherford Place* **Condo/Rental**	Built around 1900, renovated in 1987 as condo - 10 stories Landmark building	Doorman, Concierge, laundry on each floor, sundeck, apartments have high ceilings, dish-washers and sleep lofts	Studios, One-bedrooms, Two-bedrooms, Three-bedrooms	Orb Mgt. Ltd. On-site Rental Office: (212) 473-9066
Chelsea Area **56 Seventh Avenue** @ 13th/14th Street **Rental**	Post - war - 21 stories	Doorman	Studios, One-bedrooms	N/A

LUXURY DOORMAN/CONCIERGE BUILDINGS
DOWNTOWN STREETS AND AVENUES IN ALPHABETICAL ORDER

Address	Description	Amenities	Apartment Types	Managing Agent
Chelsea Area **77 Seventh Avenue** @ W 14th/15th Street *The Vermeer* Co-op	Built in the 1960's, converted in 1980 to co-op - 21 stories	Doorman, garage, solarium	Studios, One-bedrooms, Two-bedrooms, Three-bedrooms	Orsid Realty Corp.
Chelsea Area **140 Seventh Avenue** @ 18th/19th Street *Chadwin House* Condo	Built around 1960, converted in 1985 to condo - 6 stories	Doorman, concierge	Studios, One-bedrooms, Two-bedrooms	Mark Greenberg RE Co.
Chelsea Area **181 Seventh Avenue** @ West 20th/21st Street *The Atrium at Chelsea* Condo	Built in 1986 as condo - 15 stories	Doorman, balconies, sundeck	Studios, One-bedrooms, Two-bedrooms	Sandra Greer Real Estate, Inc.
Greenwich Village Area **3 Sheridan Square** @ Barrow/Grove Street *Parker Towne House* Co-op	Built in the 1960's, converted in the 1980's to co-op - 18 stories	Doorman, garage	Studios, One-bedrooms, Two-bedrooms	Tudor Realty Svs. Corp.
Greenwich Village Area **10 Sheridan Square** @ Grove/Sixth Avenue **Rental**	15 stories	Elevator operator, garage	Studios, One-bedrooms	N/A
Battery Park City **2 South End Avenue** @ West Thames/ Liberty Street *The Cove Club* **Condo/Rental**	Built in 1990 as condo - 9 stories	Doorman, health club, garage, sundeck, private garden, some balconies, high ceilings, fireplaces	Studios, One-bedrooms, Two-bedrooms, Three-bedrooms	Cooper Square Realty
Battery Park City **21 South End Avenue** @ W. Thames Street *The Regatta* Condo	Built in 1988 as condo - 9 stories	Doorman, solarium	Studios, One-bedrooms, Two-bedrooms, Three-bedrooms	American Landmark Mgt. Corp.
Battery Park City **250 South End Avenue** @ S/E/C Albany Street *Hudson View East* Condo	Built in 1985 as condo- 18 stories	Doorman, concierge, private garden, laundry on every floor	Studios, One-bedrooms, Two-bedrooms	R. Y. Mgt. Co. , Inc.
Battery Park City **375 South End Avenue** @ Liberty Street *Gateway Plaza* **Rental/Rent Stabilized**	Built in the 1980's - 35 stories	Doorman, concierge, driveway, garage, laundry on the second floor, health club and pool, sundeck	Studios, One-bedrooms, Two-bedrooms, Three-bedrooms	Owner: Lefrak Organization Gateway Plaza Mgt. On-site Rental Office: (212) 488-9456
East Village Area **111 Third Avenue** @ East 13th/14th Streets Co-op	Built around 1960, converted in the 1980's to co-op - 17 stories	Doorman	Studios, One-bedrooms, Two-bedrooms +	Majestic Rose Corp.

LUXURY DOORMAN/CONCIERGE BUILDINGS
DOWNTOWN STREETS AND AVENUES IN ALPHABETICAL ORDER

Address	Description	Amenities	Apartment Types	Managing Agent
Gramercy Park Area **205 Third Avenue** @ East 18th/19th Streets *Gramercy Park Towers* **Co-op**	Built in the 1960's, converted in 1980 to co-op - 21 stories	Doorman, garage, some balconies	Studios, One-bedrooms, Two-bedrooms+	PRC Mgt.
Gramercy Park Area **330 Third Avenue** @ East 24th Street **Co-op**	Built in the 1960's, converted in 1980's to co-op - 21 stories	Concierge, garage	Studios, One-bedrooms, Two-bedrooms	Orsid Realty Corp.
Gramercy Park Area **344 Third Avenue** @ East 25th Street *Manhattan Promenade* **Rental**	Built in 1998 - 23 stories	Doorman, balconies, bay windows, ISDN and T1 internet access	Studios, One-bedrooms, Two-bedrooms	Owner: ATA Enterprises: Mgt. Number: (212) 308-1888 Bldg. Number: (212) 684-1130
Soho Area **211 Thompson Street** @ Bleecker Street **Co-op**	Built in the 1970's - 6 stories	Doorman	Studios, One-bedrooms	Sponsor - Harold Thurman et al
East Village Area **1 Tompkins Square** Also **143 Avenue B** and **601-03 East 9th Street** *Christadora House* **Condo**	Built in the 1920's, renovated in 1985 as condo - 17 stories	Concierge	Studios, One-bedrooms, Two-bedrooms, Quadraplex P.H. of 3000 sq. ft.	Andrews Bldg. Corp.
East Village Area **1 Union Square South** @ 14th St/Fourth Ave **Rental**	Built in 1998 - 26 stories	Doorman, health club, sundeck, laundry on 10th floor, apartments have high ceilings and washer/dryers	Studios, One-bedrooms, Two-bedrooms, Three-bedrooms	Owner: The Related Companies: Leasing office on premises: (212) 253-1400
Chelsea Area **33 Union Square West** @ West 16th Street *The Decker Building.* **Rental**	Pre-war - 11 story loft building	Doorman	Studios, One-bedrooms, Two-bedrooms	N/A
Greenwich Village Area **1 University Place** @ University/Waverly **Co-op**	Post-war - 20 stories	Doorman, Elevator operator	Studios, One-bedrooms	Norsco Realty
Greenwich Village Area **40-56 University Place** also **25 East 9th Street** **Co-op**	Built in the 1920's, converted in 1980's as co-op - 13 stories	Doorman	Studios, One-bedrooms, Two-bedrooms, Three-bedrooms	Lerner Group
Greenwich Village Area **101 University Place** @ N/E/C 12th Street **Co-op**	Built around 1930 - 13 stories	Doorman	Studios, One-bedrooms, Two-bedrooms	Buchbinder & Warren

LUXURY DOORMAN/CONCIERGE BUILDINGS
DOWNTOWN STREETS AND AVENUES IN ALPHABETICAL ORDER

Address	Description	Amenities	Apartment Types	Managing Agent
Wall Street Area **45 Wall Street** @ Broad/William Street **Rental/Rent Stabilized**	Built in 1960, Renovated in 1997 - 27 stories	Doorman, concierge, garage, penthouse, lounge, free roof-top fitness center, free indoor golf center, recreation room, sundeck, fiber-optic, ISDN, and T1 wiring	Alcove Studio, One-bedroom, Two-bedroom, Three-bedroom, Duplex and Loft home/office residences	Owner: Rockrose Development On-site Rental Office: (212) 797-7000
Greenwich Village Area **88-99 Washington Place** also **126 Waverly Place** and **360 Sixth Avenue** *Washington Court* **Condo**	Built in 1986 as condo- 6 stories	Doorman, courtyard garden	One-bedrooms, Two-bedrooms	Taranto & Assoc.
Greenwich Village Area **32 Washington Square** @ N/W/C Washington Pl **Co-op**	Built in the 1920's, Co-oped in the 1940's - 16 stories	Doorman	Five rooms, Six rooms and Seven rooms+	TUC Mgt. Co. Inc.
Wall Street Area **130 Water Street** @ N/W/C Pine Street *Seaport South* **Condo**	Built in the 1950's, converted in 1983 to condo - 12 stories	Doorman, Concierge	Studios, One-bedrooms, Two-bedrooms	W.P.G./Rudd Residential Mgt.
Seaport Area **200 Water Street**	Recent construction - Scheduled to open June 1, 1999 - 32 stories	Doorman, Concierge, valet, rooftop terrace, gym, laundry facility, and wiring for the internet, spectacular views, some apartments have terraces	576 units - Studios, One-bedrooms, Two-bedrooms	Rockrose Development On-site Rental Office: (212) 697-4422
Soho Area **11 Waverly Place** @ Mercer/Greene Street **Rental/Furnished** **Short-Term Leases**	Built in the 1920's - 12 stories	Doorman, apartments have high ceilings, dishwashers and microwave ovens	Studios, One-bedrooms, Two-bedrooms	Owner: Jakobson Properties On-site Rental Office: (212) 533-1300
Tribeca Area **260 West Broadway** @ Beach/York Street *American Thread Building* **Condo**	Built around 1900, renovated in 1982 as condo - 11 stories	Doorman, health club, sundeck, laundry room on every floor	Studios, One-bedrooms, Two-bedrooms	Lawrence Properties
Soho Area **426 West Broadway** @Spring/Prince Street *Broadway House* **Condo**	Built around 1890, renovated in 1984 as condo - 6 stories	Doorman	Studios, One-bedrooms, Two-bedrooms	Taranto & Assoc.
Wall Street Area **21 West Street** @ Morris/Washington St *Le Rivage* **Rental**	Built in 1998 - 32 stories	Doorman, concierge, fitness center, sundeck, garage, laundry on every floor, high speed communications, satellite Direct TV with 200+ channels	Studios, One-bedrooms, Two-bedrooms, Three-bedrooms	On-site Rental Office: Rose Associates Inc. (212) 509-2121

NON-LUXURY ELEVATOR AND LOFT BUILDINGS

DOWNTOWN STREETS AND AVENUES IN ALPHABETICAL ORDER:

Address	Description	Amenities	Apartment Types	Managing Agent
East Village Area **85 Avenue A** @East 5th/6th St **Condo/Rental**	Built in 1998 as a condo - 8 stories	Elevator building, video security, sundeck, apartments have high ceilings, dishwashers	Studios, one-bedrooms, two-bedrooms, duplexes	Park Square Assoc. (212) 529-9595 Rental brokerage fee, one month's rent
East Village Area **97-101 Avenue B** **Co-op**	Prewar, converted in the 1980's to co-op - 6 stories	Elevator building	Studios, one-bedrooms, two-bedrooms	Siren Mgt.
East Village Area **105 Avenue B** @East 6th/7th St **Rental/Rent Stabilized**	Prewar, renovated in 1991 - 6 stories	On-site superintendent, apartments have high ceilings and exposed brick	One-bedrooms, two-bedrooms	Park Square Assoc. (212) 529-9595 Rental brokerage fee, one month's rent
Greenwich Village Area **100 Bank Street** @Greenwich/Wash. St **Co-op**	Prewar, converted in the 1980's to co-op - 6 stories	Elevator building	Studios, one-bedrooms, two-bedrooms	Plymouth Mgt. Group
Greenwich Village Area **164 Bank Street** @West/Washington St *Bank Street Home* **Condo**	Built in the 1980's as a condo - 12 stories	One passenger elevator, terraces	Studios, one-bedrooms, two-bedrooms	Gotham Properties Mgt.
Greenwich Village Area **166 Bank Street** @Washington St **Co-op**	Built around 1920, converted in 1980 to co-op - 7 stories	Elevator building	Studios, one-bedrooms, two- bedrooms	Kaled Mgt. Corp.
Greenwich Village Area **130 Barrow Street** @West/Washington St **Condo**	Built around 1930, converted in the 1980's to condo - 6 stories	Elevator building, washers and dryers in apartments	Studio, one-bedroom, and two-bedroom duplexes with sleep lofts	Charles H. Greenthal Co.
Wall Street Area **26 Beaver Street** @Broad St/ Broadway *Beaver Tower* **Co-op**	Built around 1910, converted in the 1980's to co-op - 18 stories	One passenger and one service elevator, TV security	18 full-floor lofts	Plymouth Mgt. Group
Wall Street Area **56 Beaver Street** @William/Broad St *Delmonico's Building* **Rental**	Landmark building- built around 1890, renovated in 1996- 9 stories	Elevator building, on-site superintendent, free health club, sundeck. Apartments have high ceilings, exposed brick, and fireplaces. Laundry on 3rd floor	Studio, one-bedroom, and two-bedroom live/work residences, which range from 750 to 1500 square feet.	Time Equities (212) 206-6044
Greenwich Village Area **78-80 Bedford Street** @Commerce/Barrow St *Star Corner* **Condo**	Built around 1920, converted in 1985 to condo - 5 stories	Elevator building	One-bedrooms, two-bedrooms	Buchbinder & Warren

NON-LUXURY ELEVATOR AND LOFT BUILDINGS

DOWNTOWN STREETS AND AVENUES IN ALPHABETICAL ORDER:

Address	Description	Amenities	Apartment Types	Managing Agent
South Street Seaport Area **130 Beekman Street** *Beekman Landing* **Rental**	Three prewar adjoining buildings- recently renovated to residential lofts	High ceilings, fireplaces, exposed brick walls, hardwood floors	18 luxury loft-like units of 885 to 2,300 square feet. Each apartment has a washer/dryer, and T3 communications line	Exclusive Agent: Brian Edwards, Halstead Properties (212) 253-9300 ext. 6535
Greenwich Village Area **33-37 Bethune Street** @Greenwich/Wash. St *Pickwick House* **Condo**	Built around 1880, converted in the 1980's to a condo - 5 stories	Elevator building	Studios, one bedrooms, two bedrooms	Simon A. Berman Realty Co.
East Village Area **10 Bleecker Street** @Bowery/Elizabeth St **Co-op**	Built arount 1900, converted in 1986 to a co-op - 7 stories	Elevator building	Studios, one bedrooms, two bedrooms	Superior Mgt.
Greenwich Village Area **88 Bleecker Street** @S/W/C Broadway **Co-op**	Built around 1960, converted in the 1980's to a co-op - 7 stories	Elevator building, garage	Studios, one bedrooms, two bedrooms	Charles H. Greenthal Co.
Greenwich Village Area **189-95 Bleecker Street** also **91-93 MacDougal** **Co-op**	Prewar, converted in the 1980's to a co-op - 6 stories	Elevator building	Studios, one bedrooms, two bedrooms	Buchbinder & Warren
East Village Area **1-5 Bond Street** @S/E/C Jones Alley **Condo**	Built around 1870, converted in the 1980's to a condo - 6 stories	One passenger elevator, one service elevator, TV security	18 live/work units	Andrews Building Corp.
East Village Area **7-9 Bond Street** @Lafayette/Broadway **Condo**	Built around 1900, renovated in the 1980's as a condo - 6 stories	Elevator building	20 lofts - ranging from 1200 to 1500+ square feet	Andrews Building Corp.
Lower East Side **200 Bowery Street** @Prince/Spring St *Bowery Court* **Condo**	Renovated in 1988 as a condo - 8 stories	Elevator building	Studios, one bedrooms, two bedrooms, three bedrooms	Bethel Mgt.
Wall Street Area **176 Broadway** @Maiden Ln/John St **Co-op**	Build around 1905, converted in the 1980's to a co-op - 14 stories	Elevator building, solarium	Studios, one bedrooms, two bedrooms	John J. Grogan Assoc.
Lower Manhattan **260-261 Broadway** @N/W/C Warren St **Co-op**	Built around 1915, converted in 1980 to a co-op - 12 stories	Elevator building, solarium, TV security	Studios, one bedrooms, two bedrooms	Tudor Realty Service

NON-LUXURY ELEVATOR AND LOFT BUILDINGS

DOWNTOWN STREETS AND AVENUES IN ALPHABETICAL ORDER:

Address	Description	Amenities	Apartment Types	Managing Agent
Lower Manhattan **356 Broadway** @Leonard St **Condo**	Built around 1940, converted in the 1980's to a condo - 5 stories	Elevator building	Studios, one bedrooms, two bedrooms	Andrews Building Corp.
Chinatown/Little Italy **364-66 Broadway** @N/E/C Franklin St. *Collect Pond House* **Co-op**	Built around 1920, converted in 1979 to a co-op - 12 stories	Two passenger elevators, two service elevators, TV security	Studios, one bedrooms, two bedrooms	Andrews Building Corp.
Tribeca Area **395 Broadway** @S/W/C Walker St **Condo**	Built around 1910, renovated in 1983 as a condo - 15 stories	Two passenger elevators, TV security	64 one bedrooms - 1000+ square feet	Excelsior Mgt. Co.
SoHo Area **684 Broadway** @Great Jones/East 4th St **Co-op**	Built around 1900, converted in 1979 to a co-op - 12 stories	Elevator building	Studios, one bedrooms, two bedrooms	Andrews Bldg. Corp.
East Village Area **718 Broadway** @Astor Pl/East 4th St **Co-op**	Built around 1910, converted in the 1980's to a co-op - 11 stories	Two passenger elevators and one service elevator, TV security	40 units	Charles H. Greenthal Co.
East Village Area **830-34 Broadway** @East 12th/13th St **Co-op**	Built around 1900, converted in the 1980's to a co-op - 11 stories	Two passenger and one service elevator, TV security, individual laundry facilities	19 loft units	Buchbinder & Warren
Greenwich Village Area **10 Christopher Street** @Greenwich/Gay St **Co-op**	Built around 1940, converted in the 1980's to a co-op - 7 stories	Elevator building, TV security	Studios, one bedrooms, two bedrooms	Hoffman Mgt. Co.
Lower Manhattan **249 Church Street** @Franklin/Leonard St **Condo**	Prewar - 4 stories	Loft building, keyed elevator security	Loft units	River to River Properties
Wall Street Area **1-5 Coentes Slip** @Pearl/Water St **Co-op**	Built around 1900, converted in the 1980's to a co-op - 5 stories	Elevator building, common storage space	Studios, one bedrooms, two bedrooms	Orb Mgt.
Wall Street Area **46 Commerce Street** **Co-op**	Postwar	Elevator, garage	Studios, one bedrooms, two bedrooms	N/A
East Village Area **65 Cooper Square** @E. 7th St/St. Marks Pl *Cooper Square* **Condo**	Built in 1984 as a condo - 6 stories	Elevator building, TV security	Studios and one bedrooms	Bellmarc Regal Mgt.

NON-LUXURY ELEVATOR AND LOFT BUILDINGS

DOWNTOWN STREETS AND AVENUES IN ALPHABETICAL ORDER:

Address	Description	Amenities	Apartment Types	Managing Agent
SoHo Area **18-20 Cornelia Street** @Bleecker/West 4th St **Rental/Furnished/ Short-term leases**	Built around 1880 - 6 stories	Elevator building, on-site superintendent, apartments have high ceilings, exposed brick	Studios, one bedrooms, two bedrooms	Jakobson Properties (212) 533-1300
Chinatown/Little Italy **135 Division Street** @Canal/Pike St **Condo**	Built in the 1980's - 8 stories	Elevator building	One bedrooms and two bedrooms	N/A
112 Duane Street or **72 Reade Street** **Condo**	Built in 1856 - recently renovated Italianate-style 7 story landmark building with 1,000 square foot courtyard in the center.	Private balcony or deck, 3 or 4 exposures, high ceilings, fireplaces, original cast iron columns and tin ceilings.	Eight 3,400 to 4,700 square foot lofts	72 Reade Assoc. (212) 965-6018
Tribeca Area **165 Duane Street** @N/W/C Hudson St **Duane Park Lofts** **Co-op**	Built around 1880, converted in the 1980's to a co-op - 10 stories	Elevator building, TV security	37 loft units	Tudor Realty Services
Tribeca **176 Duane Street** **Zenith Godley Building** **Condo**	Built in 1868, recently renovated to residential lofts	Wide plank floors, exposed brick and ceiling beams, central air conditioning	Four full floor lofts, each at 2,336 square feet, plus one 2,200 square foot duplex penthouse	N/A
Chelsea **77-9 Eighth Avenue** @West 14th St **The Bank Building** **Condo**	A former neo-classical bank building, recently renovated to residential lofts - 7 stories	The building will retain many of the architectural details of the bank along with motif and design of the original building	12 two to three bedroom loft spaces with 18 foot ceilings, 2.5 bathrooms, and outdoor space.	BFI Construction (212) 929-3610
Chinatown/Little Italy **122 Elizabeth Street** @Broome/Grand St **Condo**	Built in 1987 as a condo - 6 stories	Elevator building	One bedrooms, two bedrooms, three bedrooms	Longines Realty
Chinatown/Little Italy **146 Elizabeth Street** also **354 Broome Street** **Ice House** **Condo**	Built around 1925, renovated in 1989 as a condo - 6 stories	Elevator building	37 studios	Self managed
SoHo Area **301 Elizabeth Street** @East Houston St **SoHo Court** **Rental/rent stabilized**	Built in the 1990's - 11 stories	Elevator building, on-site superintendent, exercise room, private garden, apartments have high ceilings, fireplaces, and skylights	Studios, one bedrooms, two bedrooms	Zucker Organization Mgt. Office: (212) 889-1850

NON-LUXURY ELEVATOR AND LOFT BUILDINGS

DOWNTOWN STREETS AND AVENUES IN ALPHABETICAL ORDER:

Address	Description	Amenities	Apartment Types	Managing Agent
Greenwich Village Area **39 Fifth Avenue** @East 10th/11th St **Co-op**	Built around 1920, converted in the 1980's to a co-op - 17 stories	One passenger elevator	One bedrooms, two bedrooms	Samson Mgt.
Greenwich Village Area **45 Fifth Avenue** @East 11th/12th St **Co-op**	Built in the 1920's, converted in the 1980's to a co-op - 16 stories	Elevator building, TV security	One bedroom units	R.F. Stuart Realty Mgt.
Greenwich Village Area **51 Fifth Avenue** @N/E/C 12th St **Co-op**	Built around 1930, converted in the 1980's to a co-op - 15 stories	Elevator building	One bedrooms, two bedrooms, +	John J. Grogan & Assoc.
Chelsea Area **73 Fifth Avenue** @N/E/C East 15th St **Condo**	Built around 1910, converted in 1979 to a condo - 11 stories	Two passenger and one service elevator, TV security, washer/dryer in each unit	17 loft units	Self Managed
Chelsea Area **74 Fifth Avenue** @West 13th/14th St **Co-op**	Built around 1910, converted in 1980 to a co-op - 12 stories	Two passenger elevators, one service elevator, solarium, TV security, washer/dryer in each unit	Studios, one bedrooms, two bedrooms	Taranto & Assoc.
Chelsea Area **77 Fifth Avenue** @15th/16th St **Rental/Rent Stabilized**	Built in the 1980's - 19 stories	Elevator building, video security, on-site superintendent, apartments have lofts and dishwashers	Studios, one bedrooms, two bedrooms	Bettina Equities (212) 744-3330
Chelsea Area **105 Fifth Avenue** @East 18th St *Folio House* **Co-op**	Built around 1900, converted in the 1980's to a co-op - 11 stories	Two passenger elevators, one service elevator, TV security	Studios, one bedrooms, two bedrooms	Andrews Building Corp.
Chelsea Area **129-31 Fifth Avenue** @East 19th/20th St **Co-op**	Built around 1900, converted in 1980 to a co-op - 8 stories	One passenger elevator, TV security	Studios, one bedrooms, two bedrooms	Self Managed
Chelsea Area **140 Fifth Avenue** @West 17th/18th St **Co-op**	Built around 1900, converted in the 1970's to co-op - 12 stories	One passenger elevator, one service elevator, TV security	18 loft units	Gerard J. Picaso, Inc.
East Village Area **224/228 First Avenue** @East 13th/14th St *The Crossings* **Condo**	Built in 1987 as a condo - 5 stories	Elevator building, TV security	Studios, one bedrooms, two bedrooms	Bellmarc Regal Mgt. Co.

NON-LUXURY ELEVATOR AND LOFT BUILDINGS

DOWNTOWN STREETS AND AVENUES IN ALPHABETICAL ORDER:

Address	Description	Amenities	Apartment Types	Managing Agent
140 Franklin Street @Cnr Varick Street	Prewar - 6 stories Recently renovated, and scheduled for occupancy January 2000	High ceilings, central air conditioning, double glazed windows	14 finished three to four bedroom lofts, ranging from 3,000 to 6,226 square feet, with high end kitchens and baths	Franklin Equity Assoc. (212) 243-4000 ext. 235
Chinatown/Little Italy **179 Grand Street** @Mulberry/Baxter St *La Grande* **Condo**	Built in 1989 as a condo - 7 stories	One passenger elevator	Studios, one bedrooms, two bedrooms	Self managed
NoHo **27 Great Jones Street** **Condo**	Prewar - recently renovated to residential lofts	Oversize thermopane windows, wide-plank wood flooring	8 floor-through apartments and 2 penthouse apartments; All have flexible layouts and range from 2,000 to 3,100 square feet.	GMA Development
SoHo Area **95 Greene Street** @Spring/Prince St *Greene House* **Condo**	Built around 1890, renovated in 1985 as a condo - 6 stories	Elevator building	Studios, one bedrooms, two bedrooms	Washington Square Mgt.
SoHo Area **114-20 Greene Street** @Spring/Prince St *SoHo Heritage Condo* **Condo**	Built around 1880, renovated in 1988 as a condo - 6 stories	Elevator building	Studios, one bedrooms, two bedrooms	Pretium Assoc.
SoHo Area **26, 28, & 30 Greenwich Avenue** @Sixth/Seventh Ave **Rental**	Prewar - 6 stories	Elevator building, on-site superintendent, apartments have exposed brick and high ceilings	Studios, one bedrooms, two bedrooms, three bedrooms	Jakobson Properties Mgt. Office: (212) 533-1300
Tribeca Area **110 Greenwich Street** @Carlisle Street **Rental**	Built around 1920, renovated in 1998 - 14 stories	Elevator building, apartments have high ceilings, exposed brick, dishwashers, microwaves, washers and dryers	Studios, one bedrooms, two bedrooms, three bedrooms, duplexes	Jakobson Properties (212) 533-1300
Tribeca Area **335 Greenwich Street** @S/E/C Jay St *Hanover River House* **Co-op**	Built around 1930, converted in 1979 to a co-op - 13 stories	One passenger elevator; some units with terraces	28 loft units	ETC Mgt.
Tribeca Area **371-75 Greenwich Street** @N/E/C Greenwich St **Condo**	Prewar, converted in the 1980's to a condo - 8 stories	Two passenger elevators, one service elevator, all units have terraces	8 loft units	Self managed

NON-LUXURY ELEVATOR AND LOFT BUILDINGS

DOWNTOWN STREETS AND AVENUES IN ALPHABETICAL ORDER:

Address	Description	Amenities	Apartment Types	Managing Agent
387-97 Greenwich Street @Cnr. of Beach ST *Fischer Mills* **Condo**	A group of 5 brick, 19th century buildings - recently renovated to residential lofts - 7 stories	Elevator building	36 loft units, ranging in size from 1,600 to 5,000 square feet.	GMA Development
Greenwich Village Area **708 Greenwich Street** *Greenwich 10* **Co-op**	Prewar, converted in the 1980's to a co-op - 6 stories	Elevator building	Studios, one bedrooms, two bedrooms	Sequoia Property Mgt.
Greenwich Village Area **822 Greenwich Street** @Jane St **Co-op**	Built around 1900 - converted in 1984 to a co-op - 6 stories	Elevator building	Studios, one bedrooms, two bedrooms	Redman Mgt. Co.
SoHo Area **92 Grove Street** Cnr. of Sheridan Square **Rental-rent stabilized**	Prewar, renovated in 1994 - 6 stories	Elevator building, on-site superintendent, apartments have fireplaces, exposed brick, and dishwashers	Studios, one bedrooms, two bedrooms	Eberhart Brothers Mgt. Office: (212) 570-2400
East Village Area **46-50 Henry Street** @Market/Catherina St *Bishop Paul Moore Twr* **Condo**	Built around 1990 as a condo - 11 stories	Elevator building	One bedrooms, two bedrooms	Target Three Assoc.
East Village Area **48 Hester Street** @Essex/Ludlow St *Kwok Wah House* **Condo**	Built in 1988 as a condo - 9 stories	Elevator building, garage	Studios, one bedrooms	Edmar Development
Tribeca Area **16 Hudson Street** @Reade/Duane St **Co-op**	Built around 1900, converted in 1979 to a co-op - 6 stories	Elevator building	Studios, one bedrooms, two bedrooms	Self managed
Tribeca Area **55 Hudson Street** @S/W/C Jay St **Co-op**	Built around 1890, converted in the 1980's to a co-op - 10 stories	Elevator building	Studios, one bedrooms, two bedrooms	Cooper Square Realty
Tribeca Area **67-69 Hudson Street** @Jay/Harrison St *Whitehouse* **Condo**	Built around 1915, converted in 1984 to a condo - 5 stories	Elevator building	One bedrooms, two bedrooms	33 Bond Street Bldg. Mgt.
Tribeca Area **90 Hudson Street** @Leonard St **Co-op**	Built around 1915, converted in the 1980's to a co-op - 7 stories	Elevator building, TV security	Studios, one bedrooms, two bedrooms	Andrews Bldg. Corp.

NON-LUXURY ELEVATOR AND LOFT BUILDINGS

DOWNTOWN STREETS AND AVENUES IN ALPHABETICAL ORDER:

Address	Description	Amenities	Apartment Types	Managing Agent
Tribeca Area **100 Hudson Street** @Franklin/Leonard St **Co-op**	Built around 1910, converted in the 1970's to a co-op - 10 stories	Elevator building, TV security	Studios, one bedrooms, two bedrooms	Andrews Building Corp.
Tribeca Area **105 Hudson Street** @N/W/C Franklin St **Co-op**	Built around 1890, converted in the 1970's to a co-op - 11 stories	Elevator building	28 loft units	Self managed
Tribeca Area **110 Hudson Street** @N/E/C Franklin St ***Borden House*** **Condo**	Built around 1900, converted in the 1970's to a condo - 10 stories	One passenger elevator, one service elevator	14 loft units	Self managed
124-30 Hudson Street **Condo**	9 stories		Loft units, ranging from 1,500 to 3,600 square feet.	124-30 Hudson Street, LLC (212) 255-4748
Tribeca Area **181-85 Hudson Street** @N/W/C Vestry St ***Vestry Place*** **Condo**	Built around 1910, renvovated in 1984 as a condo - 8 stories	One passenger elevator, one service elevator, TV security, individual laundry facilities	20 loft units	Hoffman Mgt. Co.
Greenwich Village Area **519-525 Hudson Street** @West 10th/Charles St **Rental/Rent stabilized**	Built in the 1890's - 5 stories	Elevator building, on-site superintendent, exposed brick, fireplaces	Studios, one bedrooms	Time Equities (212) 206-6044
534 Hudson Street ***The Kimberly*** **Condo**	7 Stories		One bedroom, two bedroom, three bedroom, and four bedroom, plus a penthouse. Apartments range from 880 to 2,400 square feet.	Stillman Organization (212) 769-9835
Greenwich Village Area **652 Hudson Street** @Gansevoort/13th St **Co-op**	Built around 1900 - 6 stories	Elevator building	Studios, one bedrooms, two bedrooms	Self managed
82-84 Irving Place @East 19th St **Co-op**	Prewar, converted in the 1980's to a co-op - 6 stories	Elevator building	Studios, one bedrooms	Merlon Mgt.
Greenwich Village Area **100 Jane Street** @Greenwich St **Rental/Rent stabilized**	Built in the 1990's - 8 stories	Elevator building, video intercom security, on-site superintendent, fitness room, sundeck	Studios, one bedrooms, two bedrooms	Rockrose Dev. Rental Office: (212) 727-3500

NON-LUXURY ELEVATOR AND LOFT BUILDINGS

DOWNTOWN STREETS AND AVENUES IN ALPHABETICAL ORDER:

Address	Description	Amenities	Apartment Types	Managing Agent
Greenwich Village Area **124-132 Jane Street** @West/Washington St **Co-op**	Built around 1930, converted in the 1980's to a co-op - 6 stories	Elevator building	Studios, one bedrooms, two bedrooms	ETC Mgt.
Wall Street Area **41 John Street** @William/Nassau St **Rental**	Prewar, renovated in 1998 - 4 stories	Elevator building, voice intercom security, washer/dryers, exposed brick, high ceilings, and skylights in apartments	One bedrooms, two bedrooms	Time Equities (212) 206-6044
Wall Street Area **170-176 John Street** @South/Front St **Condo**	Landmark building, built in 1840, converted in the 1980's to a condo - 6 stories	Elevator building	15 units - mostly two and three bedroom duplexes	Self managed
SoHo Area **10 Jones Street** @West 4th/Bleecker St **Rental/Rent stabilized**	Built in the 1970's - 6 stories	Elevator building, voice intercom security, on-site superintendent, apartments have exposed brick and high ceilings	One bedroom, duplex, and triplex apartments	Abington Holdings Mgt. Office: (212) 759-5000
SoHo Area **22 Jones Street** @Bleecker/West 4th St **Rental**	Built in the 1970's - 6 stories	Elevator building, on-site superintendent, apartments have fireplaces, lofts, and exposed brick	Studios, one bedrooms, duplexes	Abington Holdings Mgt. Office: (212) 759-5000
SoHo Area **2 King Street** @S/E/C Sixth Ave **Co-op**	Built around 1960, converted in the 1980's to a co-op - 7 stories	Elevator building, garage	Studios, one bedrooms, two bedrooms	Cornerstone Mgt. Systems
SoHo Area **29 King Street** @Sixth Ave/Varick St *King Street Condo* **Condo**	Built around 1890, renovated in 1982 as a condo - 5 stories	Elevator building	Studios, one bedrooms, two bedrooms	WPG/Rudd Residential Mgt.
SoHo Area **284 Lafayette Street** @Prince St **Co-op**	Built around 1900 - 6 stories	Elevator building	Studios, one bedrooms, two bedrooms	Gerard J. Picasso
SoHo Area **285 Lafayette Street** **Condo**	A former 19th century building - recently converted to residential lofts. Three stories are being added for nine penthouse lofts	Round the clock services, set-back terraces and double height ceilings.	21 fully furnished two to four bedroom lofts, ranging from 1,800 to 4,000 square feet.	Allied Partners (212) 955-6008

NON-LUXURY ELEVATOR AND LOFT BUILDINGS

DOWNTOWN STREETS AND AVENUES IN ALPHABETICAL ORDER:

Address	Description	Amenities	Apartment Types	Managing Agent
Gramercy Park Area **61 Lexington Avenue** @N/E/C East 25th St **Co-op**	Built around 1980, converted in 1990 to a co-op - 7 stories	Elevator building	Studios, one bedrooms	New Bedford Mgt.
Gramercy Park Area **105 Lexington Avenue** @East 27th/28th St **Rental**	Built in the 1980's - 12 stories	Elevator building, on-site superintendent, TV security, apartments have high ceilings and lofts	Studios, one bedrooms, two bedrooms, duplex, triplex, and quardraplex apartments	Bettina Equities (212) 744-3330
Gramercy Park Area **151 Lexington Avenue** @East 29th St *Beta South* **Rental**	Built around 1980 - 11 stories	Elevator building, voice intercom security, apartments have eat-in-kitchens and dishwashers	Studio and one bedroom duplexes	Bettina Equities (212) 744-3330
Wall Street Area **114 Liberty Street** *The Engineering Bldg.* **Condo**	Built in 1900, recently renovated to residential lofts - 12 stories	Elevator building	Full floor lofts	N/A
SoHo Area **124 MacDougal Street** @Bleecker/West 3rd St **Rental/Furnished/ Short-term leases**	Built in the 1880's - 6 stories	High Ceilings, exposed brick	Studios, one bedrooms, two bedrooms	Jakobson Properties (212) 533-1300
East Village Area **23-29 Market Street** @S/E/C Henry St **Condo**	Built around 1990 as a condo - 15 stories	Elevator building, TV security	Studios, one bedrooms, two bedrooms	Century 21 - New Age Mgt.
Greenwich Village Area **25 Minetta Lane** @West 3rd/Bleecker St **Co-op**	Built around 1940, converted in 1990 to a co-op - 6 stories	Elevator building	Studios, one bedrooms, two bedrooms	Time Equities, Inc.
Greenwich Village Area **32 Morton Street** @Bedford St/7th Ave So **Co-op**	Built around 1920, converted in the 1980's to a co-op - 8 stories	Elevator building	Studios, one bedrooms, two bedrooms	Buchbinder & Warren
Greenwich Village Area **55 Morton Street** @Hudson/Bedford St **Co-op**	Built around 1900, converted in 1990 to a co-op - 6 stories	Elevator building	Studios, one bedrooms	Self managed
East Village Area **284 Mott Street** @Prince/Houston St *The SoHo Abbey* **Rental/Rent stabilized**	Built around 1990 - 10 stories	Elevator building, video security, garage, laundry on lobby level	Studios, one bedrooms, two bedrooms	Abington Holding Mgt. Office: (212) 759-5000

NON-LUXURY ELEVATOR AND LOFT BUILDINGS

DOWNTOWN STREETS AND AVENUES IN ALPHABETICAL ORDER:

Address	Description	Amenities	Apartment Types	Managing Agent
Wall Street Area **65 Nassau Street** @S/W/C John St **Co-op**	Built around 1900, converted in the 1980's to a co-op - 11 stories	Two passenger elevators	28 units, some with saunas	Century Realty
Wall Street Area **80 Nassau Street West** @John St **Rental**	Prewar, renovated in 1998 - 4 stories	Elevator building, on-site superintendent wall-to-wall windows, high ceilings, skylights, floating kitchens, ISDN, cable, washer/dryer, exposed brick	One bedroom, two bedroom, and three bedroom live/work lofts which range in size from 1,400 to 1,600 square feet.	Time Equities, Inc. (212) 206-6044
Wall Street Area **140 Nassau Street** @N/E/C Beekman St **Co-op**	Built around 1900, converted in the 1980's to a co-op - 15 stories	One passenger elevator and one service elevator	39 loft units	Tudor Rlty Service
Wall Street Area **145 Nassau Street** @Beekman St **Co-op**	Built around 1900, converted in the 1980's to a co-op - 11 stories	Elevator building	Studios, one bedrooms, two bedrooms	Martin J. Raynes Mgt.
East Village Area **166, 178 Norfolk Street** @Stanton/Houston St **Rental/Rent stabilized**	Prewar - 6 stories	Elevator building, apartments have high ceilings, exposed brick, and fireplaces	Studios, one bedrooms	Park Square Assoc. (212) 529-9595 Brokerage fee: one month rent
25 North Moore Street *The Atalanta Building* **Condo**	17 stories		Loft units, ranging from 1,800 to 5,000 square feet.	25 N. Moore Assoc. (212) 965-6008
27 North Moore Street *The Ice House* **Condo**	13 stories		Two to three bedroom lofts, ranging from 1,700 to 4,598 square feet	The Corcoran Group (212) 780-2441
Wall Street Area **31-37 North Moore St** @Varick St *The Merchants House* **Condo**	Built around 1900, converted in the 1990's to a condo - 8 stories	Elevator building, TV security	23 loft units	Andrews Bldg. Corp.
Gramercy Park Area **222 Park Avenue South** @N/W/C East 18th St **Co-op**	Built around 1910, converted in the 1970's to a co-op - 12 stories	Two passenger elevators, two service elevators, solarium, TV security	Studios, one bedrooms, two bedrooms	Heron Mgt. Ltd.
Gramercy Park Area **239 Park Avenue South** @East 19th/20th St **Rental**	Built in the 1970's- 12 stories	Elevator building, voice intercom security, on-site superintendent, apartments have high ceilings, and lofts	One bedrooms	Abington Holding (212) 759-5000

NON-LUXURY ELEVATOR AND LOFT BUILDINGS
DOWNTOWN STREETS AND AVENUES IN ALPHABETICAL ORDER:

Address	Description	Amenities	Apartment Types	Managing Agent
Tribeca Area **180 Park Row** @Pearl/Worth St **Co-op**	Built in the 1960's, converted in the 1980's to a co-op - 25 stories	Elevator building	Studios, one bedrooms, two bedrooms	Akam Assoc.
Wall Street Area **66 Pearl Street** also **1-5 Coenties Slip** *Coenties Slip Apts.* **Co-op/Rental**	Built around 1900, converted in 1990 to a co-op - 8 stories	Elevator building, on-site superintendent, apartments have high ceilings, exposed brick, and dishwashers	Studios, one bedrooms, two bedrooms	Orb Mgt. (212) 734-2464
SoHo Area **22 Perry Street** @7th Ave/West 4th St **Condo**	Built in the 1980's as a condo - 6 stories	Elevator building	22 units	Self managed
Greenwich Village Area **165 Perry Street** @Washington St **Co-op**	Built around 1900 - converted in 1982 to a co-op - 6 stories	Elevator building	21 units	Self managed
SoHo Area **50 Prince Street** @Cor/Mulberry St **Rental**	Built in the 1980's -7 stories	Elevator building, on-site superintendent	Studios, one bedrooms	Linmar L.P. (212) 759-5000
Tribeca Area **96-102 Reade Street** @Church/W.Broadway *Tribeca Court* **Condo**	Built around 1900, converted in 1990 to a condo - 7 stories	Elevator building	25 lofts - approx. 1000 - 1500+ square feet	N/A
Tribeca Area **97-101 Reade Street** @W.Broadway/Church *Reade Court* **Condo**	Built around 1890, converted in 1990 to a condo - 8 stories	Elevator building	Studios, one bedrooms, two bedrooms	Metro Mgt.
Tribeca Area **121 Reade Street** @West Broadway *Tribeca Abbey* **Rental/Rent stabilized**	Built in 1997 - 12 stories	Elevator building, voice intercom security, on-site superintendent, garage, laundry on lobby level	Studios, one bedrooms, two bedrooms, duplexes, triplexes	Abington Holding (212) 759-5000
Chelsea Area **245 Seventh Avenue** @West 24th St *Chelsea Atelier* **Condo**	Prewar, renovated in 1996 as a condo- 12 stories	Elevator building	Studios, one bedrooms	Manhattan Pacific Mgt. Co.
291 Seventh Avenue **Condo**	10 stories		Loft units, ranging from 3,400 to 4,400 square feet.	291 Seventh Ave Assoc. (212) 985-6008

NON-LUXURY ELEVATOR AND LOFT BUILDINGS

DOWNTOWN STREETS AND AVENUES IN ALPHABETICAL ORDER:

Address	Description	Amenities	Apartment Types	Managing Agent
Chelsea Area **315 Seventh Avenue** @West 27th/28th St **Condo**	Built in the 1920's, converted in 1989 to a condo - 21 stories	Elevator building, TV security	Studios, one bedrooms	Fashion Place Assoc.
Greenwich Village Area **1-2 Sheridan Square** @Washington Pl/ West 4th St **Condo**	Prewar, converted in 1987 to a condo- 8 stories	Elevator building	Studios, one bedrooms	Buchbinder & Warren
Greenwich Village Area **196 Sixth Avenue** @Spring/Prince St **Co-op**	Built around 1900, converted in 1983 to a co-op - 7 stories	Elevator building	Studios, one bedrooms, two bedrooms	Regal Mgt.
Greenwich Village Area **241 Sixth Avenue** @N/W/C W. Houston St *Breen Towers* **Co-op**	Built around 1950, converted in the 1980's to a co-op - 13 stories	Elevator building	Studios, one bedrooms, two bedrooms, +	Self managed
Greenwich Village Area **290 Sixth Avenue** @Bleecker/Minetta Ln **Co-op**	Built around 1940, converted in 1985 to a co-op - 6 stories	Elevator building	Studios, one bedrooms, two bedrooms	N/A
Greenwich Village Area **360 Sixth Avenue** @Waverly Pl/ Washington *Washington Court* **Condo**	Built in the 1960's, converted in the 1980's to a condo - 6 stories	Two passenger elevators, landscaped interior courtyard, balconies, fireplaces, video intercom security	One bedroom and two bedroom duplexes	Taranto & Assoc.
Greenwich Village Area **450 Sixth Avenue** @West 10th St **Rental**	Prewar, renovated in 1981 - 6 stories	Elevator building, on-site superintendent, laundry on every floor	Studios, one bedrooms, two bedrooms, lofts	Manhattan Skyline Mgt. (212) 889-1850
SoHo Area **172-176 Spring Street** @W.Broadway/ Thompson St **Rental/Rent stabilized**	Built in the 1890's- 6 stories	Elevator building, on-site superintendent, apartments have exposed brick, and eat-in-kitchens	Studios, one bedrooms, two bedrooms	Time Equities Rental Office: (212) 206-6044
East Village Area **102,128 St. Marks Pl** @Ave A/First Ave **Rental/Furn/Short-term leases**	Built around 1880 - 6 stories	Apartments have high ceilings and exposed brick	Studios, one bedrooms, two bedrooms	Jakobson Properties (212) 533-1300
SoHo Area **97-119 Sullivan Street** @Prince/Spring St **Rental/Rent stabilized**	5 stories	Elevator building, on-site superintendent, laundry on every floor	Studios, one bedrooms	Manhattan Skyline Mgt. (212) 889-1850

NON-LUXURY ELEVATOR AND LOFT BUILDINGS

DOWNTOWN STREETS AND AVENUES IN ALPHABETICAL ORDER:

Address	Description	Amenities	Apartment Types	Managing Agent
SoHo Area **240 Sullivan Street** @West 3rd St **Rental/Rent stabilized**	Built around 1880 - 7 stories	Elevator building, apartments have exposed brick	One bedrooms	Time Equities (212) 206-6044
East Village Area **64 Third Avenue** @East 10th/11th St **Rental**	Built around 1900, renovated in 1996 - 4 stories	Sun-deck, laundry on second floor, apartments have high ceilings, washer/dryers, dish- washers, microwaves	Lofts - up to 5,000 sq. ft.	Jakobson Properties (212) 533-1300
Gramercy Park Area **382 Third Avenue** @East 27th/28th St *Eastview Tower* **Rental**	Built in the 1980's- 15 stories	Elevator building, on-site superintendent	Studios, one bedrooms, two bedrooms	Abington Holding (212) 759-5000
Greenwich Village Area **180 Thompson Street** @Bleecker/Houston St **Co-op**	Built around 1900, converted in the 1980's to a co-op - 6 stories	Elevator building	Studios, one bedrooms	Marlboro Realty Assoc.
Greenwich Village Area **211 Thompson Street** @Bleecker/West 3rd St **Co-op**	Built around 1976, converted in the 1980's to a co-op - 6 stories	Elevator building	Studios, one bedrooms, two bedrooms	N/A
SoHo Area **230-234 Thompson St.** @Bleecker/West 3rd St **Rental/Rent stabilized**	Built in the 1880's- 6 stories	Elevator building, on-site superintendent, apartments have exposed brick and eat- in-kitchens	Studios, one bedrooms, two bedrooms	Time Equities Rental Office: (212) 206-6044
Gramercy Park Area **60-62 University Place** @N/W/C East 10th St **Co-op**	Built around 1920, converted in the 1980's to a co-op - 13 stories	Elevator building	Studios, one bedrooms, two bedrooms	David Eisenstein Real Estate Corp.
Greenwich Village Area **79 Washington Place** @6th Ave/Washington Square Park **Co-op**	Built around 1910, co-oped in the 1980's - 8 stories	One passenger elevator, TV security	Studios, one bedrooms, two bedrooms	Self managed
Peck Slip Area **264 Water Street** *Seaport Mews* **Rental**	Built in the 19th Century - 7 stories	Video intercom security, exposed brick walls, oak floors, exercise room	One bedrooms, two bedrooms, penthouse duplex	WPG Rudd Mgt.
(Peck Slip area) **273 Water Street** *The Captain Rose* *House* **Condo**	Beautifully restored 4 story building. Once the home of a seafaring captain and the third oldest house in Manhattan.	Voice intercom	Simplex and duplex style apartments	WPG Rudd Mgt.

NON-LUXURY ELEVATOR AND LOFT BUILDINGS

DOWNTOWN STREETS AND AVENUES IN ALPHABETICAL ORDER:

Address	Description	Amenities	Apartment Types	Managing Agent
Tribeca **130 Watts Street** *SoCa* **Condo**	Two recently renovated, side-by-side buildings of six and seven stories.	Elevator building, split-level units and ceiling heights of 10 to 14 feet.	12 Classic semi-finished lofts, ranging from 1,500 to 3,500 square feet, with complete kitchens and bathrooms.	N/A
Greenwich Village Area **23 Waverly Place** @Broadway **Co-op**	Built around 1900, converted in the 1980's to a co-op - 6 stories	Elevator building	Studios, one bedrooms	Hoffman Mgt. Co.
Greenwich Village Area **136 Waverly Place** @S/W/C Sixth Ave **Co-op**	Built around 1930, converted in the 1980's to a co-op - 16 stories	Elevator building, fireplaces in some units	One bedrooms, two bedrooms, +	Equity Mgt. Group, Inc.
Greenwich Village Area **189 Waverly Place** @West 10th St **Rental/Furnished/ Short-term leases**	Built around 1880 - 6 stories	Apartments have high ceilings, exposed brick	Studios, one bedrooms, two bedrooms	Jakobson Properties (212) 533-1300
Battery Park City Area **47 West Street** @Rector St **Rental**	Built in the 1890's, renovated in 1997 - 12 stories	Elevator building, dishwashers and washer/dryers in apartments, exposed brick, and high ceilings	Lofts - 2,000 to 6,000+ square feet	Time Equities (212) 206-6173
Greenwich Village Area **468 West Broadway** *The Arches* **Condo**	Built around 1880 - 6 stories	Elevator building	Studios, one bedrooms, two bedrooms	Buchbinder & Warren
Greenwich Village Area **433 West Street** @S/E/C Bank St **Co-op**	Prewar, converted in the 1980's to a co-op - 7 stories	One self-service elevator, TV security, washer/dryers in each unit	Studios, one bedrooms, two bedrooms	Self managed

SECTION III
ALPHABETICAL INDEX OF MANAGEMENT COMPANIES

ABC Rlty.	1775 Broadway, NY, NY	(212) 307-0500
A.J. Clarke Mgt. Corp.	1881 Broadway, NY, NY	(212) 541-4477
ATA Enterprises	800 Third Avenue, NY, NY	(212) 308-1888
Abington Trust	950 Third Avenue, NY, NY	(212) 759-5000
Advanced Mgt.	25 West 45th Street, NY, NY	(212) 382-3600
Akam Associate	420 Lexington Avenue, NY, NY	(212) 986-0001
Alchemy Properties, Inc.	600 Third Avenue, NY, NY	(212) 972-0055
Algin Mgt. Co.	315 East 21st Street, NY, NY	(212) 477-8962
Allied Partners Inc.	770 Lexington Avenue, NY, NY	(212) 935-4900
American Landmark Mgt.	700 Lexington Avenue, NY, NY	(212) 207-8000
American SIBA Corp.	580 Fifth Avenue, NY, NY	(212) 764-0700
Andrews Bldg. Corp.	666 Broadway, NY, NY	(212) 529-5688
Arnold S. Warwick Co.	129 Charles Street, NY, NY	(212) 633-6500
Argo Corp.	10 Columbus Circle, NY, NY	(212) 757-5830
Arthur Leeds R.E.	215 West 83rd Street, NY, NY	(212) 874-6400
B & D Leistner Properties		(212) 965-6008
B & L Mgt. Inc.	42-19A Bell Blvd., Bayside, NY	(718) 225-9411
Becker & Rubin	201 West 70th Street, NY, NY	(212) 580-2100
Bell Realty Mgt.	525 Northern Blvd., Great Neck, NY	(516) 829-7300
Bellmarc Regal Mgt.	352 Park Avenue South, NY, NY	(212) 252-1900
Berick Mgt.	381 Park Avenue South, NY, NY	(212) 679-8222
Bernard Gans Mgt.		(212) 570-4030
Bethel Mgt.	7 Chatham Square, NY, NY	(212) 349-5344
Bettina Equities	230 East 85th Street, NY, NY	(212) 772-8830
Big City Mgt.	160 Fifth Avenue, NY, NY	(212) 242-2657
Blue Woods Mgt.	307 Seventh Avenue, NY, NY	(212) 645-7333
Brown Harris Stevens	770 Lexington Avenue, NY, NY	(212) 508-7200
Buchbinder & Warren	1 Union Square West, NY, NY	(212) 243-6722
Cantor Mgt. Co.	7401 Ridge Blvd., Brooklyn, NY	(718) 833-6600
Cambridge Mgt.	419 Park Avenue South, NY, NY	(212) 889-3500
Caran Properties Inc.	150 East 58th Street., NY, NY	(212) 207-8118
Carlton Mgt.	87-47 Marenqo St., Holliswood, NY	(212) 575-0200
Carole Ferrara Assoc.	80 East 11th Street, NY, NY	(212) 475-8811
Casdal Realty Corp.	80 East 11th Street, NY, NY	(212) 254-8280
Century Operating Corp.	7 Penn Plaza, NY, NY	(212) 239-8800
Century 21-New Age Rlty.	6 Chatham Square, NY, NY	(212) 693-2828
Citadel Mgt. Co.	310 Madison Avenue, NY, NY	(212) 682-5938
Chou Mgt.	408 Eighth Avenue, NY, NY	(212) 629-5890
Charles H. Greenthal Mgt. Co.	4 Park Avenue, NY, NY	(212) 340-9300
Church Mgt.	1370 Sixth Avenue, NY, NY	(212) 977-1300
Cooper Square Rlty. Inc.	6 East 43rd Street, NY, NY	(212) 682-7373
Cornerstone Mgt.	271 Madison Avenue, NY, NY	(212) 661-1150
David Eisenstein Rlty.	1841 Broadway, NY, NY	(212) 582-9080

Ditmas Mgt. Corp.	505 Chestnut Street, Cedarhurst, NY	(516) 374-7000
Diversified Properties	114 East 32nd Street, NY, NY	(212) 685-4646
Dwelling Mgt.	380 Madison Avenue, NY, NY	(212) 210-6666
Eberhart Brothers Inc.	312 East 82nd Street, NY, NY	(212) 570-2400
Edmar Development	48 Hester Street, NY, NY	(212) 353-8563
Eichner Rudd Assoc.	545 Madison Avenue, NY, NY	(212) 233-1700
Elm Mgt. Assoc.	1035 Second Avenue, NY, NY	(212) 293-0300
Emanuel & Co.	110 Wall Street, NY, NY	(212)344-0590
Equity Mgt. Group	228 East 45th Street, NY, NY	(212) 808-0900
ETC Mgt.	61 West 23rd Street, NY, NY	(212) 727-0800
Excelsior Mgt. Co.	909 Third Avenue, NY, NY	(212) 751-7511
Fashion Pl. Assoc.	315 Seventh Avenue, NY, NY	(212) 924-5441
Felder Mgt. Assoc.	12 East 41st Street, NY, NY	(212) 685-5250
Frederick Lee R.E. Inc.	306 Fifth Avenue, NY, NY	(212) 736-6200
Gerard J. Picaso Inc.	1133 Broadway, NY, NY	(212) 807-6969
Goodman Mgt. Co.	2736 Independence Ave., Riverdale, NY	(718) 796-5022
Goodstein Mgt. Inc.	211 East 46th Street, NY, NY	(212) 376-8600
Gotham Property Mgt.		(212) 633-8858
Hakimian Org.	60 Madison Avenue, NY, NY	(212) 683-9292
Harper Mgt. Co.	245 East 19th Street, NY, NY	(212) 581-4180
Helmsley Spear	60 East 42nd Street, NY, NY	(212) 880-0305
Henson Mgt. Inc.	160 Fifth Avenue, NY, NY	(212) 924-4766
Herman Realty Corp.	7 Penn Plaza, NY, NY	(212) 239-3232
Heron Mgt. Ltd.	850 Third Avenue, NY, NY	(212) 753-3210
Hoffman Mgt.	300 West 55th Street, NY, NY	(212) 247-4975
Hudson Lofts Assoc.		(212) 539-4414
Insignia Residential	909 Third Avenue, NY, NY	(212) 370-9200
Irving R. Raber Co.	175 Canal Street, NY, NY	(212) 925-1950
Jal Mgt.	9437 Shore Road, Brooklyn, NY	(718) 745-3500
John J. Grogan & Assoc.	360 Lexington Avenue, NY, NY	(212) 370-1480
Jordon Cooper & Assoc	204 West 84th Street, NY, NY	(212) 362-3575
Justis Properties Mgt.	224 West 4th Street, NY, NY	(212) 807-7700
Kaled Mgt. Corp.	9525 Queens Blvd., Rego Park, NY	(718) 896-4800
Knott Harbor Corp.	575 Fifth Avenue, NY, NY	(212) 953-4000
Kreisel Co. Inc.	3333 Henry Hudson Pkwy, NY, NY	(212) 370-9200
Lawrence Properties	855 Sixth Avenue, NY, NY	(212) 868-8320
Lerner Group	404 Park Avenue South, NY, NY	(212) 686-3434
Linmor L.P.		(212) 759-5000
Longines Realty Inc.	194 Grand Street, NY, NY	(212) 941-9680
Majestic Rose Corp.	66 Cuttermill Road, Great Neck, NY	(516) 466-3100
Mark Greenberg R.E.	8 Haven Avenue, Port Washington	(516) 944-5000
Marlboro Realty Assoc.	408 West 57th Street, NY, NY	(212) 757-5220
Manhattan Skyline Mgt.	103 West 55th Street, NY, NY	(212) 977-4813
Maxwell Kates, Inc.	9 East 38th Street, NY, NY	(212) 684-8282
Mayerhauser Realty, Inc.	85 Pondfield Road, Bronxville, NY	

Merit Corp.	1212 Sixth Avenue, NY, NY	(212) 391-2770
Metro Mgt. Dev.	42-25 21st St., Long Island City, NY	(718) 706-7755
Nardoni Rlty. Inc.	305 East 24th Street, NY, NY	(212) 679-4655
New Bedford Mgt. Corp.	333 Park Avenue South, NY, NY	(212) 674-6123
Newmark & Co.	1501 Broadway, NY, NY	(212) 512-9662
Norsco Realty	118 East 28th Street, NY, NY	(212) 532-7878
NRK Mgt.	1110 Second Avenue, NY, NY	(212) 421-8400
Orb Mgt. Ltd.	421 Hudson Street, NY, NY	(212) 243-1320
Orsid Realty Corp.	156 West 56th Street, NY, NY	(212) 247-2603
Park Square Assoc.	512 Broadway, NY, NY	(212) 943-6850
Penmark Rlty. Corp.	5 East 86th Street, NY, NY	(212) 876-4200
Plymouth Mgt. Group	404 Park Avenue South, NY, NY	(212) 447-7000
PRC Mgt.	19 East 82nd Street, NY, NY	(212) 772-1108
Pretium Assoc.	270 Lafayette Street, NY, NY	(212) 334-9005
Punia & Marx Inc.	265 Lexington Avenue, NY, NY	(212) 686-9400
R.A. Cohen & Assoc.	60 East 42nd Street, NY, NY	(212) 972-5900
R.F. Stuart Realty	38 East 57th Street, NY, NY	(212) 593-5971
R.Y. Mgt.	1619 Third Avenue, NY, NY	(212) 534-7771
Regal Mgt.	1501 Broadway, NY, NY	(212) 944-5240
Related Companies	175 East 96th Street, NY, NY	(212) 996-0646
River to River Properties	86 East 10th Street, NY, NY	(212) 995-5140
Rockrose Development	309 East 45th Street, NY, NY	(212) 697-4422
Rose Assoc.	200 Madison Avenue, NY, NY	(212) 717-4379
Rudin Mgt. Co. Inc.	345 Park Avenue, NY, NY	(212) 407-2400
R.V.P Mgt. Corp.	130 Madison Avenue, NY, NY	(212) 683-3200
Salon Realty Co.	338 East 92nd Street, NY, NY	(212) 534-3131
Samson Mgt.	97-77 Queens Blvd., Forest Hills, NY	(718) 830-0131
Sandra Greer R.E.	201 East 77th Street, NY, NY	(212) 472-1878
Sequoia Property Mgt.	666 Lexington Ave., Mt. Kisco, NY	(914) 666-6860
Siren Mgt.	40 Exchange Place, NY, NY	(212) 483-0700
Simon A. Berman Realty	61 West 23rd Street, NY, NY	(212) 727-0800
Sterling Mgt.	1975 Hempstead Tpke, E. Meadow, NY	(718) 525-7607
Stillman Org.	276 Fifth Avenue, NY, NY	(212) 686-2400
Superior Mgt. Inc.	50 Bank Street, NY, NY	(212) 243-7757
Taranto & Assoc.	267 Fifth Avenue, NY, NY	(212) 686-6200
Thurcon Development	254 Park Avenue South, NY, NY	(212) 477-2700
Time Equities Inc.	55 Fifth Avenue, NY, NY	(212) 206-6000
TUC Mgt. Co. Inc.	980 Columbus Avenue, NY, NY	(212) 865-8600
Tudor Rlty. Srcs.	25 Tudor City Plc., NY, NY	(212)557-3600
Urban Assoc.	400 West 59th Street, NY, NY	(212) 245-1870
Vintage R.E. Srcs.	49 West 45th Street, NY, NY	(212) 944-5944
Wallack Mgt. Co.	18 East 64th Street, NY, NY	(212) 753-3381
Walter & Samuels, Inc.	419 Park Avenue South, NY, NY	(212) 685-6200
Weinreb Mgt. Co.	276 Riverside Drive, NY, NY	(212) 316-0045
Washington Sq. Mgt.	1356 First Avenue, NY, NY	(212) 472-3500

Wiener Rlty.	1500 Broadway, NY, NY	(212) 730-8900
William B. May & Co.	4 Park Avenue South, NY, NY	(212) 779-6000
Winoker Realty Co.	1410 Broadway, NY, NY	(212) 764-7666
Wolff Mgt.	223 West 21st Street, NY, NY	(212) 989-4390
WPG/Rudd Residential	85 John Street, NY, NY	(212) 233-0109
Z & R Mgt. Corp.	251 West 19th Street, NY, NY	(212) 691-9542

Did You Know That...

New York City, with its 7 million residents, is made up of five boroughs: Manhattan, Brooklyn, Queens, the Bronx and Staten Island. Manhattan is the smallest, a 22 square mile island that is largely a protrusion of granite, rising a few hundred feet from sea-level. The southern tip and center of the island are solid granite, while areas in Greenwich Village and Chelsea are composed of soft soil. As a result of these differences, Manhattan's tallest buildings are located on it's two large "rocky areas."

Fifth Avenue is the dividing line between east and west: 1 East 50th Street is just east of Fifth, and 1 West 50th Street just west. Avenues run north-south and streets east-west; streets increase in number as one travels uptown.

Some uptown avenues have names. For example, Eighth Avenue becomes Central Park West, Ninth Avenue becomes Columbus, Tenth Avenue is called Amsterdam, Eleventh is called West End and Twelfth is called Riverside Drive.

Manhattan was first settled by the Dutch in 1613 who named the island New Amsterdam. In 1626, Peter Minuit purchased the entire island for approximately $24. The English changed the name to New York when they took it over in 1664.

Broadway began as a meandering Native American trail known as the Weekquaesgeek Trail, and is the only major Manhattan street that twists and crosses over other avenues.

New York City became the nation's first capital in 1789 when George Washington took the presidential oath here.

The Statue of Liberty was constructed in Paris in 1886 and was a gift of the French government to the the American people. It commemorated the 1778 alliance between France and the United States.

The Brooklyn Bridge, which links Brooklyn and Manhattan, was designed by John A. Roebling. Construction began in 1869 and took 16 years to complete.

The Empire State Building, built in 1929 with a height of 1,250 feet was, until the 1970's, the tallest building in the world.

The Flatiron Building at 175 Fifth Avenue was the first self-sufficient skyscraper. Designed in 1902, it had a steel skeleton and an electric generator to provide all of its electricity and heating.

The twin towers of the World Trade Center, located at Battery Park City, are presently the tallest structures in New York. These corporate buildings provide a business center for some five hundred international companies, and spectacular views can be seen from the outdoor deck on the 110th floor.

The phrase "The Big Apple" was coined in the 1930's by jazz musicians to describe the Harlem nightclub scene. Later, the city government adopted the phrase to promote all of New York City's cultural and performing arts.

The United Nations, with its peace-keeping mission, was created in London following World War II. Today, the U.N. buildings and plaza cover fifteen acres on the bank of the East River, between 42nd and 48th Streets. Tours of the General Assembly, and the Economic and Social Council are given every half-hour.

There are nearly 12,000 licensed taxi-cabs in New York City. They are bright yellow, and signal their availability with a light on the roof. If the cab is available, the roof light will be lit; if already taken, the light will be off.

Taxi rates are posted on the side of the car. The current charges are: $2.00 initial charge, 30 cents per 1/5 mile, 20 cents per 75 seconds in slow traffic, 50 cents surcharge from 8pm-6am.

The quickest way to get around is on the subway system. The subway connects 714 miles in four buroughs; Staten Island has its own transit system. The Transit Authority also operates the buses that travel North and South along the avenues, and crosstown on major streets. One ride costs $1.50. Metrocards and tokens may be purchased in subway stations and in local shops that display a Metrocard sign in the front window.

It is illegal to smoke on all public transportation, public buildings, theatres and restaurants seating more than 35 people.

New York City has more than 3,500 churches and synagogues, 200 skyscrapers, 578 miles of waterfront and 6,400 miles of streets. There are 1,600 parks and playgrounds occupying more than 26,000 acres.

The Metropolitan Museum of Art, The Museum of Modern Art, the Whitney Museum and the Guggenheim are just a few of the many museums which contribute to the cultural life of New York.

The New York Public Library (Main Branch) on 42nd Street, at Fifth Avenue, houses more than six million volumes in its stacks.

Gracie Mansion at East 88th Street and East End Avenue has been home to New York's mayors since 1942. Its present occupant is Mayor Rudolph Giuliani.

The Staten Island Ferry runs 24 hours a day from Manhattan to Staten Island and back. At only 50 cents a ride, it is the cheapest cruise around lower Manhattan. There are great views of the Manhattan skyline and the Statue of Liberty from the ferry.

1.5 million people pass through Times Square everyday. They arrive by subway (eleven different subway trains make Times Square one of the largest hubs in NYC), bus, car and foot.

The Times Square Visitors Center at 226 West 42nd Street, between Seventh and Eighth Avenue, is the place to go for information, directions and help in finding one's way around Manhattan. The center is open seven days a week. On Fridays, at noon, a free two-hour walking tour of Times Square is given.

The Tkts Booth at 47th Street and Broadway offers half-price day-of-performance tickets to Broadway plays. Tickets for evening performances go on sale from 3 to 8 P.M. and on Sundays from noon to 8 P.M. For matinees, on Wednesdays and Saturdays, tickets can be purchased from 10 A.M. to 2 P.M.

New York City Sales Tax is 8.25% and will automatically be added to most consumer goods, as well as to the cost of food and beverages purchased in bars and restaurants. Bar hours vary, but the legal limit for closing is 4AM; the legal drinking age is 21 in New York State.